MAKING LOCAL FOOD WORK

Making Local Food Work

—— ☼ ——

THE CHALLENGES AND OPPORTUNITIES
OF TODAY'S SMALL FARMERS

——

Brandi Janssen

UNIVERSITY OF IOWA PRESS, IOWA CITY

University of Iowa Press, Iowa City 52242

Copyright © 2017 by the University of Iowa Press

www.uipress.uiowa.edu

Printed in the United States of America

Design by April Leidig

The University of Iowa Press is a member of Green Press
Initiative and is committed to preserving natural resources.

Printed on acid-free paper

Library of Congress Cataloging-in-Publication Data

Names: Janssen, Brandi, 1976– author.

Title: Making local food work : the challenges and opportunities
of today's small farmers / Brandi Janssen.

Description: Iowa City : University of Iowa Press, [2017] |
Includes bibliographical references and index.

Identifiers: LCCN 2016040303 | ISBN 978-1-60938-492-0 (pbk) |
ISBN 978-1-60938-493-7 (ebk)

Subjects: LCSH: Farms, Small—Iowa. | Local foods—
Iowa. | Community-supported agriculture—Iowa.

Classification: LCC HD1476.U6 1853 2017 |
DDC 338.109777—dc23

LC record available at https://lccn.loc.gov/2016040303

Contents

Preface vii

CHAPTER ONE
New Markets for Alternative Farmers
1

CHAPTER TWO
The Stories We Tell
13

CHAPTER THREE
Old Systems, New Farmers
31

CHAPTER FOUR
The Not-So-Direct Market
53

CHAPTER FIVE
Farm to School
81

CHAPTER SIX
Just a Simple Salad:
Purchasing Local Food for School Lunch
95

CHAPTER SEVEN
Herd Management:
Labor in Local Food Production
119

CHAPTER EIGHT

Working at Great Greens

143

CHAPTER NINE

Good Fences Make Good Neighbors

171

CHAPTER TEN

Looking Downstream

197

EPILOGUE

211

Notes 215

Index 227

Preface

IN IOWA, agriculture looms large. Nearly one hundred percent of the original tallgrass prairie has been converted to agricultural production, and the related industries of machinery manufacturing, input sales, corporate seed research, and other support services dominate the state's economy. Most years, Iowa produces more corn and soybeans than any other state in the country and boasts seven pigs per human. As a result, the state has become the epicenter of some of the most hotly contested debates about agriculture. When activists and journalists decry the current model of agriculture, it is likely that they point their finger at an Iowa cornfield or a hog confinement facility.[1] But Iowa is an agricultural state in every sense of the word—not just because Iowans are top producers of several commodities but also because a growing number of smaller scale food farms supply ever-expanding statewide and regional markets. The rhetorical tendency to pit industrial against alternative agriculture becomes complicated when those two systems coexist. In reality, Iowa has a long history of leading in the number of farmers' markets as well as hog barns per capita. The diversified farms where food and commodity crops are integrated with livestock that once dominated the landscape are only a generation in the past. Further, whether a farmer grows on three acres or one thousand, the family farm identity remains strong.

Combine with this history the newfound attention to local food, and Iowa provides a glimpse into an agricultural system that can and does produce just about everything you would want to eat. The state falls short on a few dozen products, including citrus and tropical fruits, coffee, cocoa, and avocados, but that's about it. I have spoken with many farmers in recent years who have suggested that local food is not simply a passing trend and that its presence in the food system will only continue to increase. They have been encouraged by the obvious growth in farmers' market attendance and the interest in their community-supported agriculture

(CSA) shares as well as popular books and media that have recently extolled the virtues of local food. Farm to school programming has steadily become more mainstream and was included in the 2008 and 2014 farm bills. Other organizations typically associated with conventional agriculture have turned their attention to local food, most notably land grant extension services. Farmers are not generally known to be an optimistic bunch, but this groundswell of support has suggested to them that there is some hope for a sustainable local food system.

In addition to optimistic farmers, the attention to local food comes from consumers who have become disenchanted with the conventional food system. In particular, highly publicized food safety scares, such as the 2011 recall of thirty-six million pounds of ground turkey contaminated with salmonella or a thirty-nine–state recall of bagged spinach in February 2013, suggested to some consumers that local food systems may be safer. One beef producer chuckled as he told me, "every time there's an *E. coli* scare, my phone starts ringing." In these cases, local food becomes the safer and healthier alternative to the dominant system.

Not everyone is positive about the current national dialogue around food and agriculture. Large-scale agribusiness has begun to take notice, especially of those who want to overhaul the food system. In 2010, the president of the American Farm Bureau Federation claimed that criticism of conventional agriculture was the number one threat to American farmers. Conventional agriculture faces a number of challenges, including volatile oil prices, climate change, and international trade agreements that exclude genetically modified crops. For the Farm Bureau, arguably the most powerful voice for conventional agriculture, to fear criticism above all other challenges suggests that the call by journalists and filmmakers to "vote with your fork" has made an impact.

It is in this context that I have conducted research in Iowa since 2008. I came into the topic not really thinking about food but rather as someone interested in the changing structure of agriculture over the past few generations. I grew up on a beef cattle farm in the Missouri Ozarks in the 1980s, a decade when farm families across the country were at risk of foreclosure. I spent many days in my youth at farm auctions as we picked over the remains of others' livelihoods. Sales were often highly stressful for the farmer whose possessions were being auctioned. One apocryphal story in our family involves my father as he returned to pick up a piece of equipment he had purchased at a farm sale earlier in the day. He was met at the gate by the farmer, armed with a shotgun and prepared to protect his possessions. While there was no resulting violence, the farmer's desperation was clear. Although a foreclosure sale may appear to simply liquidate a business, in reality farms are also homes, and farming is as much an identity as a job.

Later in my life, while making annual visits to a local apple orchard and pumpkin farm with my young children, I was surprised to find working farms opened to the public. I could not imagine the Ozark farmers from my childhood allowing strangers such access to their homes. These experiences led me to wonder about how small farms maintained profitability in the midst of increasing vertical integration in agriculture. The variety of direct market and alternative farming strategies, especially related to fruits and vegetables, were largely unknown to me at the time.

I started out wanting to understand this new kind of farming, in which small-scale farmers interact directly with their customers. I wondered about how they learned how to farm vegetables, as opposed to corn and soybeans, in Iowa. I wondered if they were driven to compete against other vegetable farmers, or if there were enough customers to go around. I also wondered how much they thought—or cared—about the rest of agriculture, those thousand-acre grain farms for which Iowa is known.

It was somewhat of a surprise to me to eventually realize that this research was also about food. Given the trajectory of midwestern agriculture over the past decades, in which farms have become larger and more specialized in grain production, the distance between the farmer and the consumer has become greater. The commodities produced on Iowa's farms—primarily corn, soy, and pork—go through many phases of processing and packaging before they ever reach the dinner table. Consumers have been trained to look at nutritional labels and wonder about food additives or fat content rather than agricultural practices.

Local food attempts to change that habit by reengaging consumers with agriculture. Now eaters are expected to know their farmer and investigate how the food they eat was grown or raised. By reestablishing links between farms and eaters, the local food movement hopes to make agriculture more environmentally friendly and create a food system that is both healthier for consumers and more profitable for small farmers. Thus, my research was not just about agricultural production and practices—it was about food production. The farmers I spoke with frequently emphasized that point, that they produce fresh, healthy food—not faceless commodities that go on for further processing.

This book attempts to understand the balance between farm profitability and community improvement through agriculture. Can farms be environmentally sustainable, produce healthy food, and support farmers' livelihoods all at the same time? Is local food really a fundamental challenge to conventional agriculture, or is it one part of the spectrum of farming? Do local food farmers primarily want to be profitable, or do they want to build a new food system? Maybe most important: can they do both?

I learned that there are not too many clear-cut answers to these questions. This may not be entirely satisfying, but it is realistic. In some cases, local food can create new markets for farmers—especially those just starting out—and can create good jobs for at least some in rural Iowa. Local food is beginning to make its way into school food, and students at public elementary schools are benefiting from more education about agriculture. But we are far from a local food revolution; progress has been incremental.

Slow progress is better than no progress. Thus, I attempted to understand the growth of local food in Iowa, even when it came in fits and starts. This book captures a moment in time when several Iowa CSAs were entering their second decade and farmers' markets were experiencing a surge in attendance. For many growers using these marketing strategies, local food was maturing well. Many of these farmers were expanding to the point of needing outside labor and had put considerable thought into how to scale up efficiently and profitably. New and aspiring farmers, encouraged by the apparent success of these veterans, were trying to find their own niche in this new system. They were trying to access land, equipment, and knowledge. In addition, farm to school programs were just taking off, and many were experiencing some growing pains as volunteers, farmers, and administrators tried to find workable procedures for getting local food into schools. At the same time, food safety regulators, extension services, nonprofit agencies, and agricultural colleges were trying to find their own place in this burgeoning alternative farm economy.

The most striking finding during my research was that local food—even though we mostly talk about farmers and consumers—requires much more than the direct market relationship to be successful. Local food farms require support from more than just customers, and their experiences with the rest of the food system are an important indicator of how well local food is functioning. I try to show some of the hidden features of the local food system. How, in addition to farmers and consumers, there are employees, inspectors, market managers, nonprofit organizations, journalists, and others, all helping to determine what we grow and how we eat.

THIS BOOK IS BASED on qualitative anthropological research, though I have tried to write it in an accessible, mostly nonacademic, style. Except for those who are public figures, I have used pseudonyms for individuals and also for farm names to protect the identities of my informants. The location of this research is relevant, however, so I have maintained the actual names of cities, public markets, and institutions. Throughout the book, my goal has been to accurately represent the points of view of the farmers I interviewed and spent time with. Thus, I also report their perceptions of the current state of agriculture, including opinions related to agribusiness, university involvement in agriculture, genetically modified organisms, and, in some cases, the practices of their neighbors. Anthropologists often joke that our data is just someone else's gossip, in that we want to reflect how people perceive the world around them. Regardless of whether an informant is technically right about, say, how GMOs work or what the land grant extension service does, recording that person's reflection on the world around him or her is an important part of capturing the human experience.

I have many people to thank in relation to this research and book. Mike Chibnik has read multiple drafts and provided consistently excellent advice as well as the occasional tidbit of local gossip related to real estate transactions in our fair city. I also am grateful to Mike for introducing me to my editor, Catherine Cocks. A project like this cannot go from raw to cooked without considerable editorial skill, and I have been very lucky to work with Catherine and the University of Iowa Press. Her thoughtful questions and comments brought about the best possible final product.

Margaret Beck and Scott Schnell improved both my analysis and semicolon use, and Jim Throgmorton always helped me keep my eye on the big picture. I am grateful to James (Woody) Watson for his consistent advocacy of my work and, especially, his no-nonsense advice to buck up and get publishing. Most of this research was generously funded by the Wenner-Gren Foundation. In addition, the University of Iowa's Center for Global and Regional Environmental Research and the Department of Anthropology provided funding for research as well as conference travel. Of course, I am indebted to the many farmers who allowed me to visit their farms, follow them around, and ask silly questions. Many welcomed me into their homes, and even served coffee, while I took hours of their time conducting interviews. I am especially grateful to James Nisly and to Andrew and Melissa Dunham, whose friendship and advice have been central to my work. They, along with Laura Krouse, were also kind enough to review the manuscript before publication. The local farm to school team let me tag along and work with them in a number of different roles. I am especially grateful to Heather Widmayer, Jason Grimm, Diane Duncan-Goldsmith, and Alison Demory for their time and expertise.

A number of colleagues have also been helpful during coffee-shop writing sessions. I especially appreciated the opinions of Susie Donaldson and Nina Ortiz; their knowledge of rural life, social class, and diversity in Iowa always provided a useful perspective. Misha Quill's advice to include more of my own story in proposals for this project was spot-on. Deirdre Egan's encouragement and friendship has been invaluable, and Steph Leonard's enthusiasm helped me power through the final, tedious steps of the writing process. Although I am the only anthropologist in my academic department, I am lucky to work with people who have been supportive of this project. Thanks to Peter Thorne, Diane Rohlman, and Matt Nonnenmann for their encouragement to prioritize this work.

I am lucky to spend most of my free time with an assortment of musicians and artists. I am especially grateful to Al and Aleta Murphy, Patti Zwick, Chris Clark, and the most philosophical guitar player I know, Warren Hanlin. They all keep life colorful and interesting.

This project would have been impossible had Marc Janssen not been willing to pack up and move so that I could follow my interests. I am grateful for his consistent assertion that I should pursue my goals, even when it resulted in the disruption of his own work. Finally, to Maia and Lucy, who always bring me back to earth and remind me that this is really just another boring book about agriculture.

MAKING LOCAL FOOD WORK

CHAPTER ONE

New Markets for Alternative Farmers

EVERY YEAR in late February, organic farmers and foodies meet in the unassuming city of LaCrosse, Wisconsin, for the annual meeting of the Midwest Organic and Sustainable Education Service (MOSES). This is the largest organic farming conference in the United States, for which thousands brave the late Wisconsin winter and winding Mississippi River roads to listen to organic farmers, food activists, and researchers speak about the significance of organic agriculture. In 2011 keynote speaker Tom Stearns stood in front of the more than three thousand attendees and forcefully made the case against modern agriculture. He argued that the current global food system is "out of control, marinated in fossil fuels," and has resulted in environmental destruction and social inequality. Though he blames the current food system for numerous problems, including global political unrest, he also believes that food can be the solution. Stearns owns High Mowing Organic Seeds, based in Hardwick, Vermont. There he has fostered collaboration between several small-scale agricultural businesses that have given a shot in the arm to a once dying community. Stearns suggests that small, interconnected food and farm-related businesses can reinvigorate rural areas that have been degraded by the increasing centralization of agricultural production.

Stearns went on to describe the changes he has seen in Hardwick and called us all to action. As he continued to warm up during his talk, pacing back and forth and raising his arms like a revival preacher, he shouted, "Do you hate your job? Are you sick of sitting in a cubicle all day? Then become a farmer!" He described the pleasures of working outside, communing with nature, and the satisfaction of producing food for his family and his neighbors. Farmers, he pointed out, are independent from cubicle culture; they make their own hours and are their own bosses. Not only do they do noble work, feeding people, they are independent and resourceful. A dynamic and engaging speaker, Stearns had the whole room in the palm of his hand. By the end, we were all ready to storm out of the conference and farm our way to a rural revolution, one organic potato at a time.

This message was quite a contrast from what I had learned while sitting with Alan Marshall in his eastern Iowa kitchen. Alan, a lifelong farmer, and his wife Brenda had returned to his family's land to farm and to care for his aging mother. They started a small CSA farm in 2007 because, as Alan put it, "how do you make forty acres pay" in a state filled with giant row crop and livestock operations? He delivered fifteen shares every week directly to people's homes their first year. In 2008, they increased slightly to nineteen shares and had to turn down more than twenty requests. That year started with remarkable optimism; their CSA was in demand, and with one year under their belts, they felt confident in their ability to deliver the shares. But the spring rains were heavy and unrelenting that year. Alan replanted several crops that were repeatedly washed away. He had never seen so much of the farm underwater in all the time his family owned it, since 1973. He was ultimately forced to suspend his CSA deliveries after the third week. He quietly said to me, "it was the hardest thing I ever had to do."

While listening to Tom Stearns trumpet the dawn of a new agricultural era, I also thought of Frances Baumgartner. I joined her in her living room one steamy July evening to discuss the local food movement in Iowa. Another lifelong farmer, she talked about the different ways she had marketed her produce over the years. Three decades earlier, Frances sold strawberries and cabbage on a rural radio call-in show; later, she was able to sell her produce at area farmers' markets. As Frances was planning to leave a nursing career in the late 1990s, she learned in an extension brochure about something called community supported agriculture, which gave farmers new ways to directly sell their crops to consumers. Frances was immediately drawn to the idea because she thought that many people had lost their connection to the soil. Frances told me about how pleased—and surprised—she was to become a participant in the growing local food movement. She mused: "I think we've happened upon something on the cutting edge—for once in our life! . . . Because I think this is the way people want to eat."

These three stories show some of the range of experiences that farmers have had with local food. For some it is the new way to rebuild rural communities, both economically and socially. For others it posed more challenges and difficulties than expected. And for some it represents their way of life for many decades, even as they now enjoy a resurgence of interest in their products; local food feels new and promising. All three share a sense of optimism for the future, that local food can become the new normal, even when hampered by Mother Nature.

Indeed, in recent years, the production and marketing of local food has become the fastest growing segment of the natural food industry and an important part of the sustainable agriculture movement. The heightened attention to local food systems has bolstered attendance at farmers' markets and participation in CSAs, and led to the development of programs that add local foods to public school menus. Popular books such as Michael Pollan's *The Omnivore's Dilemma* and Barbara Kingsolver's *Animal, Vegetable, Miracle* call for consumers to rediscover place-based foods.[1] In doing so, the argument goes, they challenge the food industry and vote with their fork for a more sustainable system of food production in the United States. The movement has gained such popular salience that in 2007 "locavore" (defined as a person who seeks out locally grown foods) was *Oxford American Dictionary*'s word of the year.[2]

In large part, local food has galvanized journalists, food activists, and farmers because of a sales strategy that makes small, environmentally sustainable farms directly accountable to consumers. But the focus on that direct relationship neglects the many other important interactions that farmers engage in to get their products to market. The discussion also tends to portray local food only as an alternative, or as resistance, to the industrial food system. In doing so, we miss the ways that the two systems are intertwined and, importantly, what local food farmers might actually learn from or gain by taking some tricks of the trade from conventional agriculture.

In this book, I draw on the experiences of farmers in Iowa who are navigating the current local food system. This includes produce growers doing CSAs and farmers' markets, beef and poultry producers, some of whom butcher their own animals for sale, and dairy producers who are pasteurizing and packaging their own cheese. Although Iowa is much better known for its huge corn and soybean operations, as well as hog and poultry confinement facilities, local food production continues to steadily increase in the state as more farmers and customers engage in this new way to produce and buy food.

But what do we even mean by local food? The term generally refers to agricultural products, such as fruit, vegetables, meat, and cheese, that are minimally processed and grown near the final point of sale. In Iowa, local food production typically occurs on small-scale, often highly diversified, farms. A vegetable farmer, for example, may grow more than a hundred varieties of produce on less than ten acres. The phrase "local food" also encompasses the various marketing strategies that farmers use to eliminate distributors or middlemen and sell their agricultural products directly to consumers. The farmers' market may be the most common strategy; according to the U.S. Department of Agriculture (USDA), as of 2014 there were more than eight thousand active farmers' markets in the United States.[3] Another increasingly popular local food option is a CSA, in which consumers, often called shareholders, pay a fee directly to a farmer at the beginning of the growing season. The early payment provides welcome income for farmers at a time of year when cash flow is generally low. Shareholders receive weekly portions of produce from the farm throughout the season in return for their early investment. Other direct market options include U-Pick farms, where customers go to a farm to harvest their own berries or vegetables, and agritourism farms, where families can spend an afternoon purchasing products and enjoying a farm experience, such as watching cider production, seeing farm equipment, or visiting livestock.

In addition to direct-to-consumer sales, the marketing of local foods includes institutional sales, particularly to primary and secondary schools. The website of the National Farm to School Network states that such programming "enriches the connection communities have with fresh, healthy food and local food producers by changing food purchasing and education practices."[4] Other direct-to-institution sales are to hospitals, long-term care facilities, day care centers, and universities.

The aim of this book is to improve our understanding of the goals, ideologies, and economic strategies of local food farmers in Iowa, a state largely regarded as the epicenter of large-scale industrial agriculture. Local food producers set themselves apart from the conventional system in several ways. Although my focus is on the specific marketing and labor strategies they use to do so, they are also deeply embedded in the broader policy and land-use realities that affect all farmers in the state and, as a result, there is more overlap between alternative and conventional production than one would expect. During this research, I spent many hours in conversation with farmers, working on local food farms, and attending workshops and conferences aimed at making small-scale food production more feasible and profitable for farmers and local products more available for eaters. As a result, what I hope to show is the nuanced reality, both good and bad, of running a small-scale farm in a large farm state.

The farmers running those small farms and directly selling their crops to consumers are often portrayed by popular authors and even researchers as renegades railing against the system or poetic intellectuals. Marketing teams at natural food stores display artsy photos of such farmers, prominently featuring the dirt under their fingernails. These depictions suggest to consumers that they can change the face of our food system and economy through their purchases, pausing only briefly to put down their recyclable cup of fair trade coffee. Thus, local food is as much a set of values as it is an economic strategy. And as a result, it is tied to larger social and political ideas about sustainability and community. When marketers and authors show farmers as rebels, those of us who buy their products get to go along for the ride, making agriculture more sustainable, supporting small farms, or standing up to the industrial system. Consumers, without really doing much work on their own, can still claim to be part of the movement. We have focused so much on the farmers who produce and the consumers who purchase that the rest of the system is neglected. I hope to illuminate some of those hidden parts.

The emphasis on producers and consumers has resulted in a number of assumptions about how local food works. One is that the direct relationships in local food networks reconnect food buyers with the processes of production. By purchasing from farmers, consumers will automatically know more about, care more about, or advocate for sustainable agriculture. These connections seem impossible in the conventional system, with its complicated web of production, processing, and marketing. As a result, some have argued that local agricultural sales outlets may counter the processes of industrialization, and revitalize local connections that have been lost in modern life, simply by shortening the distance between the grower and the consumer.[5]

The shortened supply chains associated with local food systems have also contributed to broader discussions about new alternatives to mainstream economics. These embedded economies, in which social interactions are enhanced as a result of economic transactions, lead to a more socially cohesive community. While social scientists consistently argue that all economic systems are culturally derived, the shortened supply chains of CSA and farmers' markets have been deemed particularly useful in "illuminating the social context" of economic transactions.[6] The term "civic agriculture" is now sometimes used to describe the community-building potential of local food systems, because the social elements are an obvious and integral part of those economic transactions.[7]

Proponents of local food networks also sometimes solely emphasize economic impacts. Local food systems may provide significant potential for job creation on farms, in small-scale processing, and at farmers' markets.[8] A 2014 evaluation by The Leopold Center for Sustainable Agriculture at Iowa State University reported twenty-four million dollars in local food sales by 120 Iowa farmers plus 171 new jobs created in 2012 and 2013.[9] There are, however, limits to the extent to which local food production provides economic benefits. In many parts of the United States, such work is seasonal and volunteers or interns provide much of the production labor. The popularity of local food has encouraged young college students to spend a year working on an alternative farm. These students are often not from the area where the farm is located, eliminating any long-term wage investments in the local community.

The tendency to reduce local food systems to a farmer-consumer relationship or an economic driver has resulted in a literature that fails to sufficiently consider the challenges that direct market farmers face. One way to address this problem is to closely examine the segments of the local food system that truly set it apart from conventional farming. Rather than specializing in one or two commodities, which are sold to grain co-ops or corporate livestock buyers before the commodity moves into a complicated system of processing and distribution, direct market farmers produce whole foods that are sold to individual consumers. Selling agricultural products locally requires farmers to grow many varieties of fruits and vegetables to meet their customers' needs throughout the season. Additionally, some producers may raise livestock to diversify their product line with meat, dairy, or eggs. Even local farmers who specialize in livestock usually manage diverse breeds and sell a variety of products, such as a combination of pork, beef, and poultry.

The inherent diversity of local food farming requires a significant amount of labor. Ironically, the small scale of most Iowa fruit and vegetable farms results in high labor costs because it can be difficult to find appropriately scaled implements to mechanize such small acreages. In the Midwest, the labor needs in food farming make it distinct from commodity production. Even though agriculture is a critical segment of the economy in the American Midwest, conventional production agriculture does not create many jobs.[10] While the large-scale fruit and vegetable production typical in California remains relatively labor-intensive, often employing migrant workers, the increasing mechanization of commodity grain production in the Midwest has reduced the need for manual labor on farms. Thus, aside from crews of mostly teenaged—and a growing number of migrant and seasonal—detasselers who descend on the Corn Belt for a few weeks each summer, on-farm labor is not generally a critical component of commodity grain production. For direct market farmers, in contrast, business growth is contingent on finding a reliable source for labor.

Unlike commodity cash crops that require large economies of scale to be profitable, local food production tends to provide a higher economic return for each product. Commodity production relies on farmers selling high volumes at low prices. In this production system, farmers do not benefit from the processing and marketing of their food; instead, the product moves out of their control and into corporate supply chains. In contrast, direct market farmers shepherd their products from seed to consumer and capture the full price of whatever is sold. This high margin has made small-scale food production economically viable. Nevertheless, even the most direct-to-consumer strategies are still based on other relationships with landlords, inspectors, market managers, and equipment vendors. Further, even when farmers capture more of the final price, they become responsible for the work involved in marketing and distributing their products.

Analyzing these clear differences between local food production and conventional commodity farming, as I do in this book, clarifies some of the key challenges of direct market production and may illuminate ways to enhance local food systems. It is critically important, however, to recognize that the two systems operate simultaneously and are very closely intertwined. Local food producers in Iowa and elsewhere must deal with the daily realities of production, harvesting, and marketing in a place dominated by conventional agriculture and agribusiness. They interact with organizations that usually focus on conventional farmers, such as extension services, equipment dealers, and lending institutions. The economics of local food production must be understood in the context of broader trends in land use in Iowa, such as the increasing number of rental agreements and the ever-increasing price of land. Perhaps most important, local food producers and conventional farmers are neighbors in Iowa. As a result, even those food farmers criticizing industrial agriculture may put the equipment and expertise of conventional growers to use on their own farms. The potential for cooperation and overlap between conventional and alternative production is rarely recognized or explored. I argue that these points of convergence may shed light on how the food system can truly be transformed.

Iowa is an ideal setting to explore these relationships. Anthropologist Walter Goldschmidt wrote that Iowa "is the quintessential locale of the American farm, the very stuff of the mythic America, where motherhood and apple pie are not merely the living symbol but, one almost believes, were actually invented."[11] Certainly, Iowa's long agricultural history has led to a national reputation centered on agricultural production and rural life. Even though the majority of residents are no longer rural, agriculture and its related industries dominate the state's economy.

The quantity and value of agricultural products that Iowa produces is staggering: agricultural products sold in Iowa are worth well over thirty billion dollars, ranking Iowa second in the nation (behind California). The USDA Agricultural census, the gold standard in agricultural data conducted every five years, consistently ranks Iowa the number one producer of both corn and soybeans; more than thirteen million acres of corn and nine million acres of soybeans were harvested in 2015.[12] Iowa is also the top producer of hogs and laying hens. There are about twenty million pigs and, before the avian influenza outbreak of 2015, well over fifty million laying hens.[13]

All of this output is generated by 88,000 farms spread across 30,500,000 acres. That is a lot of farms, but not nearly as many as there used to be. In 1950, there were more than two hundred thousand, reflecting steady consolidation over time. Improvements in equipment and technology, starting with the adoption of the tractor during the first half of the twentieth century, allowed fewer people to farm more acres. Larger farmers bought or rented land from neighbors, slowly increasing their control. Technological changes such as highly productive hybrid seeds, chemical fertilizers, and an ever-growing buffet of pesticides further encouraged farmers to specialize. A farm in the early 1900s would have produced a wide variety of food and grain crops, integrating livestock for sale as well as their own family's consumption. Grain rotations of the past included corn, wheat, oats, and hay crops; now those rotations are largely reduced to two: corn and soybeans.

The overall number of pigs has not changed significantly in Iowa over the past hundred years, but they now live on fewer farms and in bigger buildings. A farmer of the past may have kept a small herd of pigs along with other livestock. Now, a hog farmer typically raises pigs in buildings that hold several thousand animals. These confined—or concentrated, depending on your perspective—animal feeding operations (CAFOs) are at the center of some of the most intense debates about agriculture. Proponents see them as modern and efficient, the only viable strategy to feed the world. Opponents see them as inhumane and environmentally destructive. Certainly, manure management is one of the most contentious issues, and a farmer planning to build a new confinement structure is required to provide documentation to county authorities showing a strategy for containing manure so that it will not leach into water sources. In many counties, advocacy groups have strongly lobbied against farmers who plan to erect new confinement buildings, as relationships between the farm and nonfarm population become ever more strained.

Despite the increasing specialization and scale, Iowa farms are not as large as some might expect: the average size has remained around 350 acres over the past ten years.[14] That reflects the land owned by farmers, not the land they rent from others, so many do farm more than the average number of acres. Even so, the last agricultural census in 2012 showed that most farms, more than 70 percent, reported annual gross income less than $350,000 (which the USDA designates as a small family farm), and another 17 percent report sales between $350,000 and $999,000; these are designated mid-size family farms.[15] The outside perception of Iowa is that of corporate or factory farms, but farmers, even those who produce on several hundreds or thousands of acres, strongly consider themselves family farmers. Iowa laws forbid corporations from owning farmland for any purposes other than research. Thus, while Monsanto may have some Iowa farmland for researching new varieties of seeds, any seed produced for sale is done though contract arrangements with individual farmers. The point is that even in the face of increasing specialization and scale, Iowa farmers do not share the view that their farms are factories or corporations.

This is the context in which local food operates in Iowa. Despite the growing attention to the potential economic and social benefits of local food systems, the production of agricultural commodities — corn, soy, and pork — dominates the landscape and the agricultural resources. If you plan to start an organic CSA in Iowa, you will likely have a neighbor with row crops, which he will spray with chemicals several times each season. You may also be in a county with a number of hog confinement operations, which may raise concerns about the water you use to irrigate your food crops and the risk of contamination from a spill.

The research that framed my interest in understanding the experiences of local food farmers in Iowa, especially how they interact with conventional agriculture. The research for this book occurred between 2008 and 2012, and the big picture hasn't changed substantially since then. Most academics who study agriculture are trained as sociologists or agricultural economists. I am an anthropologist, and that makes this work look a little different than it would if I came from one of those other disciplines. Anthropologists like to dig in and understand the details of people's daily lives. We want to understand what people do, in addition to what they tell us in an interview, and so we participate as much as we can in ordinary activities. I did interview farmers, but I also worked with some of them on their farms. I also attended several conferences, workshops, and meetings devoted to promoting local food to get an idea of what the bigger conversation about local food was like.

When I started in the summer of 2008, my work focused primarily on CSAs. I interviewed CSA farmers and spent much of the season working on two farms. That work provided a basic understanding of how growers managed their farms and the learning process that helped them develop their direct market systems. During consecutive summers, I continued to attend markets and meet farmers. I also became a member of Practical Farmers of Iowa (PFI), a nonprofit organization that supports alternative agriculture, which allowed me to attend field days during which producers gather at various farms to learn about specific issues, ranging from grazing to crop rotation to poultry butchering.

Summer is the time for farmwork, but winter is the time for farm conferences. I attended several conferences directed at alternative farmers, most of which occurred in January and February, when growers are generally less busy. These included the annual conferences of two Iowa organizations, Practical Farmers of Iowa and the Iowa Network for Community Agriculture, as well as the annual meeting of the Midwest Organic and Sustainable Education Service. The conferences provided important information about current events in farming and local food and allowed me to meet many producers. During these meetings, I had many informal conversations with producers and other participants. I also attended smaller workshops and events; some aimed to bring together producers and institutional buyers, others focused on farm management or finances. I also sat in on a series of five workshops aimed at beginning farmers, hosted in various locations throughout eastern Iowa.

Finally, I became involved in the local farm to school chapter and worked at a specialty greenhouse operation during my research. These

experiences allowed me to fully operate as a participant observer. As a
farm to school member, I assisted the group in purchasing local foods
that would be served in public school lunches. I share this experience and
discuss the potential for farm to school purchasing to scale up local food
production in chapters five and six. At the greenhouse, I worked with
the regular employees on daily operational tasks, including harvesting
and packaging items for sale. I also assisted in the owner's certified organic garden plot, harvesting asparagus and planting sweet potatoes and
cabbages.

In *Making Local Food Work: The Challenges and Opportunities of Today's Small
Farmers*, I attempt to make sense of what the local food system really looks
like from the farmer's perspective. That means thinking about how new
farmers get started in the face of increasing land prices and challenging
rental agreements. It also requires some attention to what direct marketing actually entails—whether the customer is an individual or an institution. I will also spend some time examining how the work gets done on
local food farms—as farmers spend considerable time figuring out how
to find the most efficient source of labor. Finally, we will look at how food
farmers interact with their neighbors, who usually have bigger farms, use
different strategies, and send their products into a complicated processing
system rather than driving them to a farmers' market.

Popular media and marketing portrayals of food farmers as activists
leading the charge into a new paradigm are only part of the local food
story. The reality is, as always, more complicated than the pictures on the
natural foods grocery store walls. The farmers in this book are committed to a new food system, but their approach shows the pragmatism and
level-headedness one would expect of the heartland. Certainly, there is
some fiery rhetoric and a fair amount of grumbling about being the little
guy. There is also, however, a significant amount of cooperation between
conventional and alternative farmers. We like to think that local food
begins and ends with that happy moment at the farmers' market when
the customer procures a bunch of vibrant, soil-encrusted carrots, but this
snapshot ignores the work and regulatory hoops the farmer has already
navigated to get them there. I hope that this book will open the gates to a
better understanding of how our food really gets from farm to table.

CHAPTER TWO

The Stories We Tell

STORIES ABOUT FOOD are everywhere now. Chefs have taken to the *New York Times* and other national media outlets to espouse the most current wisdom about food and agriculture. Major bookstores have not only cookbook sections but entire rows devoted to books telling the stories of food culture, history, production, and consumption. University food studies programs are sprouting like weeds, and having "food" in the title of a class ensures that it will fill quickly. This wealth of information has arguably contributed to a population that knows more about food than ever before. We recount what we have learned at dinner parties—"Did you know that the entire cacao crop in Belize is certified organic?"—as narratives recirculate again and again.[1] We put our new knowledge to work by reading labels carefully and looking for production standards that we can support.

Enter local food, with its emphasis on consumer knowledge and experience. Through local food, consumers go beyond retelling the stories of Op-Ed writers and chefs and begin to construct their own stories of food. Now, at our dinner parties, we can explain how our CSA works and what the farmer had to say that morning at the farmers' market. We describe the day we volunteered at a local farm and picked tomatoes in the heat. We share the best way to use up the kohlrabi that arrives in the CSA share box every week in the late summer.

Despite our increasing ability to have a complex discussion about food production and distribution in our everyday lives, current stories about farming tend to fall into just a couple of categories. The first is the critique of industrial agriculture and call for a new food system. This thread largely dismisses modern agriculture as inherently destructive and controlled by corporations. The second set of narratives portrays local food farming as the embodiment of the agrarian ideal of rural America and the solution to the problems with conventional agriculture. These stories promote local food farmers as heroes changing agriculture, row by row.

In both of these categories, eaters are lost sheep who need help figuring out the complicated food system. With a bit of guidance, we trust that people will do the right thing. Sometimes the tone is instructional, "eat this, not that"; other times, it is motivational, espousing the glory of a freshly dug carrot. Even when the content addresses farming or food production, the audience is nearly always the imagined consumer making a decision about whether to buy organic or conventional produce or where to shop and what to make for dinner. I want to examine some of the stories told about local food farmers and the presumed benefits of the local food system. To do this, we have to place the recent growth of local food into its proper context: largely, the critique of the mainstream food system over the past decades. We should also think about local food and what it can do for all who participate in the food system—or so the story goes.

The attention to the negative effects of conventional agriculture certainly implies that there must be significant social and environmental benefits associated with alternative models such as local food. Indeed, many scholars have suggested that local food systems, with their potential to reconnect producers and consumers, are inherently better positioned than conventional systems to revitalize agriculture and rural communities while improving consumer knowledge of health and food production. Other researchers, however, have exposed the challenges of developing a truly democratic alternative system. Terms such as sustainable and local are difficult to define. Local food systems are not inherently just or democratic, and claims of job-creation potential may be overstated in rural development literature.

I am not suggesting that the challenges negate the potential that local food has to enhance communities and create new markets for entrepreneurial farmers, distributors, and processors. Rather, I am advocating for an eyes-wide-open approach. Local food efforts will suffer if participants continue to assume that they operate in a vacuum, divorced from the rest of the food system. Step one is to realize that local food is one piece of a larger puzzle. Step two is to figure out how to take the best features of that larger system and use them to the advantage of small-scale producers.

———

WE START HEARING stories about farming before most of us can even remember them; learning "Old MacDonald Had a Farm" is a basic shared experience of American childhood. Picture books about farmers line library shelves, and most of us can remember at least one foundational story about farming read aloud to us during our childhoods. My own favorite was Arnold Lobel's *Small Pig*, in which a pig, wearied by the constant tidying by the farmer's wife (she even vacuumed up his beloved mud!), wandered off to the city. He mistook wet concrete for a mud puddle and became stuck. Only after the herculean efforts of the fire and police departments was he reunited with his farm family. Despite the mud-turned-concrete plot twist, the book follows a pretty typical narrative of childhood stories about agriculture. The farm is small and picturesque, the farmer and his wife love their animals and carefully tend their crops, and they all live happily ever after.

In truth, many of the stories told to grown-ups about agriculture, especially local food, are pretty similar. Those picture books tap into and shape our collective ideas about agrarianism and rural life, in which farmers are independent stewards of a healthy food system. We see this portrayal clearly at the grocery store, in what Michael Pollan has called "supermarket pastoral," where happy cows and small farms are shown on every product.[2] Even though the vast majority of Americans do not live—and have not ever lived—on farms, food marketers trust that we will respond to this agrarian imagery.

The agrarian story begins with Thomas Jefferson, our third president, who was burdened with maintaining a burgeoning and experimental democracy. Jefferson was tasked with building the economic base of the country while avoiding the internal unrest and revolution experienced by the country's key ally, France. Jefferson saw farmers as fundamental to strengthening a new democracy because he believed that productive, independent landowners could best make economic use of the country's vast natural resources. Thus, developing policies that distributed populations across the rural landscape and bestowed them with economic and political power was a win–win. The independent farmer became, in Jefferson's view, the cornerstone of a sustainable democratic society.[3] In addition to this functional, economic foundation, agrarianism has a moral framework based on self-sufficiency, relationship with the environment, and community. Farmers, through their economic independence and close relationship with their land, embody these fundamentally American principles.

The pastoral, agrarian ideal still has resonance in media, marketing, and politics. This is especially obvious to Iowans every four years, when presidential candidates host media events constructed to look like intimate country picnics, complete with checkered tablecloths and buttered sweet corn. These events mask the real rural challenges of depopulation, school mergers, and increasing wealth disparity, all of which critics have tied to modern agriculture. Anthropologist Katherine Marie Dudley explains that we look to our rural communities to find beauty and order, but "the realities of technology and industrial society insistently intrude, reminding us of 'the machine's increasing domination of the visible world.'"[4] Likewise, poet and farmer Wendell Berry writes, "in all this, few people whose testimony would have mattered have seen the connection between the 'modernization' of agricultural techniques and the disintegration of the culture and the communities of farming."[5] Although we still popularly ascribe to the agrarian ideal of the American countryside, where yeoman farmers embody the fundamental principles of democracy and equality, this perspective hides the realities of modern agriculture, which,[1] as many have pointed out, have negatively affected rural economies, health, and culture.

The story of local food ultimately combines our shared imagery of agrarianism, agriculture, and rural life. The first step in arguing for the superiority of local food is to critique current agricultural practices so as to expose "the machine in the garden" and the disconnect between what we want to believe and what we know about modern-day food production.[6] Although rural, agriculture life is marketed as a quaint utopia, in reality, farming is highly technological and there are relatively few people actually doing the farming. Next, local food is placed as the only path to true agrarianism because it emphasizes small scale agriculture in which plants and animals are tended with care. In this narrative, alternative production reroots agriculture in our local communities, reinvigorating rural landscapes with environmentally sensitive food production and democratic engagement.

The social science critique of modern agriculture probably began with the early work of anthropologist Walter Goldschmidt, who laid the foundation for much of the research in American agriculture during the second half of the twentieth century.[7] Goldschmidt's work in California focused on three communities, which he called Wasco, Arvin, and Dinuba. The themes that surface from this work can be seen throughout the literature that followed. Regarding Wasco, Goldschmidt links social problems, including conflict among community members and lack of resources, to what he calls "influences exerted from outside the community."[8] As corporate entities, such as distant agribusiness firms, consolidate power and resources outside the community, local people become less able to make democratic decisions about their own towns and neighborhoods.

Comparing Arvin and Dinuba, Goldschmidt presents what might be considered his most controversial assertion: larger average farm sizes in agricultural communities lead to more social problems. Conversely, smaller average farm size is associated with better quality of life in the community. Goldschmidt ultimately argues that data from his study in the 1940s is a model for the country as a whole, especially reflecting the changes in social class in rural communities. His work reflects an agrarian ideal as he states that family farms are more "conducive to democratic rural communities."[9] Like Jefferson, Goldschmidt drew parallels between landownership and engagement. Farmers who are economically independent and successful will contribute to the democratic process, empowering communities. His work was seen as an attack on modern agriculture and was broadly maligned by politicians and farm organizations in California, creating a public controversy that played out in several statewide newspapers after its publication.[10]

Many other researchers have followed Goldschmidt, looking for relationships between farming and social and economic health. Those with a social science approach have largely agreed with his results and support what has become known as the Goldschmidt hypothesis. Those whose approach is more grounded in economic analysis without social context are more likely to criticize Goldschmidt's work. Some of these studies examine the relationship between farmer and farmworker income and farm size. They find that there is a positive statistical relationship between larger farms and income for both farmers and farmworkers, though farmers' incomes remain higher than farmworkers' incomes.[11] Others point out that it is difficult to clearly and consistently measure farm structure or organization, let alone then apply those measures to other parts of the community. Farms are complex. Some researchers have questioned the utility of statistical comparisons between a farm practice and socioeconomic measures from elsewhere in the community.[12] Others suggest that the two communities he compared, Arvin and Dinuba, were less similar than Goldschmidt had claimed, making them incompatible for analysis.[13]

Although Goldschmidt's name is rarely noted outside academic circles, his critique of conventional agriculture has become well-trod ground for both journalists and popular writers. Ultimately, what Goldschmidt and his supporters have repeatedly suggested over the decades is that large-scale agriculture is not consistent with the agrarian ideals of an empowered, democratic rural society. In Jefferson's vision, landowning farmers were ideal citizens. Because of their ties to the land and power of ownership, they were the best equipped to make community level decisions. The work that criticizes the modern farming system suggests that decision-making power has been removed from farmers and others in rural communities.

Among the various critiques of the current state of agriculture, many focus on the political landscape that supports current production practices and ultimately benefits corporate interests more than farmers or rural people. Over the course of the twentieth century, American agricultural policy became consistently more favorable to corporate interests. Corporations that are vertically integrated, taking control of multiple segments of the production process, have particular advantages. A vertically integrated poultry company, for example, owns the birds and contracts with farmers who are responsible for overseeing the hatching or growing process in barns that they pay to build themselves. When the birds are mature, the company buys them from the farmer at a predetermined price and then sends them to its own processing facilities to wind up as meat with a Sara Lee or Tyson label. The corporations benefit enormously from grain prices that are held artificially low through federal subsidies—either in the form of direct payments or newer insurance plans. It is difficult to make the argument that farmers in this system are truly independent agrarians. Instead, in this example, they play the role of a contractor and are a small part of a very complicated processing network, largely under the control of federal policy and corporations.[14]

Although the agrarian ideal no longer applies to conventional farming, it has been embraced by alternative producers in search of a new agrarianism. Historian Paul Thompson suggests, however, that agrarianism is not well understood by either scholars or lay people: "As a philosophical tradition, agrarian thought emphasizes the idea that farming practices have the power to shape the moral character of the individuals who engage in them, and that a society's farming culture—its means of subsistence— reverberates through all institutions."[15] The recognition that subsistence strategies are related to other realms of social interaction is not unique to agrarianism. As an anthropologist, I often teach these ideas in introductory courses. Students clearly get how, for example, a hunter-gatherer society that has no storage capacity must rely on food sharing. That sharing ethic permeates other areas of social life. Relationships between subsistence and society today are less visible to American students, who find it hard to see how our mechanisms of food production reproduce themselves in other arenas. One aim of the contemporary local food movement is to make the relationships of conventional agriculture more visible, and then transform them into a more sustainable system.

The principles of the new agrarianism include careful land stewardship and long-term investment. Another key tenet is that of private property. The agrarian ideal emphasizes morality and encourages it in all interactions. Thus, the moral (or appropriate) use of private property ensures long-term stability and ecological enhancement rather than degradation. One must be able to care intimately and carefully. This approach encourages landowners to be the primary operators and discourages distant landlord-tenant relationships. This perspective also leads to an intense independence, a DIY ethic, and a distrust of governmental interference.

Historically, Jefferson believed that farmers were the ideal citizens because of their economic independence and ability to thrive without governmental support.[16] This presumed independence is one reason agrarianism has been linked with local food. Because local food farmers do not benefit from the direct support subsidies typical in commodity production, they appear to be more independent than conventional farmers.

Agrarians view the household as the fundamental unit of production. Centering economic activity on the household improves self-sufficiency and reduces reliance on the market. Purchasing items not produced on the farm not only reduces the landowners self-sufficiency, it also invites negative cultural influences and increased materialism through participation in modern market exchange. If complete independence is impossible, agrarians argue, a community-level system of exchange and sharing should be implemented. Resistance to outside influences is a strong thread of agrarianism that extends well beyond producing one's own food and into other areas of life. Eric Freyfogle writes that "outside the land-use realm, individual agrarians can successfully resist outside pressures they dislike — by home schooling and religious worship, for instance."[17]

The presumed moral relationship between food production and society can be difficult to apply to a modern context. Past agrarians had clear religious traditions to lean on and help direct their morality. Implicit in these traditions were clear-cut roles dictated by one's gender, race, and social status. The new agrarians now must develop a system that allows for modern sensibilities related to gender, race, and imbalances in power. Further, the agrarian tendency toward libertarian values often eliminates government regulation as a way to adjust inequality. Past mainstream American models of religious morality have not been particularly favorable to disenfranchised populations, particularly women and minorities. How, then, can the new agrarians promote a fair and just system?

Local food seems to be the answer. Many scholars and activists, even without delving specifically into agrarian ideologies, have written about the social and community benefits in local food systems. For one, the direct market relationship appears to avoid corporate markets and interests. Because farmers in this system produce food crops rather than a commodity that will go on to be processed further, they are presumed to have more self-sufficient households. The ethos of shared, community knowledge is another theme that resonates with agrarian ideology, and several scholars have pointed out that alternative agriculture is predicated on the lateral sharing of knowledge between farmers.[18]

In addition, the new agrarians argue that local food increases consumer knowledge. "People don't know where their food comes from" is a common lament in the local food movement. But when a customer goes to a farmers' market and buys tomatoes from the person who grew them, presumably that customer learns a little something about food production in the process. This is what sociologist Thomas Lyson calls "civic agriculture."[19] He envisioned a food system that is closely connected to its local community so that eaters are knowledgeable about the processes of food production and farmers are accountable to their neighbors. Thus, there is no impersonal market; instead, each economic interaction has a social component. People know one another and their interactions are a fundamental part of the monetary exchange. From Lyson's standpoint, local food systems that connect producers and consumers seem to resist the standard market model by encouraging social rather than purely economic relationships. Because farmers are accountable to their neighbors, these linkages result in agricultural production that is less environmentally destructive. In return, consumers understand and advocate for farmers by purchasing their products and supporting farm-friendly policies.[20]

Community-supported agriculture has received particular attention as a way to build relationships between farmers and eaters. Even researchers, not known for their flowery or emotional language, have written about CSA quite poetically. One notes that "a CSA is a way to bind people into a tight social group together through the shared effort, travails, and gratifications of producing their own food."[21] A study in Iowa suggests that "CSA as a community-focused food systems model transcends the conventional boundaries between producer and consumer and rural and urban."[22] Another, in Ohio, states that "CSAs are a political and philosophical statement about the relationships that should inhere between producers and consumers, between people and the land, in short, the relationships that form a community of people, embedded in place."[23] These do not sound like the typical dry statements of dispassionate scholars. They

reflect an optimism about the potential for local food to serve as a fundamentally new way for people to interact around food. Rather than simply
picking up a bell pepper at the grocery store, consumers are able to participate in the production of their own food. This engagement, according
to some, can improve people's relationships with each other and create a
community fully invested in agriculture and sustainable food production.

Farmers' markets have received their fair share of attention as well.
As keystones of a local food system, they also appear to increase social
cohesiveness and community relationships.[24] The farmers' market is the
one-stop-shop in local food. The presence of a mix of farmers along with
bakers, jam makers, and other craft people encourages diverse production in a community as each vendor sets him or herself apart from the
rest. The markets are also sites of economic transactions that have social
components, the kind that Thomas Lyson and others see as the basis for a
strong community. Further, many markets now include live music, cooking demonstrations, and activities for children. As a result, the farmers'
market becomes more than just a place to shop. It is a valuable community
space that includes opportunities for recreation and leisure in addition to
purchasing food.[25]

In short, a lot of research strongly supports local food as a fundamentally different way for consumers to interact with the food system. But
there is always the other side of the coin to consider. For example, despite
eloquent statements about CSAs, the level of customer commitment is a
constant question and challenge for growers. Overall, most CSAs often
lose up to half of their shareholders each year.[26] CSA member surveys and
interviews show that most of the shareholders are primarily interested in
the food, more so than the experience of growing it.[27] And research on
the experiences of CSA managers is somewhat bleak. Despite the ideals
of member participation and engagement, the burden ultimately falls on
the farmer to ensure that he or she produces enough food to pack the
shareholders' boxes every week. Direct marketing is simultaneously an
opportunity and a challenge. The farmer gets to keep all the dollars that
would otherwise go to a distributor, processor, or marketer. Of course,
the farmer then becomes the distributor, processor, and marketer, doing
the work of three other people in addition to the central job as farmer. In
contrast to the optimism associated with local food, CSA farmers some-

times feel exhausted and disappointed when the workload is too great and customers feel the return on investment is too low.[28]

When it comes to farmers' markets, its not always clear exactly what customers learn about agriculture or how they act on any new knowledge they do obtain. Swedish researchers interviewed farmers' market customers about their knowledge of the ecology and environmental impact of food production. They found that although customers were aware that the food at the market was produced nearby, most were not very interested in the fact that the food was local.[29] In addition, most respondents indicated that they gained very little knowledge about agricultural practices or the ecological implications of food production as a result of their interactions with farmers at the market. The researchers asserted, however, that there were numerous opportunities for learning about food, especially in the potential to develop a better understanding of seasonality and biodiversity. As they say, you can lead a horse to water, but you can't make him drink. Just because there are opportunities for learning about agriculture at the farmers' market does not mean that patrons will automatically take advantage of them.

In addition to examining the potential for knowledge change at farmers' markets, it is also important to think about who feels welcome and able to attend. A significant criticism of local food is that it is not available to the poor because it is too expensive and is limited to specialty food outlets. While local food is often seen as the ultimate win–win situation, in which farmers can use a variety of sales and marketing methods and people have better access to healthy food, low-income consumers are often at a disadvantage.[30] Food prices that will support farmers' livelihoods are often too high for low-income consumers. Farmers want to make a living, and the farmers' market or CSA may allow them to charge a high enough price to do that. For a low-income consumer, however, these local food options may be out of reach. Local food farmers and advocates often point out that Americans spend a lower percentage of their incomes on food than in the past. But Americans also now pay quite a bit more for housing, transportation, education, and childcare than a generation ago. Those who are already stretched thin do not have the flexibility to spend a higher percentage of their income on food.

Even more troubling are researchers' consistent findings that farmers'

markets and other alternative food networks are not welcoming to people
of color. Based on interviews with CSA operators and farmers' market
managers, Julie Guthman found that a widespread spirit of universalism,
the idea that local food is for everyone, actually reinforces the whiteness
of alternative food outlets and, in her study, especially marginalizes African Americans. For example, markets tend to be located in more affluent
neighborhoods, which are also overwhelmingly white. People from outside
the neighborhood, especially those who stand out because of their race, do
not find these settings to be inclusive. But when asked why people of color
do not participate in farmers' markets and CSAs, the market managers
noted that people would eat better if they only knew how their food was
produced. Instead of realizing that the market may be unwelcoming, they
identified the population as ignorant. Another common reason given for
people of color not participating is that it is not part of their culture or lifestyle. Guthman points out that this view automatically portrays the other
lifestyle as less progressive and less ethical than that of the usually white
speaker. Finally, the assumption that local food markets are inherently
welcoming, that what we present attracts all, relieves the managers of the
responsibility of reaching out to potential African American consumers.[31]

Researchers in Memphis found that even when markets and county-
level health departments specifically attempt to alleviate inequality by
implementing programs such as the Supplemental Nutrition Assistance
Program (SNAP) or the Senior Farmers Market Nutritional Program
(SFMNP) at farmers' markets, the results are sometimes unexpected. Because of a number of complications with rolling out a new program, the
implementation of SFMNP in Memphis only allowed the use of vouchers
at the large, mostly white and more affluent, downtown market. Only
after voucher users protested by making repeated calls to the county office
did policies change to better serve the older, mostly African American,
population as intended.[32] Like Guthman, the Memphis researchers found
that local food markets are not inherently welcoming for all; instead, in-
clusiveness may only be achieved by making barriers and marginalization
obvious. Despite these challenges, the growth in farmers' markets and alternative food outlets has not been solely for the benefit of the white middle
class. Programs such as Growing Power, run by Will Allen in Milwaukee,

and SAAFON (Southeastern African American Farmers' Organic Network) as well as thriving historic Chinatown markets in San Francisco and Seattle and an increasing number of Hmong refugee vendors in Minneapolis all indicate broader local food activism and success.

These issues related to inclusion and consumer knowledge are part of the overall context of community enhancement and relationships. Ultimately, promoting local food as a way to build community relationships presumes that communities, even the smallest ones, are of one mind about how to solve the problems they face. We tend to assume that a food system that is managed locally will be more reflective of the community's needs than a larger scale structure that serves global markets. In reality, diversity in experiences and opinions often leads to community-level disagreement. Further, because there are populations that remain marginalized at the local level, just as they are marginalized in other contexts, local disputes often result in inequitable outcomes. Disputes over pesticide drift in California, for example, disproportionately emphasize the burden of drift on suburban and exurban, largely white communities and ignore farmworkers, who have much higher rates of pesticide exposure.[33] We assume that a global system is somehow fundamentally different than a local one because the larger systems are only motivated by profit and people do not know one another. But local systems are equally imperfect, and some people are valued more than others even at the local level. A better approach is to recognize that just because something is local does not mean that it automatically resists all the problems associated with national and global food distribution."[34] Instead, both are imperfect and they often resemble and react with each other. Put simply, the local and global are more related than they are opposed.

Researchers in Canada provide an example of how local systems do not automatically result in community enhancement. They assessed the extent to which local food initiatives have the potential to improve the social economy and increase the presence of social justice and equity in Vancouver, British Columbia, and Edmonton, Alberta. As in the United States, the current popularity and salience of local food make developing a local food infrastructure attractive to city planners and policymakers. The authors found, however, that when cities try to increase local food, social justice takes a backseat to economic growth. Ultimately, the commitment to the market and ideologies of profit and entrepreneurship are inconsistent with principles of sustainability and justice that are the supposed basis of local food systems. For example, producers were wary of risking their own businesses and taking responsibility for investing in the necessary infrastructure. If a farm or market is looking for investors to fund an expansion, they have to prove that the business will be profitable, not that it will be socially responsible. Investors want to see risk management and profitability, not food access or economic restructuring. Even social-justice–minded farmers end up conforming to the conventions of economic growth to ensure the survival of their business.[35]

Ultimately, the pastoral utopia associated with agriculture often obscures the extent to which food production, for both global and local outlets, remains deeply embedded in a capitalist market philosophy. Local politics are frequently exclusionary and decisions continue to be made by those who have access to the most resources. Community-supported agriculture and farmers' markets are often only supported by and available to the wealthiest community members. Even when institutions attempt to be for everyone, they often inadvertently exclude marginalized populations.

Although the social ideals of local food may fall short, the economic argument is becoming more forceful. Those who have taken an unapologetically economic approach appear optimistic about the potential for local food to make a positive impact. Smaller farms that produce labor-intensive crops such as fruits and vegetables may provide more on-farm jobs than grain farms that require very little human labor. Despite the high workload, economists also point out that farmers who "assume responsibility for additional supply chain functions, such as processing, distribution, and marketing, capture revenue that would otherwise accrue to a third party."[36] Rather than sharing the price of a tomato with the distributors who move it from one place to the next and the grocery store that sells it, the local farmer keeps the entire sale price for him or herself.

Another way to study the economic impact of local food is to look at its community impact, especially with regard to job creation and, to some extent, social improvement. Community impact studies provide data that tends to be regionally specific, making it difficult to generalize nationally.

But many studies have found that people are optimistic about the social and economic benefits of local food systems.[37] Farmers' market managers who were surveyed in the mid-Atlantic region reported that their markets enhanced the community by providing a place for social activity in addition to a sales outlet for small farmers.[38] In Michigan, researchers used remarkably specific economic modeling to project up to 1,889 new jobs if "existing producers double or triple the amount of fruits and vegetables they sell into fresh produce markets."[39] The authors suggest that their calculations are conservative, and even more jobs could be generated as farms continue to expand and food entrepreneurs innovate. A similar analysis in Mississippi was less optimistic about job creation, noting that the seasonality of farmers' markets limits consistent job availability. In addition, the authors point out that the potential for any market to generate jobs depends on the size of that market and the willingness of local governments to provide some infrastructure or support.[40] Thus, the potential for job creation at farmers' markets depends on the location and popularity of the market as well as the ability—or perhaps willingness—of vendors to increase their production and/or innovate by developing new products.

A report by the Union of Concerned Scientists attempts to develop some generalizable national numbers and asserts a high estimate of 5.4 jobs created per farmers' market and a low estimate of 2.4 jobs per market. These numbers represent full-time equivalent (FTE) jobs, which means that several part-time or temporary positions could add up to the equivalent of 5.4 forty-hour-a-week, year-round positions.[41] The report adds a rare caveat, pointing out the difficulty of nationalizing regional assumptions and noting that "there is no evidence that the job implications of farmers' markets in, say, Oklahoma or West Virginia are representative of the job growth that could be expected in other regions."[42] Furthermore, this report is one of the few that addresses the prevalence of volunteer labor in local food systems. Although using volunteer labor is a common strategy among farmers and is heavily promoted by local food advocates, it is rarely addressed critically in the literature on local food. Proponents see two key benefits in volunteer labor. First, farmers save money by replacing costly employees with free labor. Second, the community becomes more agriculturally literate as people who are not farmers learn about food production. Volunteer labor does not, however, make any economic contribution to a local community, nor does it encourage consumers to pay the real cost for their food. The failure of researchers to include volunteer labor in their work is an important shortcoming if the goal is to truly understand the economic impact of local food.

In Iowa, the potential for local food as a rural development strategy has engaged both academics and policymakers. Dairy farmer and recent candidate for Iowa Secretary of Agriculture Francis Thicke claimed that local food could be a multibillion dollar opportunity creating thousands of jobs.[43] A report for the Iowa Department of Agriculture and Land Stewardship attributed 374 direct jobs and 200 indirect jobs to farmers' markets in 2009, with an overall estimated sales of $38.4 million.[44] While these numbers appear small, particularly the number of jobs created, the report contends that local food is important to Iowa's economy. Economist Dave Swenson has done extensive modeling of the potential impact of local food in Iowa. In one scenario, he estimates that if Iowa farmers were to meet the daily fruit and vegetable needs of the state's residents (with the highly unlikely assumption that Iowans will regularly consume five servings of fruit and vegetables a day), it would sustain "$331.2 million in total economic output, $123.3 million in total labor income and 4,484 total jobs in Iowa," far outstripping the estimates of the researchers in Michigan.[45] Even economists can wax poetic about the community benefits of local food. Noting that face-to-face interactions between producers and consumers develop cohesive communities, Swenson writes, that "mere economic gains may be the least of the reasons for promoting local foods production and consumption among community members."[46]

The number of stories about local food has grown nearly as quickly as the number of people attending farmers' markets, and like local food itself, the stories are diverse and sometimes contradictory. It is clear that we need a better understanding of both community and economic benefits. Local food may, indeed, develop new knowledge and social relationships, but it does so within the context of our market economy. Examining only the number of potential FTEs misses important social components, but looking at farmers' markets primarily as social events is equally limiting.

The possibility that social change may happen within a market context can be uncomfortable for some; locavores like to imagine that food production is unsullied by the machine in the garden or the invisible hand of the market. But for better or worse, "the market is where society increasingly spends its time and attention" and social movements will occur as much within the market place as elsewhere.[47]

An inclusive approach requires a clear understanding of local food producers, including how they relate to the industrial system, how they approach business decisions about scale and labor, and how they interact with the various markets available to them. We have to tell their stories thoroughly. In the next chapters, I hope to illuminate some of the hidden portions of the system. Local food farmers interact with market managers and regulations, county and state regulators, meat lockers, and the media. When selling to institutions, farmers contend with another layer of regulations and bureaucracy. Finding and maintaining farm labor is another key component, one that shows how the social aspects of civic agriculture can be applied beyond the producer-consumer interaction. All of these interactions are ignored when we focus on agrarian self-sufficiency or farmers' interactions with their buyers. In the next chapter, I look at Iowa's agricultural history. From the start, agricultural policy helped to create a farm state that, far from being self-reliant, has always leaned on federal and state support structures, lenders, and outside agricultural research to exist.

CHAPTER THREE

Old Systems, New Farmers

WHEN YOU TELL stories about farmers, you quickly learn that it is never just about farmers. As I began interviewing growers and working on farms, I anticipated hearing about how they learned new production strategies or first understood how to operate a CSA. Maybe I would hear about someone figuring out, through trial and error, that the sandy soil on his or her farm was ideally suited for carrots. I thought I would hear a lot about how direct market farmers figured out how to most efficiently pack a CSA share or get their products to a farmers' market. And I did hear about those things quite a bit. But I also heard a lot about the Iowa State University Extension and Outreach Service, nonprofits such as Practical Farmers of Iowa and the Women's Food and Agriculture Network (WFAN), plus USDA agencies such as the Natural Resource Conservation Service (NRCS) and the Resource Conservation and Development (RC&D) programs. I quickly realized that farmers are as conversant in agricultural acronyms as they are in soil health. Part of figuring out how to farm also means figuring out what programs are available to you, and which, if any, will actually be beneficial. I also heard about access to land, which is one of the biggest barriers to start or expand a farm. With fully half of all Iowa farmland under some sort of rental agreement, growers looking to start or expand their own farm compete with other renters and potential buyers. From growers just starting out, I heard about the financial programs and low-interest loans available to beginning farmers. Farmers also talked about their rental arrangements and the sometimes complicated negotiations with their landlords.

In this chapter, I look at the various ways in which local food farmers interact with the many, many agencies that purport to offer some form of agricultural support, either through loan and grant programs, workshops, and education or through technical consulting offered by Iowa State University Extension and Outreach. Agriculture has always been a complex industry, with many interrelated components, including legislators, corporate interests, university researchers, agricultural degree programs, lenders, equipment dealers, and nonprofit and producers' associations dedicated to enhancing agriculture in some way. Many direct market farmers first come into contact with these organizations as they begin their operations and start the process of accessing land and equipment. Those who have been in local food production longer recounted to me the ways that organizations have, over time and with varied success, provided support for the changing local food movement. In many cases, both new and experienced food farmers have difficulty finding their fit within all of these organizations. There is a long trajectory of support for conventional commodity production in Iowa, which often ignores the needs of a CSA or a small-scale direct market beef producer.

When we tell the story of agriculture in Iowa, we tend to focus on its high productivity and look for easy, straightforward explanations. Why does Iowa produce more corn and soybeans than any other state? Because the soil is excellent and our farmers work hard. What about all those hogs? Conveniently, they like to eat the corn. Both of these things are true, but they do not fully explain why agriculture looks the way it does. A complex history of political and business interests has literally shaped the landscape since the state was first opened for settlement in 1832. It is well known that agricultural policy and agribusiness have been most friendly to large-scale farming. Even as the state was being settled, the earliest land purchases tended to promote high debt loads and labor-intensive family management. The fencerow-to-fencerow policies of the 1970s, along with improvements in equipment and chemical inputs, which reduced the need for family labor, further encouraged land consolidation and increased farm size.

There is enormous historic momentum and power behind the conventional system. Despite our tendency to revert to simplistic stories about hard-working farmers who singlehandedly transformed the Iowa prairie into a productive landscape, agriculture would not exist in its current form if not for extensive public investment. It is true that the soil is excellent for farming. Thanks to the residue from the last glacier that receded about twelve thousand years ago, followed by thousands of years of tall grass prairie whose annual cycles of dormancy and decomposition further enriched the topsoil, Iowa agricultural land is some of the best. It is true as well that farmers have tended to be a hard-working lot. They are also historically tied to debt. The state was largely settled before the Homestead Act of 1852, which means that early settlers purchased their land rather than claiming it. But at $1.25 per acre, or two hundred dollars per quarter section, the cost was prohibitive for many individual settlers. As a result, speculators and lenders bought land and raised interest rates to astronomical levels. Theoretically, the high price of land should have resulted in corporate rather than individual or family ownership. But the prairie did not go down without a fight, and the heavy labor necessary to turn prairie sod into agricultural land was best accomplished by a family. Hired labor was cost-prohibitive for corporations, in part because many potential laborers, rather than remain employed by others, worked just long enough to afford their own farms. Historian W. G. Murray declared a "clean-cut victory" of family farms over the large-scale corporate unit. The high cost of land also built a system based on mortgage and debt, making those very same farm families vulnerable to the boom-bust cycle that characterized the 1900s.[1]

Even if the family farm prevailed over corporate interests in the early days of settlement thanks to the family members' individual hard work, investments in commercial agriculture during the last century have laid the groundwork for the current system. The early 1900s saw the development of irrigation projects in the West and the addition of rural delivery by the US Postal Service and the Federal Post Roads Act in 1916, which supported the creation of rural highways. In addition, government regulated credit systems, foreign and domestic trade, and subsidized early fertilizer imports, which later gave way to direct commodity subsidies, enhanced markets, and credit opportunities for farmers. So-called intangible investments in research, education, and information were also critical. The most fundamental of these was the land-grant university system, which provided the intangible elements of research and education as well as direct outreach to farmers to enhance their productive capacity.[2]

The land-grant university system was founded by the Land-Grant Col-

lege Act of 1862 (also known as the Morrill Act) and was later complimented
by the Hatch Act of 1887, which appropriated funds for agricultural experiment stations. One of the land-grant colleges, Iowa State University
(Iowa State College until 1959), has long been recognized as a major center
of agricultural research. The interaction of research, industry, and federal
policy, however, has often drawn criticism. While the land-grant university
system was created by a federal mandate, ostensibly each institution is beholden to the people of the individual state. The realities of federal funding
often call state loyalties into question, particularly during times of national
need such as war or economic crisis. Nobel Prize–winning agricultural
economist Theodore W. Schultz was ultimately forced to resign his post at
Iowa State College in 1943 after overseeing a publication suggesting that
margarine could be an effective butter substitute in the context of wartime
rationing. Iowa dairy producers saw the publication as a political move
that would promote cotton production rather than their own homegrown
products (cottonseed oil was a key ingredient in margarine). This public
attack on academic research from the dairy industry and the Iowa State
Farm Bureau raised the question of the appropriate function of research
in a land-grant university.[3]

That question has been asked repeatedly throughout the twentieth century as social scientists and alternative agriculture advocates continuously
pointed out that corporate involvement in land-grant universities affects
how research is carried out and disseminated to the public.[4] Corporate
fundraising in particular—for instance, an agribusiness firm's gift of a
million dollars to the Iowa State University College of Agriculture for
building renovation or its contribution to graduate student scholarships
aimed at genetic seed research—causes some to wonder whether the University can truly carry out legitimate, unbiased scientific research that
serves Iowa's farmers. Of course, land-grant universities are feeling the
reduction in state and federal funding just like other public institutions
nationwide. Like many others, therefore, they largely turn to private funding to support their research programs. As a result, both the research and
outreach missions of land-grant universities have dovetailed nicely with
the interests of agribusiness.

Corporations also exert influence more directly by serving on advisory boards for agricultural colleges and departments. Representatives from both Monsanto and Pioneer Hi-Bred (a DuPont company that merged with Dow Chemical in late 2015) are on the advisory board of the Plant Science Institute at Iowa State University. Faculty have received millions in grant support from various agribusinesses, and the funder effect, in which research conclusions tend to be favorable to private funders, has been repeatedly found in research throughout the food and agriculture sectors.[5] Ultimately, the research conducted at a land-grant university tends to support the funding agency (possibly a corporation) and also to trickle down through extension services. Thus, if corporate-sponsored research supports the use of a genetically modified crop or new herbicide, farmers will hear about it from both their corporate seed salesman and their extension agent. These behind-the-scenes relationships and influences lead to an agricultural industry that appears monolithic, with corporate interests, research agendas, and outreach services in lockstep.

Iowa's land-grant institution continues to play a huge role in agriculture throughout the state. Most producers come into contact with Iowa State University through its extension and outreach service. When it comes to local food production, the farmers I spoke with had mixed reviews. Certified organic producer Renee Johnson-Berry referenced the extension service's historic ties to chemically intensive conventional agriculture but notes that it has gotten much better. She explains:

> When I started out, extension service was very chemically oriented, hugely chemically oriented, and so they were helpful in some respects, like what varieties were good, trees and stuff like that. But I didn't find them exceptionally helpful in, you know, pest management . . . but they've made huge, huge, huge strides. When you say the word organic, they don't go, you know, "What?!" I mean I've come from a place from where organic was a completely foreign word, nobody knew what it was, to now . . . it's at HyVee.

Johnson-Berry spent many years advocating for organic certification standards in Iowa and nationally. Her comment points to another element of the extension service's history: although extension services across the country have been complicit in the development of conventional agriculture, they have been almost completely absent, until recently, in organic production.

Some producers are openly antagonistic toward ISU Extension and Outreach. One family would not allow any representative from ISU on their farm and only agreed to let me visit them after they were reassured several times by a mutual friend that I was not affiliated in any way with ISU or the extension service. Another CSA producer recounted to me that he alienated the local extension agent by openly disagreeing about a planned community garden space. During a public discussion about what varieties of tomatoes to plant in a formerly flooded area, the agent automatically proposed hybrids, arguing that they were sturdier and more productive. The CSA grower contradicted him, pointing out that heirloom varieties are often more hardy because they have developed in more biodiverse environments and have had to be competitive. The agent didn't like this and has not had further interaction with the CSA farm.

Other producers had less antagonistic relationships but simply felt the service had nothing to offer them. When asked about whether he interacted with it, one hog producer, stated: "If they had something to offer I might. But they don't have anything to offer. What do they have to offer me? Nothing!" Neal Jackson, a specialty microgreens grower, is well acquainted with his local agent; however, the agent has not been particularly useful in Neal's operation: "There's been times when I've talked to him or people in the plant pathology department in Ames about different [issues], like mold and disease in the crops. Primarily their response is, 'well, you know more about it than I do so . . .' They helped identify some things, but as far as what to do about it, they haven't really been able to help me out much at all." The mixed reactions of alternative farmers to the extension service is consistent with those who suggest that the land-grant approach tends to favor large producers. There was a general sense among most farmers I talked to that the service simply does not work for their type of farming. Agents, trained to promote the best practices of ISU and its industry partners, are sometimes at a loss when it comes to advising small-scale or organic growers.

Our agricultural systems did not sprout and grow without significant tending by political and corporate interests. To continue the analogy, we reap what we sow. Though federal dollars supported the earliest infrastructure, private interests have slowly picked up the slack. Now, the industry is a complex articulation between policy, research, and corporate interests. By and large, extension services distill and disseminate information and advice that reflect the dominant paradigm of large-scale commodity production. As a result, alternative and local food farmers sometimes find it hard to find their place in this system. It is clear that there is momentum behind local food, but it is difficult for the behemoth of conventional agriculture to nimbly shift to supporting alternative production in a meaningful way.

It is no secret that agriculture has trended big over the past decades. It is also trending old, with the average age of a farmer now at about fifty-eight years of age. In 2007, landowners over the age of seventy-four held 28 percent of Iowa's farmland—a higher percentage than any other group. This statistic in particular has the attention of policymakers who want to ensure that agricultural land in the state remains in the hands of Iowa farmers rather than out-of-state landowners. As a result, there has been significant attention to developing a population of new and beginning farmers in the state. All the agricultural acronyms referenced so far have some programming devoted to beginning farmers, related to both conventional and alternative production.

The emphasis on developing new farmers is especially relevant to the local food movement, which, if it is to continue to grow, requires both farmers and farms dedicated to direct market production. As Iowa State economists Duffy and Smith point out, "the age of a landowner affects probabilities of land transfer in the future. Land ownership turnover is of interest to state and local leaders because it may reflect conditions in the agricultural economy and carries implications for agriculture's future in the state."[6] Put another way, it matters who purchases and owns Iowa's farmland because that will affect the kind of agriculture that is practiced. Local food advocates understand this and know that training new farmers and helping them access farmland is critical to the development of a viable local food system in Iowa.

Agricultural census data categorize landowners into three groups: those older than 65 (late stage), between 35 and 64 (midstage), and younger than

35 (early stage). The proportion of land owned by those older than 65 years of age has increased from 29 percent in 1982 to 56 percent in 2012.[7] In fact, in 2012, the specific age group that owned the largest percentage of land (30 percent) was landowners over 74 years of age.[8] Simultaneously, the percentage of land owned by early stage owners has plummeted from 11 percent in 1982 to just 4 percent in 2007.[9] Although the overall trends show increasing ownership by older owners, landownership by early stage owners did more recently increase, from just under 3 percent in 2007 to 4 percent in 2012.[10]

These numbers reflect all agricultural land in the state and do not solely focus on local food or alternative production. Given the recent interest in local food production, it is reasonable to assume that at least some agricultural land will transition out of commodity production and into food production in the coming decades. The 2007 agricultural census reported an increase in the number of small farms nationwide between 2002 and 2007, though, according to the most recent census, those numbers have leveled off.[11] The potential for more land to transition into food production provides an exciting opportunity for the local food movement, but only if there are farmers who can access land and who have the skills to develop a viable local food operation.

But how does a new farmer really get started in Iowa? Given the availability of resources, it seems as if it should be easy. A number of financial incentives, including state and federal loan programs, target beginning farmers. These loan programs offer low interest rates on major purchases such as land and equipment to potential producers who have evidence of farming experience. To encourage rental agreements that open opportunities for new farmers, there are tax credits for landowners who rent to beginning farmers. For beginning farmers there are also a wide array of workshops and field days that explain machinery, fencing, land use, production practices, and livestock handling. Some organizations offer direct mentorship programs that pair experienced farmers with new farmers.

Beginning farmers, like most of the rest of us, have heard the stories of the agrarian utopia of the countryside. Those who wish to go into alternative production have the additional pressure of being the ones who will fundamentally change the food system through local food or organic methods. There is great excitement surrounding new farmers, and they are receiving a lot of attention in Iowa. Their actual stories, however, can be sobering, and beginning farmer programs, especially those developed by organizations traditionally beholden to conventional production, may miss the mark for alternative producers. The existence of such programs does not inherently mean that they are helpful or that farmers will be able to use them. State and federal opportunities often require lengthy and detailed applications or proposals with restrictions on how funds are used. Even local programs can be daunting, especially for a young farmer going into business for the first time. These farmers operate in an agricultural system that has historically promoted large-scale commodity production. Even though the largest organizations, such as land-grant university agricultural schools and extension services, are now promoting local food as a viable agricultural practice, seeing real change is like trying to turn the *Titanic*.

In fact, the very range and variety of organizations and programs can be daunting for a new farmer. During the spring of 2010 I attended an event at the Leopold Center for Sustainable Agriculture, an Iowa research and outreach center located at Iowa State University whose mission is "to identify and develop new ways to farm profitably while conserving natural resources as well as reducing negative environmental and social impacts."[12] While there, I had a conversation with a beginning farmer about the resources available to her. She is a graduate of a liberal arts college in Iowa and now manages a small CSA in the central part of the state. She told me that she is regularly confused about who she should contact for assistance with her farm. In particular, she wants help with production and marketing strategies. The new trend of web-based training does not work for her because she lacks reliable Internet access at her farm. She has also found the extension service to be very unhelpful. She reported that when she calls an agent, that person often sends her to someone else, who may or may not call her back. She said she was attending the meeting that day to try to figure out what the Leopold Center really does. Her preference is to have another farmer tell — or better, show — her how to do something. In years past, she noted, Practical Farmers of Iowa had organized days for farmers to get together for coffee during the winter. These meetings were beneficial for her because she could directly ask questions of more experienced farmers.

Other beginning farmers have had nearly the opposite experience and indicate that they are overwhelmed by the volume of information available to them. One new grower from central Iowa told me he was scared to death at the annual meeting of the Midwest Organic and Sustainable Education Service. He had just completed a daylong session led by growers from a diversified vegetable farm in upstate New York. Their presentation emphasized for him the extensive details to which a farmer must attend. He commented that farmers have to be highly skilled in many areas and that a "good enough attitude will not do it." Similarly, a potential beginning farmer who recently inherited forty acres from his grandparents attended the 2011 Practical Farmers of Iowa conference to generate some ideas about how to best use his land. He commented that some of the presentations, particularly on rotational grazing, were so detailed that it was "like they were speaking a different language." Two experienced CSA growers agreed that for new farmers the amount of information provided at farming conferences is overwhelming. One stated that most of it likely "goes over their heads."

Most farming organizations, however, provide more resources than an annual conference. The programs available are diverse and speak to the difficulties of being a new farmer. It is true that any new job has a learning curve, but farming tends to stand out as an especially complicated occupation. Not only does it require significant initial investments in land and equipment, it requires detailed knowledge of plant and animal health and behavior, soil science, some mechanical and engineering skills, a bit of fortitude and, sometimes, just good luck. For the local food community in Iowa, there is the added component of creating an alternative marketing and distribution framework in a state dominated by commodity production. Thus, extension or traditionally trained agronomic, financial, or legal experts attempting to support beginning food farmers may not be well equipped to advise a new farmer trying to convince a landowner that a CSA is a better model than corn production or provide advice on how to profitably grow and sell lettuce.

Practical Farmers of Iowa is a nonprofit educational organization started in 1985. Its mission is to strengthen "farms and communities through farmer-led investigation and information sharing."[13] The organization now has more than two thousand members, both farmers and nonfarmers in and outside Iowa, and has multiple opportunities for beginning and aspiring farmers, perhaps the most diverse and comprehensive of any organization in the state. The group fosters mentor-mentee relationships and also offers financial incentives to new farmers. There is a dedicated program manager, the Next Generation Coordinator, who regularly communicates with beginning farmer members by email and online farminars. In addition, PFI hosts an annual retreat for beginning farmers during the early winter months. The annual PFI conference in January 2011 kicked off with a lunch for new farmers and included several sessions directed at beginning farmers.

PFI's emphasis on farmer-led learning is evident in many of their events. During a beginning farmer session, the Next Generation coordinator hung several large sheets of butcher paper on the walls with headings such as Grazier, Grain, Vegetable Production, Flowers, Poultry, and Unsure. He asked the group to write their top concerns for the upcoming season on the sheets. The coordinator indicated that their responses would go to his office so that he could best determine programming for the year, all based on actual issues. The entries were diverse. Graziers wrote topics such as access to quality pasture, business planning, and beef breeds. Grain farmers were concerned about crop diversity and stability, improving soil health, and finding mentors. The unsure category included entries such as profitability and marketing and beginning farming networking in Iowa.

Throughout the year, the coordinator contacted beginning farmer members by email, notifying them about upcoming field days and events that might be of interest. In addition, during that January session, the group discussed the Savings Incentive Program (SIP) at PFI. This program is funded by established members who donate to the SIP fund. A beginning farmer who has existing farm sales, even if he or she does not own land, can obtain matching funds for savings. Over a period of two years, the farmer saves a hundred dollars a month and PFI fully matches those dollars. The producer has to show that the savings will go toward a capital farm investment, such as new equipment, livestock, or farm infrastructure. In 2010, PFI had $140,000 in matching funds available, enough for ninety-four applicants. While the financial incentives for new farmers are part of PFI's broader strategy to diversify their programming for farmers, they remain essentially a member-based networking group that emphasizes farmer-led learning and research.

Iowa State University Extension has services for beginning farmers, which also attend to retiring farmers and the complicated process of farm succession. In some cases, a family may have an identified heir who is interested in taking over the farm. It is becoming more common, however, for all of the children in a farm family to move away from the farm and find employment elsewhere. The ISU Extension Beginning Farmer Center, in particular, offers resources for farm succession planning and attempts to match new and retiring farmers in the cases that lack a family succession plan. A useful online tool called Farm On links beginning farmers without land to retiring farmers who do not have heirs. After applying to the program, a retiring farmer will be visited by someone from the center who will provide information about potential financial incentives available in the transition process. In addition, during the interview, the agent will ask the farmer about expectations for their land, including what type of beginning farmer they envision for the future of their farm. The retiring farmer will also be able to view the applications of several beginning farmers to begin finding a suitable candidate. The program requires the retiring and beginning farmer to meet and personally develop a succession plan that includes both financial and production management strategies.

While extension services are often criticized for being distant and universal, this particular program recognizes the importance of personal relationships in the succession process. One woman told the story of her sister and brother-in-law, who have been trying to buy land. She noted that it is difficult to explain stewardship and new practices to an old farmer who is only interested in dollars and asked: "How do you tell them you're going to be a better land steward than they are?" Given that much of Iowa's land is in commodity production, any purchase made by a local food farmer is likely to result in a significant change in land-use strategies. The ISU Extension matching program, while not necessarily aimed at small-scale producers, takes this into account by including interviews and meetings between farmers and buyers as part of the process.

The Iowa Valley Resource Conservation and Development (IVRC&D) office in eastern Iowa also has addressed new farmer needs. The Resource Conservation and Development (RC&D) program is part of the USDA, established by the Agriculture Act of 1962. Each local program is run by a council of local leaders who represent both public and private organizations. Historically, their activities have focused on soil conservation and land management as well as community development initiatives. The IVRC&D employs a dedicated food systems planner, who received grant funding to host a series of workshops aimed at beginning farmers in 2011. Held on five Saturday afternoons from January through March, the workshops addressed such topics as land acquisition strategies, crop production practices, market analysis, and business management. Each meeting had a designated presenter, usually an extension agent, and between five and fifteen beginning farmer participants. Many of the workshops were specifically designed to support beginning local food producers. The session on marketing and market analysis, for example, was focused entirely on direct market strategies and included information on conducting market research and on farm to firm (institutional) sales.

In some cases, however, the workshops illuminated a surprising lack of knowledge among state agencies, such as the ISU Extension and Outreach and the Farm Service Agency (FSA), about local food farming. At the presentation on business management and decision making, the extension agent (who, not long after this meeting, moved into a new statewide position supporting small-scale and direct market farmers) explained the importance of using benchmarks to compare an individual farm's production to average production standards. He provided details about how to calculate debt to asset ratios, operating profit ratios, and operating expense ratios. Then, he pointed out the usefulness of benchmarks, generally developed and provided through the extension service, to compare one's own ratios to the statewide average. At this point he sheepishly noted, however, that current benchmarks do not exist for diversified vegetable producers in Iowa. A nearby CSA farmer shook his head in disgust at this statement. The lack of production benchmarks for vegetable growers is especially problematic because without them the FSA, which is responsible for crop insurance, is unable to insure diversified vegetable growers. In early 2011, the FSA estimated that vegetable growers could expect crop revenues to reach about $10,000 per acre. David Evans, an experienced CSA grower, reported to me that his crop revenues were closer to $22,000 per acre.

Likewise, in a presentation on Production Management given by a local Extension Field Agronomist, much of the time was spent on understanding how commercial fertilizers are produced and how to test for appropriate nitrogen, phosphorus, and potassium (NPK) levels in soil. When asked about nitrates in the groundwater in Iowa, the presenter responded: "nitrate is nitrate . . . we actually get some of it right from the air and in rainwater. Whether it's manure or commercial fertilizer, when you detect nitrates, you don't really know where it's coming from. There were nitrates in the water long before man was here." In a later conversation with two growers about the presentation about nitrates and water quality at the workshop, one responded, "Oh yeah? That's B.S." The other farmer was subtler, stating, "Yeah, some of these classes you go to—you don't know what angle they're going to come from. You could tell that guy was a . . . I sensed that he was a regular ISU, you know, agronomist. He was a row-crop, NPK, type." Despite the recent increased attention to local food systems, extension agents may still lack information relevant to small-scale farmers or those producing specialty crops, such as vegetables, as opposed to commodities.

Despite the growing number of programs available to beginning farmers, many still suggest that it is difficult to find good resources, particularly through statewide agencies. In some cases, beginning farmers feel as though they are shut out because of their small scale. Robert Tomanek, a part-time beef producer, stated: "They don't always make a guy feel welcome, you know what I'm saying. It's kind of hard to explain." He went on:

> 'Cause I've called before, there was this Iowa Innovation thing I found once, and they talked about how they were supposed to help new people starting out. I called them, and they just acted like—I felt like they were treating me like I was just some whacked out guy. They said, what do you want to do? And I kind of told them some ideas,

and I said I'm not a full-time farmer. I've thought about some custom things, maybe selling equipment or supplements — or anything. And even like custom haying or something. And he just gave me the cold shoulder, and I knew I wasn't getting anywhere. When you hang up the phone you kind of feel depressed, you know. It's crazy.

An individual who manages only a few head of cattle or acres of vegetables may feel out of place in a support organization primarily devoted to the state's dominant system of large-scale farming, in which 2,500-head hog confinements and thousand-acre grain farms are common. In this context, the differences between conventional agriculture and local food production appear particularly stark. Farmers are well acquainted with the support structures available to them, but those structures have been developed with one kind of farming in mind.

Even conservation agencies, which are promoting diversified farming and sustainable agriculture, can be difficult for small or part-time farmers to relate to. Sarah Miller is a part-time farmer and baker. She sells her baked goods at various farmers' markets and, in 2011, initiated a collaborative CSA with several other producers. In addition, she hopes to add grass-fed beef to her operation. In the spring of 2011, she had a herd of fourteen cattle and planned to turn a twenty-acre pasture into a series of grazing paddocks. She contacted the local Natural Resources and Conservation Service (NRCS) grazing and pasture specialist. Though she was pleased with his analysis and suggestions, she recognized that to take advantage of any of the financial incentives the state offers for sustainable grazing would require her to enter a contract and follow their recommendations and program exactly. She said, "We'll just use our own money to do it." In this case, the available knowledge was useful, even if the overall program was not.

The rigidity of universal farm programs may not allow the flexibility that a small farmer needs. Even if farmers understand and can navigate the programs available to them, they still have to have some land to farm. The majority of land in Iowa (64 percent) is held by either sole or joint owners, usually an individual or a couple. Despite popular attention to corporate farms, only about 9 percent of all farmland is held by corporations, which includes family-owned corporations as well as nonprofits. In fact, Iowa law restricts most types of private corporation from owning land for production purposes, which means that the vast majority of farms in the state, even if they are large, are still family farms. Furthermore, despite the tendency of early settlers to acquire land based on high debt load, the majority of land is now owned outright, with no debt burden. This trend has strengthened over time: 62 percent of farmland in 1982 was owned debt-free, increasing by 2007 to 75 percent.[14] Given the mostly steady appreciation in land values, which encourages families to hold onto their land, and the increasing age of farmers, it is not surprising that mortgages are slowly being paid off.

The long-term holding of land by farm families, coupled with the increasing age of landowners, means that many farmers access their land through rental agreements. Now, more than half of all of Iowa's farmland is under rental agreement. Over the past decades, the amount of land under rental agreement has not changed significantly, but the nature of the rental agreements has.[15] There are two major rental categories: crop share arrangements and cash rent. With a crop share lease, the tenant and owner split some or all of the costs associated with managing the land and then split the yield at the end of the season. Most crop share arrangements are fifty-fifty, meaning that the tenant and owner split the input costs and the yield equally. The other option is to simply pay cash rent per acre. In the past years, cash rent arrangements have been increasing, while crop share rental agreements have declined.

Beginning farmer Robert Tomanek is navigating his way through assistance programs and rental agreements. A veteran of the first Iraq war, he is employed full time for an eastern Iowa engineering and technology firm. Though he did not grow up on a farm, both his mother's and father's parents were farmers, and he spent many childhood summers on their farms. He has fond memories of those experiences: "You know, spending the time out there—I don't know, I think just as a kid I felt more at home out there . . . I still was a kid and did the town thing. But my aunts and uncles also had a big influence on me." In 1994, he purchased a house and barn on eight acres. He says at that point he "kind of dabbled in it. The big divide for me was Iraq. I got deployed over in Iraq in '03 and '04,

came back in '05." At that point, he retired from the Army Reserves because the job "demanded a lot of my time, and I really wanted to go play
in the dirt and exercise my desire to farm." Since 2006, he has purchased
between six and ten steers each year to finish, have processed, and sell.
"I've always liked cattle," he says. "I don't know, probably because of my
cousins. I knew I didn't want to do dairy—I mean that's interesting and
cool, but . . . it takes the right person to do that. You know, my cousins
always had cattle or my grandparents. And I like beef! I like steak!"

Along with the eight acres he owns, Robert rents other parcels for pasture and hay. "I've always wanted to expand into pork and poultry more.
But you can only bite off so much at a time. I feel like I need to get the
livestock thing squared away first. I'm just now getting access to land."
He notes that it is difficult to find land to rent, especially if one is not well
known in the area. Personal relationships are key to finding land, and it
is hard to predict when, after expressing interest in renting, a landowner
will indicate willingness to rent. For example, regarding the land he now
rents for hay, he says: "Well, it's the neighbor's, the guy I hunt with. He
knows I've done this, and [one of the] two places I got the hay first was
an old retired farmer up the way here. I used to bale like a fifty-fifty or
pay him or whatever. The other guy's got horses, and the other guy that
lived there had goats. Then he got rid of his goats, and that guy just sold
me the hay 'cause the old boy didn't want to do it anymore. So that's the
first place I got into." Thus, Robert's first opportunity to obtain hay came
from his custom farming contacts and a crop share arrangement in which
he would use his equipment to bale hay and split it with the landowner. In
addition, when one farmer no longer raised goats, the other farmer needed
a buyer for his hay. In this case, he was simply a buyer, however. Robert
indicates that slowly building these relationships has allowed him to build
credibility in the area and has opened more opportunities:

> And then . . . just being around here. I think I asked around once in
> a while. There's a guy in town that owns sixty acres out here, and I
> mentioned something to him once and nothing ever happened. But
> then, you know, two, three years later, John, his name was, walks up
> and says, 'there's fifteen acres back there, do you want to hay that?' I

was like, sure, and he's actually renting it to me for a very reasonable
price, just 'cause he doesn't want to have to mow it. And I've also got
to cross the same crick that runs through my place—it's not very
far, it's all in the same area—and then kind of drive up a ridgeline,
so it's time consuming. You know, I think that's another reason he's
not charging me a lot. I think he's charging me like fifteen dollars a
round bale and that's cheap.

Relationships in Robert's farming community are built slowly over time;
it was only after several years that someone approached him with a rental
opportunity. Even though the land is not ideal—there is the creek to cross
to access it—it provided an important point of entry for Robert.

In addition to renting the fifteen acres of hay ground from John, Robert
rents another twenty-five acres. Currently, that plot is also used for hay,
though he hopes to graze cattle on it eventually. He does not actually rent
these acres directly from the landowner but is subleasing the pasture from
another long-term renter. During a Beginning Farmer workshop devoted
to land acquisition, Robert explained his situation to the presenters, one
of whom worked for the ISU Extension Beginning Farmer Center, and
the other was an attorney with the ISU Center for Agricultural Law and
Taxation. Both presenters were skeptical of the benefits of Robert's situation. One stated that "this could get complicated, if his contract doesn't
allow subleasing, it could cause problems." The attorney added, "I hate
to see you get in a situation where it's your livelihood and the other person
comes in and says you can't sublease at all." Throughout the presentation,
the speakers strongly urged renters and potential renters to have written agreements for leased land. Many of the beginning farmers, however,
were hesitant. One stated that "when you get started, a verbal agreement
seems like the way to go because you don't want to tick off the landlord."

The subleased land that Robert hopes to graze requires some fencing
improvements before it is ready for cattle. He hopes that by showing the
care he puts into the property and the infrastructure improvements he
plans to make, the landlord (in this case also a renter) will share the cost
of the improvements or allow him more use of the existing infrastructure.
"I think I'll hit 'em up one of these days," he says. "When it's all done and

I've got cattle up there, I'll say 'you've seen the fence, what I've put into it, what are we talking'? Or I might use it as leverage to use some of the buildings up top, you know what I mean?" Robert's strategy is to "show him that I'm willing and capable of doing it, knowing that there's a risk I could get burnt."

It is not uncommon for farmers to have some combination of owned and rented land. The rental process, however, is not straightforward and may be contingent on one's standing in the community. This can cause difficulties for new farmers, who may be less familiar to their neighbors. In addition, alternative farmers who wish to rent land typically used for conventional agriculture may offend their potential landlords. In Robert Tomanek's case, he has made infrastructure improvements on rented land, all at his own expense. His hope that these risks will pay off in the form of more access to land or lower costs has not yet been realized.

Rental trends are an area of interest for agricultural researchers and demographers in the state, and they have implications for the local food system as well. Landowners and tenants are regularly surveyed about rental practices and researchers assume that the nature of rental agreements, like the age of farmers and land transitions, affects what kind of agriculture is practiced. Policymakers and sustainability advocates look to long-term rental agreements with good communication between the landowner and tenant for community and environmental sustainability. The assumption is that the longer a renter farms the same ground, the more invested he or she will be in conservation practices. Cash rent agreements tend to be shorter than crop share agreements, in part because the increasing number of cash rent agreements has had less time to solidify. In 2007 and 2012, the majority of both crop share and cash leases have been in effect for more than five years and almost two-thirds of crop share leases have had the same tenant for more than ten years, while only 44 percent (2007) and 43 percent (2012) of cash leases have had the same tenant for that amount of time.[16]

The shift toward cash rental agreements is noteworthy, in part, because of the assumption that tenants who farm for shorter durations may be less invested in the health of the soil. A second reason for attention is that cash rental agreements can put beginning farmers, frequently the renters, at a disadvantage. A crop share lease helps distribute the financial risks of farming more evenly between the landlord and the tenant. This is beneficial to beginning farmers who have fewer resources available to manage risk. In theory, crop share arrangements should require more communication between landowner and tenant because the details of splitting costs and profits must be negotiated. In reality, surveys of Iowa landlords and tenants show that landlords who have a crop share arrangement visit their leased land about half as often as landlords who have cash renters.[17]

Of course, even if crop share arrangements reduce risk for beginning farmers, it is somewhat unclear whether they are appropriate for a direct market farm. The extensive agricultural data on grains and grazing allows for a landlord and tenant to work out a fairly straightforward agreement. Chemical costs, for example, are known up front, and decades of data show the average yields for pretty much every acre of corn in the state. Likewise, the hay yield per acre and the rates of growth of cattle on a particular pasture mix are fairly standard. But how does one calculate a crop share arrangement for a CSA or market farm? The lack of benchmarks and the less predictable nature of vegetable production may make cash rentals more attractive for local food operations.

Rental arrangements also have implications beyond the landlord-tenant negotiations. Given the population loss in rural areas over the past decades, looking at land-use arrangements may shed light on the social and economic health of a community. Rental transactions result in economic flows within and outside Iowa counties, so agricultural researchers pay close attention to who owns land in the state. A recent survey showed that 54 percent of landlords lived in the county where their land was located, but 21 percent lived out of state. The other 25 percent were dispersed between adjacent counties (12 percent), elsewhere in Iowa (10 percent) or were corporations (3 percent).[18] The cash paid to the landowners living in different counties or states than their farmland means the money they receive for cash rents does not benefit the community that includes that farmland.[19] There are other considerations, such as property taxes and possible in-flows of resources as landowners visit their properties or invest in equipment or infrastructure for their properties using local dealers.[20] But for local food, for which one of the claimed benefits is the potential to revitalize rural areas, paying cash rent to a nonlocal landowner potentially lowers the economic impact in the immediate area. Further, considering Robert Tomanek's experience of slowly getting to know his local landlords, those new in a community may have even more difficulty finding land that is owned by nonlocal people they do not know.

Survey data reveals that relationships between tenants and landlords decline with geographical distance and when landlords are not connected to farming. In a survey of landlord-tenant experiences, respondents were questioned about both physical distance from the rented land as well as cultural connection to farming among landlords to attempt to better understand how invested landlords were in farming practices and their tenants. As noted in the preceding paragraph, 54 percent of the landlords in the survey lived within the county where their land was rented. In addition, 41 percent of the landlords were former farmers, and 36 percent were heirs of a farm estate. Thirteen percent of landowners were spouses of former farmers, and 9 percent were investors with no family ties to the land.[21] The survey results indicate that overall the "landlord connection to farming remains fairly strong." The author, assuming that the spouses "were involved in the farm operation to some degree," concludes that "a majority of Iowa landlords do have a strong cultural connection to farming."[22]

Of course, it is difficult to ascertain subjective ideas about cultural connections to farming from a survey. The author notes that "with heirs of farm estates, the question of cultural connection to farming is less clear. If we assume that heirs have a family connection to the land, then some 90 percent of landlords in Iowa have a family history of farming."[23] In addition, the survey results show that among the categories of landowners, former farmers and spouses of former farmers are also the most likely to live in the county where the land was rented. This finding further suggests that, among these groups, connections to the land are relatively strong. Overall, tenants reported strong relationships with their landowners, on average estimating that they communicated about farming practices eight times a year (although 49 percent indicated that they communicated with landowners about farming practices three or fewer times a year, and 11 percent reported having no communication).[24] The length of tenancies are long as well.[25] Nevertheless, tenants "appeared to be much more confident in their relationships with landlords who lived close by than those who lived far away."[26]

Ultimately, we do not know as much as we should about the social and environmental effects of land rental relationships in the state. Agricultural economists worry that rental arrangements may negatively affect beginning farmers. Robert Tomanek's story shows some of the difficulties of finding a landowner or another renter who is willing to rent land. He has certainly taken on a lot of risk by investing his own money in improvements and renting from another renter. But at a statewide level, it is harder to determine the advantages or disadvantages of being both a beginning farmer and a renter. In addition, the extent to which nonoperator landowners are concerned about conservation and good farming practices is not clear. It is clear, however, that there are growing numbers of landlords who do not live in Iowa or within the counties in which they own land. Will this group want to rent to local food farmers? Will crop share arrangements, which require more communication and are usually more accessible for beginning farmers, become viable in the local food system?

If a local food system rests on farmers, they need access to land and resources that will support their operations and their own professional development. While many agricultural organizations specifically court beginning farmers and develop programming aimed at increasing this population, in some cases, such as with extension services, most of the expertise is more useful for commodity producers than for local food farmers. Further, some alternative producers, like Robert Tomanek, may feel excluded because they are only part-time farmers or farm on a very small scale. In addition, state experts in agriculture may not have the knowledge most useful to alternative producers, such as benchmarks for vegetable production or knowledge of organic practices. Tellingly, at the RC&D beginning farmer workshop focused on land acquisition and legal strategies, the presenter was unable to explain the concept of community supported agriculture.

Access to land and knowledge of educational opportunities and loan programs are critical for a farm's successful start-up. After that comes the real work of actually farming. In the next chapter, we examine a whole new set of regulations and procedures that farmers have to navigate to market their products, even directly to consumers.

———— ☼ ————

CHAPTER FOUR

The Not-So-Direct Market

U SUALLY, THOSE WHO write about local food focus on direct marketing, in which producers sell their agricultural products to consumers without the engagement of a formal distribution structure
or middleman. Just as we rarely hear about the lenders, nonprofit organizations, and public agencies that provide services to farmers looking to start
or change their operations, we also rarely hear about the inspectors, market
managers, or media who work on the other end of the spectrum, at the point
of sale. Local food has privileged the producer-consumer relationship as
the key point of differentiation from the conventional food system. Promo-
tions such as the USDA's "know your farmer, know your food" campaign
reinforce this relational perspective. All the consumer needs to know about
his or her food is who produced it. Knowing your farmer has become code
for being an informed and conscientious eater. But knowing one's farmer
does not generally extend to knowing how that farmer navigates the state
or market regulations or what other entities have played a part in making
the producer visible to the consumer in the first place.

This is part of the hidden reality of local food. The focus on the direct-
to-consumer dimension hides much of the regulatory infrastructure at
the state, county, or city level that is ultimately responsible for the success or failure of a local food system. Further, given the diversity of local
food production and marketing strategies, there is not just one system or
set of rules to which a farmer must attend. CSA growers experience the
fewest regulatory constraints and are generally free to sell their products
without interference from local health departments or inspectors. Those
who sell at farmers' markets, however, deal with rules that are specific to
each market and that can affect how they package, display, and sell their

produce. In addition to the costs of specialized equipment, meat and dairy producers deal with the most extensive regulations, especially in the case of poultry or dairy. When we assume that consumer demand is the only factor that will influence the growth of local food, we miss many of the ways in which local food systems actually mimic the processing chains and regulatory structures of conventional systems.

This chapter addresses the broader systems on which direct marketing strategies rely. I tell the story of a small CSA farm and a market farmer and also give examples drawn from the experiences of meat and dairy producers. In all of these cases, the producers' success is based on more than simply developing a customer base, though this is important. CSA farms, while mostly avoiding regulatory oversight, benefit from the activities of nonprofit groups and media. Farmers' market vendors may be constrained by market policies and locations, even as they benefit from a market's popularity and advertising. Meat and dairy producers, in particular, must navigate a very complex structure of regulations and processors, all before they are able to sell their first steak or ounce of cheese.

Community-Supported Agriculture

The community-supported agriculture movement in the United States began in the mid-1980s. The concept was originally developed in 1971 in Japan by a group of women who were concerned about chemicals in their food. They contracted with a local farmer and worked out a cooperative agreement, sparking the teikei movement — commonly referred to as "food with the farmer's face on it" (*teikei* literally means "cooperation" or "partnership"). Cooperative farming arrangements were also developing in Switzerland, where farmers had asked their customers to support their farms' spring expenses in return for weekly shares of produce. It was this model that was proposed to Robyn Van En in western Massachusetts in 1985 as she started the first CSA in the United States. Four years later, there were thirty-seven identifiable CSA farms in the United States and Canada.[1] The USDA reports that more than twelve thousand farms in the United States reported marketing at least some of their products through a CSA arrangement in 2012.[2]

Van En believed that consumers should share the costs to share the harvest, creating a model that is based on relationships and risks between farmers and consumers. CSA customers, often called members or shareholders, pay farmers a flat fee before the growing season begins and, in return, receive weekly shares of products from the farm. This early payment benefits the producer in two ways. First, growers are guaranteed the sale of their produce before the season begins, alleviating the possibility that items will be produced but not sold. Second, the payment comes at a crucial time for vegetable growers, when they are purchasing seeds, treatments, or fertilizers and normally are not earning farm income. The consumers, then, through their early investments, take on a share of the risk inherent in farming. If the harvest is poor, the amount of produce will suffer; in a good year, however, the shareholders benefit without paying more for the increased yield.

The CSA model does require some coordination between customers and farmers and therefore varies somewhat from farm to farm. In Iowa, arrangements for packaging and delivery vary. Some CSA operators deliver shares to their customers' homes or set up a central weekly meeting place for shareholders to pick up their products. Others may require that the shareholders come to the farm to pick up shares, and in some cases fill their own boxes or select their own produce. The season length and contents of a weekly share vary based on local geography, farm capabilities, and consumer wishes. Iowa CSA farms generally offer vegetable shares but may include honey, baked goods, or cut flowers. A few CSAs in the state offer animal products, such as meat, eggs, or wool.[3] Most of the CSAs in eastern Iowa are managed by one producer, though the collaborative CSA, often abbreviated cCSA, is becoming more popular. In this model, several growers, usually on different farms, cooperatively produce for one group of shareholders.

In 2011, sixteen CSA farms served the area in eastern Iowa where I did most of my research, ranging widely in size from about twenty shareholders to 250. Most had multiple delivery methods. Shareholders usually had the option to pick up at the farm, some farmers did home delivery, and some had central drop sites at a business or farmers' market. Share prices also varied considerably, and the price of a standard share ranged from

$275 for a sixteen-week season to $500 for a twenty-two-week season. Additionally, several growers offered multiple share sizes or an early spring share along with a standard, full share. Five CSAs were certified organic. Although most growers advertised that they practice organic methods, they did not necessarily carry official certification.

Most growers engage in multiple strategies to generate income, both on and off their farms. Some do custom farmwork in which they use their equipment to work for another farmer, baling hay, planting, or harvesting; others have acreage in conventional row crops. Others combine direct market meat or farmers' market sales with their CSA. As in conventional farming, many also have partners who work off the farm to provide benefits and extra income. In 2008, I focused on gaining a better understanding of how CSA farms maintain success. This was an especially interesting year to focus on small farmers in the area because we experienced record flooding early in the summer. The wet year challenged the notion that on-farm diversity is an adequate insurance solution. Some farms, like Alan Marshall's (mentioned in chapter 1), struggled to stay in business. Walnut Acres Subscription Produce, however, exemplifies the benefits of flexibility in a small CSA; even during the disastrous 2008 summer, this CSA provided important income to two lifelong farmers, Frances and Tom Baumgartner. Walnut Acres's success is based not only on operational changes that improved efficiency but also on the contribution of local media and nonprofit organizations to marketing CSAs and local food.

Frances and Tom grew up on small, diversified Iowa farms. Both farms are now designated Heritage Farms by the Iowa Department of Agriculture and Land Stewardship's Heritage Farm Program, which recognizes farms that have been owned by the same family for more than 150 years. Tom and Frances's family-based operations included livestock, row crops, and gardens and produced much of the food for their families each year. Frances's father was avidly against using chemicals on his farm, although Tom's family used them when necessary. Tom and Frances met in high school and married soon after. They initially bought a home with one acre but soon outgrew it as the trees and gardens Frances planted filled the space. At that point, the couple moved to their current location.

Though Frances worked full time as a nurse and Tom was a mainte-

The contents of a late-season CSA share.

nance worker for a nearby municipality, they planted extensive gardens each year and kept chickens for fresh eggs and meat. Through the years, Frances and her mother occasionally sold items at various farmers' markets. Her mother would bring baked goods, and Frances would bring garden produce. They were generally successful, but Frances always found the extensive preparation time frustrating, particularly on slow days when she would come home with unsold produce. She has also sold extra strawberries and cabbage on local radio farm sales when she had excess. Frances notes, "when you think about it that way, I guess I've been kind of dabbling in this in different ways all through the years." For Tom and Frances, local food has not necessarily been a new way to farm, and their experience is a reminder that there have been direct market systems in place for many decades.

In 1998, Frances was beginning to become dissatisfied with her job as a nurse. The hospital was undergoing significant changes, and like many of her colleagues, she was concerned about her job stability. She had been involved with the local extension and 4–H programs with her children for several years. She also served on the Farm Bureau Board as well as the Sheep and Wool Growers Board, so she stayed up to date with current farm literature. In 1999, she received an extension mailing promoting CSA as a new direct marketing strategy for small farms. She was immediately interested, knowing that it was a model that would mesh well with her background in gardening and experience with direct marketing.

Her husband, however, was not convinced. He thought it inconceivable that people in Iowa would pay in advance for a box of vegetables. Frances realized that she and her husband, as people who had grown up on farms and continued to grow much of their own food, were unusual. She did not think it unreasonable that those who lacked the time or ability to produce for themselves would be willing to pay for a steady supply of fresh, local vegetables. Despite her husband's misgivings, she was ready to try a CSA. She cut back her hours at the hospital and started with one share in 2000 just "to see if I could do it." Within three years, the CSA income was paying for the property taxes. By 2007, she had thirty-seven shares, and in 2008 she had fifty-one. Frances found that the CSA was a good economic niche for the two of them. Her major economic frustration with farmers' markets was alleviated, as all the CSA produce is presold, and it is work that they can do together.

Walnut Acres produces its shares on a surprisingly small area. Frances estimates that they have only one acre in vegetables and one acre in orchards. From those two acres, she produces enough potatoes, onions, sugar snap peas, lettuce, spinach, broccoli, cabbage, bell peppers, sweet corn, green beans, carrots, tomatoes, asparagus, okra, kohlrabi, beets, horseradish, cucumbers, summer squash, strawberries, raspberries, peaches, and plums to feed her household and fifty-one shareholders. They use their small space efficiently, planting consecutive crops in each space. She also grows several varieties of herbs in containers around the house. She likes this arrangement because she can monitor the plants closely, and herbs, like fruit, serve as a useful way to fill out the shares if other crops are thin.

Frances does not guarantee a specific size of share each week; she refers to share sizes in terms of baskets. Thus, if she has a large group of shareholders, she can adjust the basket size accordingly. Additionally, she keeps track of customers' likes and dislikes. "This is not an exact science," she says, "so if something comes out a little uneven, and we have a little plot of spinach left but not enough for everybody we give it to the ones who like spinach." Additionally, she includes recipes in each basket every week and sends out a comment card at the end of the season to get feedback from the shareholders

Over the years, the couple has settled into an annual routine, though they make small changes every season. Frances sends out their agreement sheet, or contract, early in the year to the past year's shareholders. The basic form is consistent: shareholders fill out their contact information and note any special requests. In 2008, Frances included a statement that fruit is an addition to the share when available but should not be expected to make up the bulk of the share baskets each week. As long as she has a few people signed up early in the year, she feels comfortable ordering seeds. Her primary goal is to get her seed order in early enough to qualify for a discount. She always plans for more than last year but rarely thinks about concrete numbers. In 2008, a major growth year for the CSA, she also had three weddings in her family to prepare for. Thus, she originally intended to decrease her shares to ten or twelve for the 2008 season, but as more and more people called, she realized that the bills from the family weddings were significantly increasing and the extra income would be helpful.

Tom, after being diagnosed with an Alzheimer's-like disability, took early retirement from his city job in 2006. He now helps with the CSA full time. Though Frances manages the bulk of the business, including all the planning and bookwork, she says that it would not succeed without Tom's help. He does most of the plowing and heavy labor under her direction. She feels that their arrangement is good for his health. His disability makes it challenging for him to complete tasks that require complicated instructions, but he thrives when engaging in repetitive tasks that are familiar to him. As a lifelong farmer, he is comfortable with equipment maintenance, tillage, weeding, and soil health.

Despite the significant increase in shares, Frances felt that 2008 was the least stressful year she had experienced with the CSA. Those who promote CSA as a way to encourage new farm operations do not readily discuss the issues of stress and burnout. Overall, the statewide number of

CSA farms has steadily grown. In 2006, the Leopold Center for Sustainable Agriculture reported fifty CSA farms in Iowa. By 2015, there were eighty-five. Fewer than twenty of those reported in 2015, however, had been in existence in 2006. This means that at least thirty of the original fifty had transitioned out of CSA or out of farming altogether. Many farmers discussed the burden of responsibility in CSA. One grower from northeast Iowa noted: "CSA is not for the faint of heart. You're essentially taking a loan from your customers, and they're paying you in advance for your product. That adds a lot of stress."

Frances attributed her smooth transition to a larger customer base to three changes she made in their operation. First, they reduced delivery to three days each week. Previously, they delivered the majority of shares directly to customers' homes on a day that suited the customer. As a result, some seasons they were delivering shares every day of the week in opposite ends of their territory. In 2008, they divided their territory up into three areas and targeted one area each day. Before the season started, they informed customers which day they would be in their area for delivery. Frances was surprised that no one complained about the change in policy. She notes that they have probably saved a lot of gas as well as time, but they have not quantified their savings. The second significant change involved starting later in the season. They used to make their first deliveries in the second week of May. In 2008, the spring was exceptionally cold, and they were unable to get into the gardens until April. Additionally, their family weddings all fell in the springtime, taking up much of their time. As a result, they started their deliveries during the first week of June. Frances was surprised to find that just a two-week delay made a major difference in the early weeks of the season. Iowa springs are generally unpredictable, and CSA shares are frequently light in May. Frances realized that starting later in the season "alleviates a lot of stress in the early spring when there usually isn't much to pick from. It's hard to fill out a basket." Pushing back just two weeks allowed her to deliver fuller baskets, which improved her overall outlook on the season. Third, she made an effort to include more fruit. Despite warning shareholders that fruit should not be expected as the bulk of the share, fruit are a popular way to fill out the basket. In a somewhat dry year, fruit will often thrive when vegetables will not. In

2008, she started with cherries in the share baskets. Shareholders were very positive about fruit, and their inclusion can offset disappointment if vegetables are scarce. Frances's diversified model serves her well, and in a difficult year the wide variety of produce ensures at least some successes.

The changes in Walnut Acres procedures were not made with the customers' convenience in mind. Arguably, this is consistent with the overall perspective of CSA, in which customers are expected to share the risk. Walnut Acres shareholders lost a bit of control over the day of the week their shares were delivered and when they received their first share. Frances reports that there were no complaints about their new strategies. In theory, local food consumers are supposed to give up some of the choices they are accustomed to when they shop at conventional grocery stores, which sell out-of-season produce and cater to their every whim. Frances's customers seem perfectly willing to give up the benefits of delivery-on-demand and an early spring start. But why are consumers suddenly more willing to abdicate their control over the timing and content of their household food purchases? During our discussions, Frances alluded to another current dimension of local food: the high level of attention and investment by third parties, including the media and nonprofits. The promotion of local food in Iowa, which often reminds people to buy seasonally rather than eating those strawberries in December, suggests to consumers that their immediate preferences should not be central in our food system.

Frances discussed her observations about the steady increase in interest in local foods during the first eight years of her CSA. Despite not advertising at all, shareholder numbers have gone up every season. She attributes this to increased media attention, what she calls the "green movement," and the work of the area nonprofit Local Foods Connection (LFC). A donation-based organization, LFC purchases CSA shares for low-income families. In addition, the nonprofit has organized and hosted an annual CSA fair and maintains a directory of CSA farms.[4] Frances and Tom have never attended the fair, but the information for Walnut Acres Subscription Produce is included in the directory put out by Local Foods Connection. The LFC directory has been Frances's major source of new shareholders. Before 2015, LFC did not charge farmers to participate in the CSA fair or to be listed in the directory. These activities have provided a significant

benefit to farmers like Tom and Frances who can then focus more on production than marketing.

Frances notes that her customers are very appreciative of the service
she provides. She feels that most would grow their own food if they had
the skills or time. From her perspective, people have grown disconnected
from the land. When she was young, most people she knew grew their
own food; now very few do. She believes that the current interest in local
foods is one way that people try to reconnect to their local environment.
As someone who has seen direct market agriculture go from a few extra
pints of strawberries sold over the radio to the current level of enthusiasm,
Frances is confident that the CSA model, and local food overall, have real
staying power.

Frances and Tom's success story shows the interaction between smart
procedural details and the effect of a broader structure that supports local
food and encourages consumers to take the plunge with a CSA. Walnut
Acres's shareholders were willing to be flexible about when they received
their shares, and they are always forewarned that popular items, such as
fruit, may not be available in a given year. This flexibility is not what we
generally expect of American consumers, who have been deemed "always
right" in nearly every other retail setting. Promotion of CSA by organizations such as Local Foods Connection provides an important service in
educating community members about what to expect out of a CSA.

Consumer demand does not happen in a vacuum. We know that the
mainstream food system relies on teams of well-paid marketers who subtly
—and sometimes not so subtly—encourage consumers to move toward a
particular product because it is healthy, convenient, inexpensive, or fulfills
some other perceived need. Although it is not as centralized, local food
benefits from the same process. Instead of paid marketers, nonfarming
local food advocates, such as those who work with Local Foods Connection, nudge consumers to try a CSA or to get to know their farmer. The
tendency to solely congratulate consumers for their superior food choices
erases much of the work done by other entities that affect and reaffirm
those choices.

Farmers' Markets

For consumers, the local farmers' market may be the first thing that comes to mind when they think of local food. Nationally, farmers' market attendance has been growing at a steady rate. In 1994, when the USDA first began tracking and publishing farmers' market numbers, there were 1,755 in the United States; in 2014, there were 8,268.[5] Iowa has also seen steady growth and ranks high in the number of markets compared to other states. IDALS lists 228 farmers' markets in Iowa, making the state fourth in the overall number of farmers' markets and second per capita.[6] The most recent economic analysis of Iowa farmers' markets indicates that weekly attendance at markets increased 44 percent between 2004 and 2009. In 2009, nearly 99,400 Iowans shopped at a farmers' market each week, resulting in 2.2 million consumer visits for the entire season. The estimated statewide total sales in 2009 was $38.4 million.[7]

In eastern Iowa, the two major market locations are in Iowa City and Cedar Rapids. A number of smaller markets are scattered within a sixty-mile radius. The Iowa City Farmers Market is managed by the city's Parks and Recreation Department and has been in operation since 1972. Consistently ranked among the most popular farmers' markets in the country, the twice-weekly event, held in a parking structure near the downtown business district, is well attended and festive. The city of Cedar Rapids also hosts multiple markets throughout the week. Small markets around the downtown area are held on Monday, Tuesday, Wednesday, and Friday evenings and on Saturday mornings. In addition, the Cedar Rapids Downtown Association coordinates another large market two Saturdays each month, May through September.

Most producers use multiple marketing strategies, and there is some disagreement about whether CSAs or farmers' markets are the more risky marketing outlet. Some whose primary focus is CSA suggested that farmers' markets are actually the easier strategy because you start fresh every week. One grower, whose primary outlet is now a CSA, reported that he sold only six dollars worth of produce at the first market he attended, and those purchases came from other vendors who took pity on him. Even with this low return, he notes, "the farmers' market is a good place to

A small farmers' market in eastern Iowa.

learn those lessons" about providing a good product and understanding what consumers want. Ultimately, "the lessons you learn at a farmers' market will cost you a lot less than if you fail at a CSA. A farmers' market is a clean slate every year, in some cases every week, so if you have a bad year, you can come back the next with very little repercussions. A CSA can't recover that quickly." Because a CSA requires a season-long relationship with shareholders, a poor year can have severe consequences: your customers may decide to go elsewhere in future seasons.

The key risk at a farmers' market is that one might have to leave each week with unsold produce. Growers often cite this particular concern as a reason to avoid farmers' markets entirely. The guaranteed sales in a CSA often make it worth the added stress of filling the box every week. Vegetable grower Faye Jefferson notes that with a CSA "in some ways it's a whole lot easier because you know exactly that you're going to get rid of everything and everything is going to sell because it just gets divvied up, and if you have extra you just give them extra." In addition, the popularity of farmers' markets has resulted in waiting lists for vendors at the locations with the highest traffic. Faye, who has transitioned to a full-time CSA, spent her first eight years growing solely for farmers' markets. Some of her success depended on the location and individual management of the markets. In other cases, her observations of customers' needs and product niches benefited her sales.

Faye started her farmers' market career after retiring from a local engineering firm. Not comfortable with the term "farmer," she declares herself a city girl and an avid gardener. "I grew up in the city. I'm a city girl completely. When I retired, I still felt like there was something I wanted to do. And I thought that what we had here, what we had going for us, was just an awful lot of land that was just grass. And so there was plenty of room to do gardening, and I've always been a gardener, but I've never done it on a very big scale. And so I decided that farmers' market was something that I'd really like to do." She hoped to have a stall in the Iowa City market because she "thought it would be a better fit," but there were no spaces available. Her property is located between Cedar Rapids and Iowa City, so the Cedar Rapids market was the next best choice for her. At the time, the market was located near the river and had about thirty vendors. "It was kind of interesting—most of them were related. Most of the vendors had been there for years, and they were all from the same family, huge extended family. They sort of competed with each other, but they sort of didn't either. And they were really into chemicals. They loved malathion, and they did not go the organic route at all. I was probably the only one there that was doing organic at the time."

While her relationships with the other vendors were collegial, she did not find many who shared her perspectives on organic growing practices. In addition, because she produced on a smaller scale than some of the other Cedar Rapids vendors, they assumed she was less committed to farming. "There was an old guy, he's passed now, from Cedar Rapids . . . He was a big vendor and he called me a fly-by-nighter. And he wasn't being mean or anything . . . I'd usually show up about the same time he did, and he was always the one that raised the shutters on the roundhouse. I'd try to help him, and he says, 'who are you? Oh yeah, you're one of the fly-by-nighters.' And he said, 'I'll be surprised if you stick it out more than one season.'" She noted that he did eventually realize that she was a serious grower and she slowly gained legitimacy among the vendors; however, she never felt fully part of the community.

When the city decided to move that market away from its original location, Faye attended the meetings and participated in the process. She
reports that the vendors were not in favor of moving the market, primarily
because the new location would be in an open parking lot rather than a
covered facility. The exposure to the elements affects sales on days with
inclement weather, as fewer customers will brave a rainy day to shop at
the market. Some customers were disappointed by the move, but only in
part because of the location. The market also increased in size when it
moved and began to include more crafts and nonfood items. Faye found
it to be an improvement overall but noted that it felt less like a traditional
farmers' market. "My customers," she commented, "would say things like
'it's so hard to shop at the downtown market in Cedar Rapids because
you have to walk so far to get your vegetables,' because they didn't put all
the vegetable vendors in one place. They had them scattered all over the
place, and they felt that was kind of inconvenient and it took too long for
them to do their shopping."

Faye eventually developed a strong customer base at the Cedar Rapids
market. But, as with showing her commitment to her fellow vendors, it
took time. For example, she has always had good luck growing greens
such as kale and chard and feels that the health value of these foods is
significant. Unfortunately, Cedar Rapids customers were not interested in
buying dark greens, "even though I would go on and on about it and how
good it was and how you fix it." Instead, customers were more inclined
to purchase green beans and tomatoes "when I had tomatoes that looked
like what people were used to." Faye's experience suggests that simply
knowing your farmer may not be enough to drive a diverse and healthy
food system. Instead of customers taking the initiative to try new items and
develop new tastes, Faye had to take the tactics of those food marketers
and sell her products to an initially unwilling customer base. She did the
work of getting to know her customer rather than the other way around.

Faye's dedication eventually paid off, and she remained committed to
selling leafy greens because she noticed that other vendors did not sell
them. "People weren't coming with lettuce or Asian greens, or they weren't
coming with kale or anything like that. So I started doing that, and it took
a lot of talking to get people to try stuff—not the lettuce of course, that

sold right away. I even noticed that there wasn't much spinach, so I started doing that a lot." Customers were also not initially interested in organic methods. She had to educate shoppers as to why it might cost more and explain the benefits of growing without chemicals. Her strategy of selling unique items, providing samples (especially of items such as heirloom tomatoes, which would get people hooked) and trying to talk to customers about how to prepare unfamiliar vegetables eventually helped her to develop a strong following at the market.

When the Saturday morning Iowa City market expanded by adding nearly thirty stalls, Fay was able to secure a space. She found that both the vendors and the customers were more receptive to her products: "Oh, it was a totally different atmosphere. They expect you to be organic and there are a lot of organic vendors, even some of the big ones are. The norm is organic produce, and they expect it—the customers do. It's just a different vibe, totally." Unlike in the Cedar Rapids market, there were many small vendors, and the difference in the size of the farms was less obvious. "You could tell because the big ones have more than one booth. If you've got three stalls, you're a big operation. But when I was there, there were maybe three or four bigs, and the rest were small. When you've got the same amount of space and you cover your table, nobody can tell how big your operation is."

Even more striking, however, were the friendly relationships between the vendors. Faye noticed the difference: "In the Cedar Rapids market most of the big vendors wouldn't even talk to me. I'd be next to them, and they wouldn't even chat. I'd ask questions because I was trying to learn, and they really weren't interested in talking to me. But in the Iowa City market everybody talks to everybody. And a couple of the big vendors actually came and wanted to know what I was selling. Wanted me to explain to them how you grow this because they weren't growing it. So that was a revelation!" In addition, the customers in Iowa City were more receptive to her products: "The customer base in Iowa City was a whole lot easier to work with—much more sophisticated. They understood what organic was, and most of them understood what it meant to be seasonal." In particular, the difficulties she experienced selling greens in Cedar Rapids were less prevalent in Iowa City. "In Iowa City people not only knew what it was, but they wanted to know what kind of kale it was. You know? And they understood, um, the concept of an heirloom tomato and the fact that just because a tomato isn't perfectly round and red doesn't mean it isn't a tomato. It was just easier." In addition, the cultural diversity in Iowa City benefited Faye's business. "Indian and Asian customers, they will buy a lot of the greens that other people won't buy because they recognize them, they're from home, and because they're a lot more vegetable-oriented, I think, than most Americans. So that was good too—to have customers who would buy the things that I wanted to grow anyway, just for us, and they would actually buy it. It's difficult to get people to buy things like mustard or tatsoi or things like that, Asian greens."

Of course, just as Frances's CSA benefited from the Local Foods Connection advertising, Faye's farmers' market success in Iowa City was also the result of some factors outside her control. The long-standing popularity of the market ensured a regular customer base. It helps that the Iowa City market remains under a covered structure, so that the negative effect of a rainy day is not significant. The presence of a well-known grocery cooperative that has promoted organic food since the 1970s and a high level of community attention to the environmental and health benefits of local food also support a robust market, benefiting all sellers.

During Faye's time as a vendor at two large markets over the years, she slowly developed a display and packaging system that worked best for her products. During her first years at the Cedar Rapids market, she had little flexibility in packaging because of market regulations. "When I started at the Cedar Rapids market, I packaged everything because I think that was what they sort of wanted you to do. Because they didn't allow scales, or the scale that they would allow had to be very expensive—it had to be a certified scale, and I wasn't sure I wanted to spend $250 on a scale at that time—and I never did." Thus, her greens, green beans, and tomatoes were sold by the bag to avoid having to weigh products at the market. This required her to spend a lot of time packaging items before each market, and it was more difficult to pack her produce in the car to take it to market. When she moved to the Iowa City market, she started selling items in bulk. Rather than bagging her greens and lettuce, she would bring it in large bins and put it in the bags as it was purchased. "It took me several years to get this figured out, but when I started in the Iowa City market I started like that in the beginning and it just worked better." The initial reason behind the transition was to simplify her work. "I was spending so much time packaging it, and I thought, why shouldn't that be part of the market experience? That's what made me do it. It was just to make it easier, but then I realized that customers liked it."

Concerns about fair scales were still an issue, however, and market policies were generally not in favor of having vendors use scales. Faye was one of the few vendors selling bulk items "because when you join the market they give you a sheet that tells you how to do things, and they definitely did not want you using scales, because they didn't figure people would be using fair scales. Well, then they decided that you could use a scale, but they had the right to inspect it and come look at it. But nobody ever did, and nobody ever questioned it." Faye's strategy was to frequently show customers the accuracy of the scale. "When I had my scale there, I had a can that had a precise weight on it so that I could put it on the scale and show people that it is a fair scale." This way, she was comfortable selling all of her items by the pound at the market. The bulk presentation was less work for her, and also more visually appealing. "It's kind of impressive when you have your table with all these big bins so people can see it all. It's pretty."

The farmers' market scales provide a good example of how the focus on the direct part of direct marketing obscures the interventions between farmers and consumers. The market recognizes that customers may be at some risk when purchasing local food. An inaccurate scale could result in their paying more than the advertised price for a product. For the vendor who is competing with neighboring stalls, presenting bulk items is a good marketing strategy that, in Faye's case, helped her products stand out while requiring less work on her part. Finding the ideal balance between consumer protection, workload, and visual appeal is a challenge for market managers, vendors, and consumers. The structure of the market provides some security for customers by ensuring consistency, but it can hamper farmers' flexibility in packaging and marketing.

Eventually, Faye was ready to transition out of farmers' markets entirely. "I just got up one morning in the winter between the last time I did the market in Iowa City and thought, you know I just really don't want to do this again. Because, it's just such hard work, getting up that early." The market bell rang in Iowa City at 7:30 A.M., requiring her to rise in time to pack all of her materials in her car, drive the twenty-five minutes to the market, then unload and set her table up before the market opening. Over the years, she had developed a strong customer base and had an active website and mailing list. "I thought that I had enough people responding to my website and paying attention to my emails that a CSA would work. So what I did was, I had a fairly good email list, a mailing list, and I sent it out to everyone asking what they thought if I decided to go the CSA route instead. And I was surprised at how many people actually signed up right away." Since then, she has managed a small membership of twenty shareholders who pick up their shares at a grocery store near her home. Her travel time is less than it was to market, and she is no longer tied to the early morning market schedule.

Relationships among vendors and with customers are also specific to each market, as Faye's experience shows. In Cedar Rapids, the vendors were a small social group who were somewhat reluctant to welcome new producers. In Iowa City, her experience was much different because vendors were curious about each other's growing practices and less dismissive of small producers. The more sophisticated and diverse clientele in Iowa City was beneficial for Faye, who grows specialty items such as Asian greens and uses organic practices. Even though the individual producers develop their own customer base, they do so within the structure and location of the specific market. They are able to direct market only during the times and in the space dictated by market policies. It was ultimately the rigid schedule and the heavy workload that caused her to leave farmers' markets entirely in favor of a CSA. Her steady customer development strategies and niche products ensured that she did not go home with unsold produce, a common concern among growers. Still, the early mornings and inflexible schedule of the market, along with the work of selling the entire weeks' worth of harvested product in one session, made the flexibility of a CSA more attractive for her.

Faye's story also shows the interplay of market policies, vendor relationships, and specific customer groups. The popular markets are still difficult for vendors to enter; in Iowa City there is a waiting list every year, despite another expansion in 2011. Many vendors resort to part-time sales, in which they fill a spot, sometimes on very short notice, if a permanent vendor is unable to attend the market. There are ever-present concerns about accurate scales and fair competition. The Iowa City document outlining rules for vendors runs twelve pages and includes language about scales—which are still prohibited unless the market manager is notified and the scale is inspected by the Iowa Department of Agriculture and Land Stewardship, Weights and Measures Bureau. In addition, all products must be displayed at least six inches from the ground, and vendors may not loudly hawk their products or distribute low cost or free items, other than small samples, that would undercut other vendors.

Ultimately, the market provides the appearance of a farmer-consumer relationship unfettered by a middleman or regulatory agency. In reality, the market recreates regulatory structures typical in conventional food production and shapes the interactions between farmers and consumers. Restrictions on specific types of display (height, for example) and marketing (no loud calling out) create a specific environment for the customer. Of course, consumers are mostly unaware of the regulatory structure of the market, making it appear as though their interactions with farmers are the central organizing principle of the system.

Meat and Dairy

Fruits and vegetables are the simplest products to market directly to consumers because there are few regulatory constraints. During the course of my research, I spoke with far more vegetable farmers than meat and dairy producers, who face greater challenges. Selling beef and pork requires access to a processor, and dairy adds additional challenges in the form of on-site licensing and inspections. These regulatory hurdles are burdensome and the start-up costs for livestock production can also be high. Investing in packages of seed at the beginning of a growing season is much less daunting than purchasing several steers that will take nearly two years to finish on pasture. The loss of one member of a small animal herd is a significant financial blow that cannot be remedied in a season. Even in the

most difficult growing seasons, vegetable producers often have the ability
to replant or to sow a replacement crop. A farmer whose flock of broiler
chickens is killed by a rogue raccoon cannot so easily recoup that loss.

Farmers' market producers work within regulatory systems that create
a space for the appearance of a relatively unencumbered direct market.
Meat and dairy producers encounter an entirely different scenario. In
their case, the system does not even pretend to create a direct market
space. Instead, they must fit their operations, no matter how small, into a
structure that only recognizes the largest of producers. The result is that
local meat and dairy products are often not readily available to consumers.

Meat processing accounted for 3.7 percent of Iowa's gross domestic
product in 2008 and is an important component of the agricultural industry in the state.[8] In 2010, there were 277 meat-processing plants; of
these, 115 are federally inspected, meaning that their products can be sold
nationally and internationally. The seventy-one state-inspected plants'
products are sold only within the state of Iowa. Finally, ninety-one of the
plants are custom-only processing. These facilities can only process meat
for the owner of the carcass—usually beef, pork, or venison. All meat
from these processors is marked "not for sale" and cannot be sold by the
producer to a third party. It can be returned to the producer for his or
her own consumption or sold by the processor directly to consumers. Of
these plants, 56 percent are fairly small, with fewer than ten employees.[9]

Most of the producers I spoke with worked with either a state-inspected
facility or a custom-only processor. Colloquially, these small plants are
called lockers, a term that harkens back to the 1940s, before household
freezers became standard. The lockers would butcher livestock from
area farmers and customers would rent storage space in the large walk-in
freezer (the locker), to hold their meat. As more families acquired their
own freezers, the communal locker became obsolete, but the term remains. Instead of storing frozen meats for customers, small processors now
tend to offer special cuts and products such as sausages or cured meats.
Many have retail operations for selling their own variety of specialty products and other grocery items.

The national trend in meat processing mirrors that of agriculture overall, with increasing concentration and scale. The vast majority of meat

processing now takes place in slaughterhouses that process more than a hundred thousand animals a year. By contrast, the USDA defines a small federally inspected plant as one that processes fewer than ten thousand animals each year.[10] These small plants are better able to receive a few animals at a time to process, and they can separate one individual producer's meat from another so that the product can be sold with that producer's specific label. Federally inspected plants of this size are rare; in Iowa, the 115 federally inspected plants are owned by Tyson, Smithfield, and other giant corporations. These facilities do not cater to small farmers.

Thus, for any producer planning to market meat directly, access to a processor is a key consideration. In eastern Iowa, beef, pork, and lamb producers have several lockers to choose from, both state-inspected and custom processors. There are eleven custom and/or state-inspected lockers in and near the county where I conducted most of my research. While custom-processed meat cannot be sold by the farmer or other third party, the meat locker can sell it directly to consumers. In these arrangements, the customer pays for the animal in advance by paying a fee to the farmer. Then, the customer works with the processor to decide how the meat is to be cut and pays a separate fee to the locker. Benjamin Garber, a producer who makes his entire living from producing beef, lamb, and poultry, sells all of his beef and lamb using this method. When working with a custom locker, the producer is not responsible for any processing and distribution beyond delivering the live animal to the locker. Growers who use a state-inspected locker can resell individual cuts of meat to their customers. They are then responsible for maintaining state-inspected freezers at their farms or when they travel to sell at a farmers' market. In this case, they may also need to follow further requirements for each individual market. For a grower like Sarah Miller, who already has an inspected commercial kitchen on her property to support her baking business, this is not a significant barrier. For producers who may not want to store or distribute individual cuts, using custom processing is usually the best option.

Poultry is handled quite differently from beef, pork, and lamb. Only two poultry processors in the eastern part of the state will process small batches of birds, and only one of those will do specialty birds such as ducks. Neither of the lockers is very accessible to farmers who are located

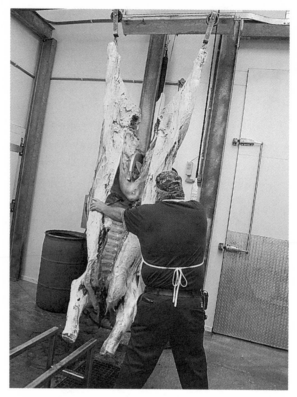

A meat locker employee splits a beef carcass
in eastern Iowa.

in east-central Iowa: one is located more than a hundred miles south and
the other is 130 miles to the north. The long distance is a concern for
farmers not only because of the significant travel time for them but also
because of the potential stress on the animals before processing. Poultry,
however, can be processed on a farm and sold directly to the consumer if
no more than a thousand birds are slaughtered per calendar year. Birds
can also be sold live with no licensing regulations, though I do not know
of any farmer in eastern Iowa who regularly does this.

    Although each producer's method for processing varies somewhat, most
follow similar procedures. Benjamin Garber, for example, processes birds
four times per year. He sends a customer letter out early in the year indicating the processing dates, usually a Saturday. His customers indicate on

a form how many birds they would like to pick up on each date. He then sends a reminder email out a week or so before butchering day and reminds customers of the time. On some days he may process as many as 170 birds, usually with a crew of about four or five people. Benjamin sets up an assembly line in a small pole shed on his property. He uses stock tanks filled with cold water to chill the birds after they are butchered. Before the birds are ready to be put into bags, he places them upright on orange caution cones to drain. Then they are bagged and stored in large coolers in a second building, where they are weighed as customers pick them up.

Although processing poultry in this way is undeniably a great deal of work, and the producer will likely need to pay for at least some labor, it relieves him or her of traveling to a locker and ensures control over the process. One area beef producer raised broilers for the first time in 2011 and had them processed at a locker 115 miles from his farm. Several birds returned with torn skin and dislocated thighs, indicating rough treatment during processing (likely during the plucking stage). On-farm processing may be more labor intensive, but it may also result in more careful handling of the birds. (I will describe poultry processing in greater detail in chapter 7.)

Unfortunately, dairy producers do not enjoy the same level of flexibility in processing options as meat producers. Because there are no custom-processing facilities for fluid milk, those who wish to direct market their products must process and pasteurize their milk and cheese on their own farms. Most commercial dairies produce on contract for a specific milk distributor, such as Roberts Dairy or Kalona Organics in Iowa. These producers are only responsible for storing the raw milk for a short time before the company picks it up.

The history of milk consumption in the United States is a fascinating story that blends American beliefs about health and child nutrition with sanitation movements and a healthy dose of political intervention to ensure the perfect food, as described by E. Melanie DuPuis in her comprehensive work on the subject.[11] Ultimately, the dairy industry has consistently moved toward centralization as local and regional networks of the past have given way to national and even international distribution of a highly perishable fluid product. The dairy industry can now rely on high-heat pasteurization and refrigerated transport to consolidate into ever-larger distribution chains. As in the meat industry, these distribution chains are not scaled for small producers, and the regulatory system has not maintained a structure that supports smaller producers who sell directly to consumers.

Fluid milk receives more stringent regulatory attention than other dairy products because of its perishability. Dairy products are divided into two classes: Grade A is milk is that will be consumed as fluid milk, yogurt, or cottage cheese; Grade B refers to cheese, cheese products, butter, and ice cream. Iowa defers to the federal standards for dairy production and processing, and both Grade A and B facilities (including farms, plants, and distributors) must be state inspected and certified. Iowa is one of sixteen states that completely prohibit raw milk sales, though some producers quietly sell raw milk to neighbors or acquaintances. Nearly every year, there is a legislative attempt to legalize raw milk sales in some form, either on farms or in retail outlets, so far without success. A few small-scale dairies in Iowa pasteurize their own fluid milk for very limited distribution, but this is an expensive and labor-intensive endeavor.

Cheese, as a Grade B product, is somewhat more manageable for a small-scale producer. Even so, the combination of regulations, most often developed for large-scale producers, and the high cost of equipment required to fulfill them can be a major barrier. The Murphy family started a goat cheese business to supplement their row-crop farm and because one of their nine children had a severe allergy to cow's milk. Their first goat was a gift from a neighbor, and they soon added a second. At this point, the goats were producing more milk than they could drink, and so the family started experimenting with making goat cheese. Soon after, they visited a small goat dairy in central Iowa and struck up a friendship with the farmer. The oldest daughter, Brittany, started learning from the central Iowa farmer and perfecting her cheese recipe. Her mother, Kerry said,

> We spent the whole winter, "Should we make cheese?" "Should we just milk goats?" We were talking about that too. My husband works off farm. He would like to work just on farm, so we've always tried to angle things that way, exploring different avenues of being able to

make a living from the farm, with everybody home working together. So anyway, we explored the idea of a large goat dairy and selling the milk to Vermont Chevre or something like that, and then we toyed around with selling milk and making cheese, and then, well why don't we start really small and see if we like this. Once we started the ball rolling, we started shelling out money for this and that, and it was a huge expensive project, and then, a year and a half, we looked back and wondered, if we had known all that, would we still have done this?

Just before I interviewed the Murphys, a family interested in starting a cheese business had visited them. Kerry reported: "We just real honestly told them what the process was, I mean as far as getting up and running and cost and everything. It felt like we scared them off—we didn't intend to at all." Because the Murphys' farm had some existing infrastructure, including a barn and milking parlor, Kerry initially thought that adding a small goat dairy would not be a complicated process. "We thought we would renovate part of the old barn because there was a milking parlor in there, and the milk room, but it was old. We thought, oh, with a little bit of effort we can make this the milk room and the parlor and then add on a cheese room on the side of the barn." They quickly learned, however, that simply having the space was not sufficient. They were already milking fifteen goats by hand and experimenting with cheese recipes. What they did not consume at home, they shared with friends and neighbors. According to Kerry, "after speaking to inspectors we realized we should start from the ground up. This is going to cost as much as building a new building so let's just do it fast and efficient and get a building up. But that whole building process took a year."

During this time they experimented with recipes and production before becoming licensed and inspected to sell cheese; in the process, they learned a lot about how to make cheese well and also about sanitary production. Brittany noted that they had learned that any milk containing *E. coli* would not produce good cheese. Instead, it resulted in "a big rubber, bubbly disgusting thing." When they read that bloated cheese was caused by *E. coli,* they wondered what could have suddenly caused the problem.

Kerry reported: "They had put the water tub on the inside of the pen rather than the outside of the pen, so the goats weren't leaning over, the water was inside. They must have been defecating in it, that's the only thing we figured. So we moved the water tub out, and then the cheese was good again!" As the family moved toward a commercial business, they had to pasteurize the milk, which would kill the *E. coli* present in the raw product.

One key regulation relates to antibiotic residue in milk. The milk from any dairy animal that has recently received antibiotics cannot be sold. Producers are required to remove an animal receiving antibiotics or discard the milk for a period of time, usually seventy-two hours. The Murphys learned that any antibiotic residue in the milk will kill the culture, and the milk will not turn into cheese. Their experiments led them to suggest that the high levels of testing that state regulations require may be unnecessary because the existence of some contaminants in the goats' milk will inhibit the cheesemaking. In addition, the small size of their business reduces the likelihood that milk contaminated with antibiotics will accidentally make its way into the process. "Well, we have twenty-four goats. We know if we would treat an animal that we would not keep that milk. If you have five hundred goats and five employees, I can see that maybe a goat hops a fence and you get a little confused, and some antibiotic milk would get in there. But you have to test each batch of milk before you make cheese to see if there's antibiotics in the milk. This lab equipment, sold by one vendor, costs four thousand dollars to test antibiotics for our twenty-four goats." Their small size makes sourcing equipment difficult as well. Kelly reported that only three vendors in the country have small-scale equipment. Another option is to source from smaller European dairies, many of which are going out of business, but the distance and shipping adds even more expense.

During the winter that the Murphys built the new building, they developed a business plan. Kerry used the state inspectors as a source of information to better understand the written regulations. "We'd been talking to inspectors—and they'd been coming out. But it's like Greek all those regulations. So we'd have to read it and read it again—and maybe some more would sink in—and try to understand what does this mean, it's written so broadly, and then you have to talk to the inspector." The number of permits required was also daunting:

They come get a milk sample every month, our local inspector does. And before we ever started up, they came to do the farm inspection, because there's one permit for the dairy farm and the parlor and the goats, and he inspects the milk room with that too. So that's one permit, and another permit is the lab permit. So the dairy micro-biology people come and show you how to run the equipment. The vendor did too, but they wanted to see that we knew how to run the lab equipment to test for antibiotics. So there's a permit for that, and that gets inspected every two years. And then there's the cheesemak-ing permit—I thought there were four permits—oh, the sampler. He comes and takes a milk sample, but he can't sample it, I have to sample it, so I have to get a permit for that, which costs money to pull the sample, which he then carries off. And then, one more, for the cheesemaking, so that's a yearly one. We'll have to get inspected in the spring to make sure all the equipment is in compliance and calibrate the thermometers with the state's thermometers. And then they test the cheese at some point to make sure there's nothing bad in it—or, no, that was the microbiology people—anyway.

These permits and inspections, however, only cover the farm and the busi-ness. Kerry added that "each place we sell the cheese, each county, each farmers' market, the health department for that county also wants to see all the paperwork before we can sell the cheese there. And some counties have their own, and some are under the state—so like Cedar Rapids and Iowa City have their own health department, whereas the county where we live and a lot of the other rural counties are under some sort of state area."

In addition to extensive regulations, many farmers consider a dairy to be the most labor-intensive kind of farm. Whether animals are milked by hand or machine, they must be milked twice every day. The Murphy's large family of home-schooled children benefited their business because there were always people available to help. The oldest son remained at home, their second oldest child when I interviewed them managed the goat herd and did most of the milking, while Brittany made the cheese along with her younger sister. Kerry helped develop recipes and package the cheese, and "everybody helps load up and sell."

While dairy may be the most regulated food industry, dairy products are in high demand. The Murphys quickly became well known at both large markets they attended and regularly sold out of their product. In addition, they sold some cheese through a local cooperative grocery store, and their products did not remain long on store shelves. Despite their frustrations with the expense and challenge of permit processes and regulations, labor was the major concern for the family, even with so many available people. When their second son left for college in 2011, they lost their primary milker and herd manager because none of the remaining boys were old enough to take on the role. This change was so significant that they put the cheese operation on hold during the 2012 season until some of the younger children became old enough to help more.

A COMMON CRITIQUE of the conventional food system is that much of it is hidden from consumers. Local food, by contrast, is presumed to be highly visible. These examples suggest, however, that direct marketing is more complex than a simple transaction between a producer and consumer. Depending on the product, the farmer may have to engage with a broader food structure that closely resembles conventional food chains to sell his or her product. Even the direct food market takes a rather long regulatory detour before the food arrives on consumers' plates. Emphasizing these interactions forces us to take a step back and consider the big picture rather than myopically focusing on only one component.

If the direct-to-consumer food system is still embedded in a complicated set of regulations, what happens when the consumer is someone other than an individual eater? Regulation in local food systems occurs during production and distribution, but once the consumer makes a purchase for his or her personal use, that oversight ends. In the next chapters, we see that directly marketing to institutions invites even more complications.

CHAPTER FIVE

Farm to School

IF MARKETING FOOD directly to individuals relies on more than just the farmer and the customer, what does it take to get local food onto the plates of students, hospital patients, or nursing home residents? These institutions, in theory, have the ability to make local food available to populations who would otherwise not be able to obtain it and could create steady new markets for farmers.[1] Schools have been identified as especially important, both because of their consistent demands for food and as a primary food service outlet for children, who would benefit from an expanded menu of healthy food offerings. Farm to school programs have received widespread, positive attention in the popular press and media. Chelsea Simpson of the National Farm to School Network declared that farm to school "will save our food system" in a 2013 *Huffington Post* piece.[2] The potential for local farmers to feed their neighborhood school children is the perfect story. Kids need healthy food at school, and farmers need new and larger marketing opportunities.

The recent growth in farm to school programming nationwide, heavily supported by state and federal legislative efforts, is an interesting development in institutional purchasing of local food. Despite the optimism of journalists and food activists, working with farmers in Iowa illuminated for me some of the challenges in scaling up local food production and marketing. Farm to school, particularly in a public school setting, pushes local food out of its direct-to-consumer comfort zone and introduces a new set of bureaucratic hurdles, most of which had not occurred to me until I started trying to source local food for my own kids' school district.

The context of food in school has changed some over the years, but the political wrangling and assumptions that school food is bad have not. While initial efforts to implement school feeding programs revolved around malnutrition—stemming from the realization that young men were unfit to serve in the military as a result of hunger—the current conversation focuses on overnutrition, particularly childhood obesity. These concerns have resulted in a number of initiatives, including Michelle Obama's Let's Move! campaign, another redesign of the food pyramid into the "my plate" concept that encourages us to fill our plates with a higher proportion of vegetables, and ever more criticism of junk food advertising to children. School food has always been an easy target. Regardless of one's political stance or worldview, most people have a complaint or two about school lunch. For proponents of farm to school programs, a key complaint about school lunch is its reliance on prepackaged and processed items. For others, it is tasteless, boring, and unhealthy, and possibly a case of government's overstepping its bounds into our daily lives.

Within this national conversation, farm to school has risen to the top as a key strategy to improve the nutritional content of school lunches, engage kids in physical activity through school gardens, and increase knowledge about nutrition and food production. Despite their popularity, as evidenced by increasing federal and state funding, however, farm to school programs suffer from many of the same political challenges as any other broad initiative that aims to create systemic change in our well-entrenched systems of education or food production.

The history of school feeding programs is rife with contradictions and competing interests. The National School Lunch Program (NSLP) delicately knits together the interests of agriculture lobbyists and social reformers. Up until the Great Depression, school lunches were managed locally, usually by women's groups or charities outside the school system. These groups were motivated by the moral call to feed the poor as well as by teachers' concerns that their students were too hungry to learn effectively. Mandatory school attendance significantly increased the number of poor children in schools, and burgeoning hygiene and home economics activism called attention to the low nutritional quality and safety of street foods often vended to school children. Nationwide, the activities of antihunger advocates and devotees of nutrition science assisted the development of school feeding programs in most of the nation's largest cities.[3] The National School Lunch Act (Public Law 396) was signed in 1946 by President Harry Truman. Twenty years later, the first Child Nutrition Act passed. These two foundational pieces of legislation are reauthorized, usually with many updates and continued political arguments, with each Farm Bill.[4]

The current system is the result of many iterations and reauthorizations. Its complicated bureaucracy puzzles even the most well-informed experts on procurement and nutrition. In Iowa, this confusion trickles down to local situations in which the tensions between agriculture and education advocates are mirrored in statewide farm to school interactions. Proponents of local agriculture, who want better prices for farmers, are sometimes at odds with procurement experts at the Department of Education, who recognize that food service buyers operate on budgets counted down to the pennies. Farmers, for their part, often resist changing their delivery schedules or packaging to satisfy the needs of an institutional kitchen.

This chapter provides an overview of farm to school efforts nationally and in Iowa. I began my research as the statewide farm to school effort was just beginning to take off. I worked closely with an emergent public school program. (I describe some of those adventures more fully in the next chapter.) The public reaction to the chapter start-up was enormously positive, to the extent that there was a city-wide argument among parents about which elementary school should host the first farmer fair, an event that invited local farmers and nutrition educators into the school for an afternoon event. While the farmer fairs and school garden component of farm to school was an easy sell in this particular district, lunch procurement was much slower to develop. The experience of my group was consistent with that of many others across the state.

Iowa producers tended to be supportive of the goals of farm to school but were frequently unable or unwilling to tailor their diversified operations to meet the needs of school kitchens. Optimistic claims that farm to school will save the food system are rarely borne out because most programs are able to source only a very small amount of food for a school feeding program.

National Farm to School Program

The National Farm to School traces its beginnings back to a few small pilot initiatives in Berkeley, California, and north Florida during the mid-1990s. By 2000, the USDA's Initiative for Future Agricultural and Food Systems (IFAFS) funded the National Farm to School Program to enable program and policy development and research. Members of the new National Farm to School Program attempted to gain more legislative support by including a geographic preference clause in the 2002 Farm Bill. This clause, which was not included in the final legislation, would have allowed school food service directors to specify that the requested item should come from within a predetermined distance in their bid specifications, thereby prioritizing local products. Marion Kalb, a policy specialist for the Community Food Security Coalition and an advisor for the National Farm to School Network at the time, explains: "In the beginning stages of farm to school, one of the biggest barriers was that food service directors didn't know if they could purchase local products. Some folks in New York started to purchase locally but were shut down by the state Education Department. So this legislation was to really give credibility to buying local, and provide the written authority to do so."[5]

The National Farm to School Program was established as part of the 2004 Child Nutrition and WIC Reauthorization Act, which included a seed grant fund for schools to set up farm to school programs and authorized ten million dollars for the program. But the funds were never appropriated, creating a program in name only. The initial legislation did include a mandate that all schools participating in the National School Lunch Program establish a local wellness policy by the 2006–2007 school year.[6] While the development of a local wellness policy was not necessarily related to local food or farm to school, one of the criteria was that wellness policies develop a plan to display the nutritional content for foods available in schools. As a result, many districts ambitiously attempted to use the mandate as a way to make improvements to schools' overall health environments. In these cases, the wellness policies moved beyond the nutritional value of items in the lunchroom and vending machines to address the frequency of classroom parties, treats, and the use of food as a reward in classrooms.[7]

By 2008, the situation really started to improve for the movement; the passage of that year's Farm Bill finally included the geographic preference clause, allowing school food service buyers to prioritize unprocessed local foods. This category included fresh, whole fruits and vegetables, bagged greens, butchered poultry and livestock, and milk and dairy products. Activists affiliated with the Farm to School Network requested that minimally processed foods also be included, such as diced onions, cut lettuce, and shredded cabbage or carrots. As a result, the USDA Food and Nutrition Services expanded the definition of unprocessed in 2009 to include some of these items that have been cut but not substantially altered from their natural state. The 2010 reauthorization of the Child Nutrition Act, passed as the Healthy, Hunger-Free Kids Act, included a funded farm to school program. Beginning in October 2012, the program had access to five million dollars a year, which was disbursed as start-up grants for new farm to school chapters nationwide. The 2014 reauthorization established a pilot program in which up to eight states can work with the USDA to develop procurement systems focusing on locally grown produce.

The legislative mandates enacted in 2004 and 2010, particularly wellness policies and increased fruit and vegetable offerings, "have dovetailed with the sustainable agriculture movement's ongoing interest in developing institutional markets and with national-level farm to school advocacy work by the National Farm to School Network, the Community Food Security Coalition and other groups."[8] This confluence has resulted in some remarkable optimism about the ability of farm to school to make a meaningful change in the school food environment and enhance local food. Some advocates hope that farm to school programs will increase fresh fruit and vegetable offerings in schools and spark broader education about food production.[9] Public health professionals also promote the programs as an early intervention for obesity prevention.[10] All we can say with certainty is that the number of farm to school programs is increasing nationwide. Less clear is the impact on child nutrition or obesity. Few studies have been peer reviewed, and data on individual farm to school programs has not been collected in a systematic way, making it very difficult to synthesize or draw conclusions.[11]

Most farm to school chapters are funded at the state or federal level, but each program looks a little different depending on the capacities of an individual district or school building. Different districts have varying space for school gardens and different kitchen arrangements for school lunch. In some cases, programs are largely parent driven; in others, school food service personnel take a lead role. This inherent localization has led some to argue that farm to school programs may provide a space for civic engagement and social justice, in which the local community becomes more deeply involved in a school district. Indeed, the high level of parent volunteerism in schools may help drive farm to school programming forward. That engagement could, in turn, encourage change at the state or federal level.[12] Of course, both financial resources and parent engagement in public school systems are unevenly distributed. In addition, as I will show in the next chapter, it is difficult for an individual volunteer-driven farm to school program to make a meaningful impact on school lunches.

Ultimately, the existence of scattered, individual farm to school programs does not eliminate every perceived shortcoming of school lunches. Kate Adamick, the first director of New York City's School Food Plus collaboration points out that replacing a regular side with a local side does not improve the entire lunch. She further cautions against assuming that a school's lunch problems are solved because the district has a farm to school program.[13] Farm to school programs also face criticism from anti-hunger activists, who are concerned that programming largely benefits only the most privileged districts. The overwhelming reliance on external funding only reinforces existing social discrepancies by privileging those schools and districts that have skilled volunteer resources. The public funding that has been made available is largely in the form of program grants. This requires that a school have access to someone with the time and ability to write a—frankly—complicated and confusing grant and submit it through the very user-unfriendly grants.gov system. A more equitable model would make public funding available across the board to schools by embedding it into district budgets.[14]

Although the research on farm to school is inconsistent and somewhat scarce, there has been some attention to identifying barriers to developing a program. Cost is usually one of the first and most important issues raised. The cost of the specific ingredients is only partially responsible; there may also be increased labor costs to food service departments because whole raw products require more preparation, new delivery and invoicing systems may be required to work with local farmers, and food service storage may be inadequate.[15] But items purchased locally in season may be cheaper than products sourced from a national distributor. Some researchers have found that food service directors see cost benefits when the supply chain is shortened, in that transportation and shipping costs are usually included in the price of an item from their distributor. Thus, when schools deal with a local grower, those costs may be lower.[16] Limiting packaging may also reduce costs. Large-scale distributors may line cardboard boxes with cardboard inserts or foam liners to protect the product, while local products, which are transported and handled less, may be packed loosely in food-grade boxes that cost less. In Iowa, however, flexible packaging options have been occasionally problematic. A food service director from a small northeast Iowa district reported to me that a producer once delivered green beans in a laundry basket, forcing her to explain the importance of using packaging that is designated food grade to ensure that the produce is protected from damage and that the packaging will not transfer any chemical or other contaminants to the food.

While the cost of local food may be either a barrier or a benefit, depending on the specific local situation, other features of institutional cooking more clearly impede the ability of schools to use local products. Food safety concerns, in particular, may inhibit food service buyers from purchasing local food. Children younger than nine are considered a high-risk population for food-borne illness. The Child Nutrition Reauthorization Act of 2004 required all schools participating in the NSLP to use food safety procedures based on the Hazard Analysis and Critical Control Point (HACCP) system, a comprehensive food safety program for processors and institutional kitchens. This program emphasizes identifying the points throughout the processing and service chain where food contamination could occur. These include food handling and transport as well as cooking and service procedures. Preventative procedures, such as wearing gloves, hand washing, and temperature control are implemented throughout the process. A significant portion of HACCP procedures involves careful monitoring and recording of food, oven, and walk-in cooler temperatures. In particular, foods should be kept out of the danger zone

(41°F–135°F); cold foods should remain below forty-one degrees; hot foods should always be above 135 degrees.

While meat has long been identified with food-borne illness, particularly infections caused by *E. coli* bacteria, well-publicized outbreaks related to spinach, tomatoes, and cantaloupe have increased concerns about fresh produce as well. Concerns about food safety have, to some extent, been responsible for the tendency to use precooked meats, including beef or chicken patties and ground beef crumbles, in school kitchens. Fresh produce is both received and often served as a raw agricultural product; therefore, there is no kill step to eliminate pathogens. Large distributors provide assurances about the safety of the food they sell and buffer food service buyers from the responsibility of ensuring food safety practices during production and processing. When food service buyers purchase directly from farms, however, they become responsible for ensuring that the food was produced in a safe environment, in addition to overseeing HACCP regulations in their kitchens.

Farm to School in Iowa

In Iowa, as in the national context, farm to school programs are subject to food safety protocols as well as a delicate balancing act between food, labor, and transportation costs. The Iowa farm to school program was created by legislation passed in 2007. Senate file 452 asserted that the newly created program was to be used to promote "the purchase of locally and regionally produced or processed food in order to improve child nutrition and strengthen local and regional farm economies." The Iowa legislature, like other state governments, saw potential for farm to school programs to simultaneously address childhood obesity and diversify the farm economy, always an important statewide topic.[17] The legislation directed the Iowa Department of Agriculture and Land Stewardship (IDALS) to hire a coordinator to oversee the program and created a seven-member farm to school council. The coordinator was charged with a number of tasks, including facilitating communication between producers and school food service buyers, promoting the program in local communities, and developing workshops and training sessions that provide assistance to schools and producers. In addition, the Department of Human Services, the Department of Education, and the Department of Public Health were directed to cooperate with IDALS by providing staff and administrative support for the program. The legislature allocated eighty thousand dollars from Iowa's general fund to be used for salaries, support, and maintenance in the 2007 fiscal year. The state funding trickles down to individual districts through start-up grants and resource materials such as menu planning tools for food service directors and reusable delivery containers for growers.

The statewide program also encourages individual districts to create locally managed farm to school chapters. Chapters are required to have at least seven members, who work solely to meet the program mission and objectives. The programming should reflect the statewide objectives, and all funding flows through a school or school district. By spring 2014, there were more than twenty-five chapters in the state. The Iowa farm to school program provides start-up funds for new chapters and resources for purchasing local produce, tools, and materials for school gardens.

Another task of the statewide program, as designated by the original legislation, is to host workshops and training sessions for producers, educators, and food service buyers. I attended two statewide gatherings in 2011, one hosted jointly by the Department of Education and IDALS and one hosted solely by IDALS. While these sessions aim to clarify the complicated procedures of procurement and food safety, in some cases, participants report that they leave confused and disheartened about the process.

In particular, the complicated regulations for school food procurement are a constant source of confusion for food service buyers who wish to purchase locally. In Iowa, school food buyers are required to solicit at least three bids for any purchase that will be reimbursed with federal funds. Procurement procedures may be either by formal or informal bids. Federal regulations require a formal bid process whenever the spending is greater than a hundred thousand dollars, though individual districts may designate a lower threshold for a formal bid. A formal bid procedure requires publicly advertised bid requests, followed with sealed, written bid submissions from vendors. Generally, local purchases remain small enough to require only an informal bid. Buyers must still solicit at least three bids and document them by recording the time, date, and amount of the bid, but they do not have to be submitted sealed or in writing. Federal requirements stipulate that the buyer accept the lowest bid submitted, though he or she can accept a higher bid if the reason is documented. The geographic preference clause, for example, may be used as justification for accepting a higher bid.

Applying procurement regulations to local products becomes problematic, however, when the food service buyer does not know which growers to contact for specific products. At one workshop facilitated by the Iowa Department of Education and the IDALS, many food service directors, as well as the representatives from IDALS, had questions about how to apply procurement regulations to local purchasing. In particular, the staff members and IDALS representatives were unsure how to proceed if there were not three vendors available who grow the requested item. The presenter, a representative from the Department of Education, cautioned the audience to carefully follow the procurement rules.

One audience member asked, "How much do you have to know about the grower? If they don't meet the specs, is that OK, or does it look like you're purposely not following the rules?" The presenter responded that the food service buyer is responsible for finding out whether the grower fits the specification. An exasperated food service employee sitting nearby exclaimed, "How?!" One suggestion was to use online price guides as bids. In an informal bid process, a buyer can look at public price listings of distributors or from the Chicago Board of Produce to compare prices with those of local growers. The mention of the Chicago Board of Produce caused a wave of protests from the IDALS representatives, who pointed out that local growers are not likely to be able to compete with commodity pricing. The interaction showed the tension between IDALS, which advocates for fair prices for local farmers, and the Department of Education, whose procedural constraints leave little flexibility for food service buyers.

One goal of farm to school programs at both the national and state level is to increase markets for small- to medium-sized farm operations. In Iowa, some producers are interested in selling directly to schools, though others find the process too complicated and prefer other markets. One diversified vegetable and flower producer, whose family has sold at farmers' markets for more than fifteen years, sees institutional sales as a good new market. He noted that the work and risk involved in farmers' markets is significant and that over the past five years, his family has seen market sales decrease, despite the recent surge in farmers' markets nationwide. He attributes the reduced sales to a number of factors, including lack of advertising and low investment by his city in the market, as well as a stand location that is in a low-traffic area. He notes that institutional sales are new to him; he does not have a refrigerated truck for deliveries, nor does he have adequate packaging for institutional needs. Although he's willing to make some investments in equipment, large items such as a refrigerated truck are currently beyond his budget.

Other producers suggest that the strict requirements related to product packaging and delivery in schools and other institutional kitchens makes them less attractive customers than are individual families and market consumers. An organic dairy farmer from northeast Iowa, whose family operates a retail ice cream store and sells fluid milk as well, expressed concerns about increasing size. "We could expand and add nine million dollars to the business, but what about quality? School budgets are not set up for local milk. It costs more to set up than fish sticks and tuna stars . . . You can't always bridge the gap; we can only deliver once each week. This is a problem for buyers who expect you to deliver three times per week." A produce and poultry producer expressed similar sentiments: "I have one pickup truck. I'm not going to buy a second one and hire someone to drive it. Maybe we'll come to a point where we'll do this. The demand will increase and we'll adapt, or someone else will get into the game."

The comment about "fish sticks and tuna stars" got a chuckle from the group that day, and it underscores the subtle disapproval of the quality of school food. Local food farmers repeatedly note that the food they grow is better—fresher, healthier, cleaner—than other foods. School food, in particular, tends to be viewed as substandard in comparison. But on a more practical level, these producers have not developed their businesses with institutions in mind, and they will have to make some fairly significant changes to make it worthwhile to sell their products to schools. Likewise, school kitchens are not always set up for local products. Constraints on storage space require milk deliveries several times per week rather than a large quantity once during the week. For a dairy farmer with limited delivery schedules, this would not work. Enthusiastic volunteers and legislatures often miss this point. Farm to school almost always looks good on paper—where the marriage between increasing markets for local farmers and increasing fresher meal options for students seems obvious. When we start examining how farmers respond to farm to school, however, some potentially irreconcilable differences arise.

Schools also have expectations about produce size standards that are not important, or even intelligible, to farmers. The USDA has standardized size designations to which small produce growers rarely have to comply when selling at farmers' markets or through CSA. Nationally distributed apples, for example, are sold by size according to how many can fit into a forty-pound case. Large apples may have as few as forty-eight apples in a case, while a case of small apples might hold up to 163. At a local food summit aimed at bringing together producers and institutional buyers, a produce grower expressed frustration about this issue, noting that not only does she not understand why institutions require her peppers to conform to a specific number per box, she has no idea how to make her product fit these specifications. A school food service director sitting in on the session explained that the sizing helps define her portion sizes and is very important to her meal planning. She needs to know how many slices you're going to get out of an apple.

For producers, the desire to have local produce conform to USDA standards seems like a push to make the local food system act more like the industrialized food system. The organic agriculture program director for IDALS points out that conforming to the USDA standards is voluntary and cautioned food service directors, "if you're going to require that, you won't have any growers." The local food system was not designed with institutions in mind. The conflict between growers and school buyers also illuminates the challenge of scale and supply in local food. For pepper or apple growers to be able to size their produce according to the USDA standards, they have to have a large enough supply to sort for different markets. If a school requires two hundred pounds of 113-count apples, a producer has to have enough variety (or a very consistent harvest) to fill that order. He may have two hundred pounds of apples, but not enough to fill the specific size requirement. That producer also has to have someone available to do the sorting and packaging of those 113-count apples.

A final concern for producers is price. Direct marketing to consumers is generally more profitable than institutional or wholesale sales. One grower, who operates a two-hundred-member CSA, indicates that she would rather donate overages to a local food pantry than sell them at wholesale prices. She regularly has more onions than her shareholders require, and she admits that she could sell them to a school district or a wholesale distributor. She points out that onions are incredibly labor intensive: "You plant every seed, then weed them at least twice, pull each one individually, you haul them to the hoop [house] to cure, then individually cut the tops off of each one." Grocery store onions are often a dollar per pound or less, and she cannot compete with those prices. Donating the onions to food pantries and free lunch programs, to her, is a better investment of her labor than selling at the low end of the price scale. Another grower, when contacted about potentially growing potatoes for an eastern Iowa school district, expressed reservations based on past experiences with the food service buyer, who he felt had been consistently inflexible and unreasonable on price. He initially resisted even considering the idea, assuming that she would not meet his price.

Many producers have stable and predictable customers with their current marketing strategies. By and large, they are satisfied with their existing level of production. They recognize that, while institutional sales may decrease their marketing costs by, for example, eliminating the labor required to vend at a farmers' market, they anticipate that schools will be unable to meet their prices. Additionally, many would have to increase production to meet the needs of larger districts. Farmers are well aware of the extra labor and infrastructure costs involved in increasing production and may be unwilling to risk expansion for institutional prices. This standoff has resulted in somewhat of a stalemate. Farmers will have to scale up to meet the larger supply needs of institutions, but they are wary of the stringent requirements of these new markets. Institutions appear interested in purchasing from local farmers, but only if they can guarantee the appropriate supply, packaging, delivery, and consistency of the product. At some point, one of these groups must take a risk, either by becoming a more flexible buyer or by significantly shifting production strategies to a wholesale model.

In the next chapter, I will dig a little deeper into the specific experiences of a newly formed farm to school program as its members attempted to purchase local foods for school lunches. Their initial experience resulted in many lessons learned, including how farmers and food service buyers have very different views on what constitutes clean or healthy food.

CHAPTER SIX

Just a Simple Salad

PURCHASING LOCAL FOOD
FOR SCHOOL LUNCH

D ESPITE THE CHALLENGES and political wrangling discussed in the last chapter, the national political and popular attention paid to farm to school remains strong. The programs are easy for parents and policymakers of all stripes to support, in that they presumably increase children's consumption of fresh foods and enhance farmers' bottom lines. Nevertheless, the process of getting local food into public school districts remains challenging. This chapter examines a farm to school program in one midsized school district in Iowa. I focus on the process of purchasing local items for school lunches, usually the holy grail of farm to school programming. Nutrition education and gardening are important, but if farm to school is going to help expand local food systems, institutions have to incorporate local products in their regular menus.

The story I tell in this chapter shows that small farms and institutional kitchens sometimes have divergent values and goals beyond just knowing how many servings you can get out of an apple. Nevertheless, the district has slowly developed a fairly small selection of local fresh produce items that it regularly purchases. It all started with a salad that turned out to be not so simple. Later, as the program matured, watermelons and sweet potatoes became two success stories. The farm to school group learned over time how to source items that are available in large quantities, easy to process, and palatable to the schools' finicky customers.

I begin with an enthusiastic farm to school team and a simple salad. A school food service buyer can purchase several menus worth of chopped, ready-to-eat lettuce for salads online or by phone in a matter of minutes.

But purchasing and preparing local lettuce for use in one day's worth of school lunch salads took several months of planning, included a number of unexpected challenges, and required a small army of volunteers. The group had to contend with the weather, inadequate local supplies, the often opposing views of the farmers and the food service director, and the labor-intensive reality of washing and cutting nearly three hundred pounds of lettuce.

The Midwestern Community School District (MCSD) farm to school chapter was chartered in September of 2010. It involved a local non-profit agency, which paid an administrative coordinator, and the area's Resource Conservation and Development (RC&D) office as well as the district's food service staff. Each new chapter is provided an automatic grant for $900 from the Iowa Department of Agriculture and Land Stewardship (IDALS) for start-up costs and initial projects. This was the tenth farm to school chapter started in Iowa; by 2014 there were more than twenty-five chapters across the state. The objectives of MCSD F2S are to "get kids thinking about where their food comes from and how it is grown; provide hands-on food activities for school students such as school gardens, in-class cooking demonstrations and composting systems; help kids make healthy food choices; add more local foods to school meals and snacks, and; support the local food economy."[1]

In addition to the paid coordinator, there were a handful of volunteers, some of them permanent chapter members, while others assisted only sporadically with special projects. I became involved when my children's elementary school became the site of the first farmer fair, organized by the MCSD farm to school program. Farmer fairs serve as in-school field trips for students. Instead of traveling to farms, several farmers visit the school to give presentations or demonstrations about their businesses. Students also have the opportunity to taste-test local foods and rate them on a scorecard. At the first farmer fair, a producer gave a presentation on his heirloom popcorn, another talked about CSA, and a third participant demonstrated how to set up a worm-based composting system. As a parent and as someone known for an interest in farming and local food, I was asked to be on the planning committee for the farmer fair. Subsequently, Amy Weber, the coordinator, asked me to become a chapter member.

In January 2011, when I started attending chapter meetings, the group was still trying to define its goals and plans for the upcoming year. The farmer fair had been very successful, and most people agreed that the chapter should offer the fairs at more schools in the area. The group was less clear about how to proceed with other projects; several ideas were presented, including developing composting systems at schools, school gardens, and local food in school lunches and snacks. Amy sent out a chart outlining seven potential projects and ten goals of the chapter. Members were asked to fill in the chart and rank the extent to which each potential project fulfilled the ten goals. In the end, the group opted to conduct two or three more farmer fairs in 2011, move forward with a school garden committee, and have a group look into the feasibility of serving more local foods in school lunches.

I opted to serve on the committee assessing school lunches, along with Amy, the RC&D food system planner Gregg Jung, grocery manager Mark Schulte, producer Neal Jackson, and MCSD food service director Carol Hendel-Patterson. While this subcommittee formed a cohesive group, there was always the sense that the food service director was somewhat separate from the rest of us. In casual conversation, the other participants often called the meetings of the school food study group "meetings with Carol." We met on her territory, at the district offices. It was clear that she was our gatekeeper, and she would approve (or not) any projects we had in mind. Our first step was to gain a better understanding of how school lunch worked in the MCSD. We initially had little idea of what local items Carol might want or be able to use. For my part, I was not sure whether Carol, who had been at every farm to school chapter meeting I had attended, really supported the program or saw it as just another challenge in the course of her job. The first food study group meeting, or meeting with Carol, occurred in late January 2011.

At the time, the district consisted of twenty-four schools: three high schools, three junior high schools, and eighteen elementary schools. That year, there were about twelve thousand students in the district, who ate 6,500 school lunches and about a thousand breakfasts each day. There were, and still are, five production kitchens in the district, one at each of the three junior high buildings and one in each of the two larger high schools. Lunches are delivered to the rest of the buildings in the mornings on seven delivery routes. The rounds are repeated in the afternoons to pick up leftovers, food carts, and trays.

Like most school lunch programs, the MCSD school lunch program is completely self-supported and is not part of the district's general operating fund. There are three school lunch categories, a full-price meal, a reduced-price meal, and a free meal. In 2010–2011, a full-price school lunch cost a student $1.85; a reduced-price lunch was forty cents. Eligibility for reduced-price and free lunch is set at the federal level. In 2011, a family with an income of up to 30 percent above the poverty line qualified for a free lunch, and up to 85 percent above the federal poverty level qualified for a reduced-price lunch. The federal government then reimburses school districts to cover the cost of the meal's production.

The cost of production for lunch during the 2011 school year was about $2.75. Federal funding made up only a small part of that disparity, with reimbursements of $2.72 for each free lunch and $2.32 for each reduced-price lunch, creating a gap of three cents per meal (given that the reduced-price students paid forty cents for their meals). Full-price meals are also subsidized; the government provided twenty-six cents for each full-price lunch, for which students paid $1.85. Thus, even when students paid full price for their lunch, the school lost sixty-four cents per meal served. Like most public systems, MCSD is able to operate in the black thanks to à la carte lunch offerings at the junior and senior high school levels. These extras, which include a sandwich and entrée salad line, are separate from the regular school lunches. The profits from these sales make up the gap between the cost of producing a school lunch and the price a student pays.

One often cited challenge of farm to school programs is that whole produce takes longer and requires specific skills to prepare. To reduce their labor costs, institutional kitchens often purchase lettuces already washed and chopped, carrots already shredded or cut into sticks, and celery already in manageable stalks. Carol, who had been the food service director since 1986, regularly pointed out to the farm to school team that in the past she had always purchased lettuces, carrots, and celery whole, and her staff had done the work to get them ready to eat. In an interview, I asked her about the reasons for the shift to precut vegetables and found that they were complex. She pointed out that when she started, the district had only nineteen buildings (fifteen elementary schools, two high schools, and two junior high schools) and served about four thousand meals, as opposed to 6,500. Carol said that despite the increase in numbers, "essentially our facilities are still the same. We just added more serving sites." The increase also requires more food to be purchased, which puts storage space at a premium. Carol pointed out that whole lettuce takes up more space in the cooler than precut lettuce, and "that would actually be one of the first issues of getting lettuce in — we get produce in once per week, do we have room for all these uncut items?"

Finally, the regulations for what must be offered in a school lunch have changed over time. Carol often referenced "offer versus serve" in relation to her serving guidelines. When Carol started her job, students were served a tray of food with one entrée, one fruit, one vegetable, and one grain serving. Those of us who enjoyed school lunches before the new millennium likely remember being handed those trays already filled with the day's menu. Now, she is required to offer two choices of fruit and two choices of vegetable, and students should select at least one fruit or vegetable item from those four choices. Carol notes that "hopefully, with the choices, that encourages them to take something they like"; however, it adds to her staff's preparation work. She told me that one of the major benefits of precut vegetables is that it gives her staff more time to prepare the other side dishes. "If you have lettuce that's ready to go, you can make the coleslaw, make the potato salad, do some of those other things — macaroni salads, fresh vegetable salads — some of those things that have a recipe and take a little more time." Add to all these issues a base labor cost of $11.15 per hour, and it becomes clearer why ready-to-eat items provide a significant benefit.

In addition to learning about these issues during our meetings with Carol, we were introduced to the nuances of school food procurement and learned that a school board member had recently proposed outsourcing the entire food service system, putting Carol's job in danger. Carol did not seem at all opposed to purchasing local food; in fact, she had purchased apples from a local orchard during the fall of 2010. Unfortunately, the grower could only supply three menus worth of apples before he risked diminishing his supply for regular customers. Carol reminded us of her large supply needs; one day's requirement of apples, lettuce, or melons may be more than some local growers produce all season long. In addition, because of food safety concerns, she was not open to purchasing local meat products. She purchases all precooked meats, such as cooked hamburger patties or crumbles and breaded chicken. Using raw meat would require her to thaw it before cooking, then cool and reheat it before the delivery (there would not be time to cook from scratch and deliver the meat the morning it would be served). This process would put the meat repeatedly in the HACCP-designated temperature danger zone that might encourage bacteria growth.

We left our initial meetings with a lot of new information but no concrete plan to proceed. The RC&D, in conjunction with the local cooperative grocery store, had scheduled a Come to the Table summit in February to try to introduce producers and institutional buyers. We projected that the meeting might help us find producers who would be interested or able to supply products. In addition, Carol would be leading a short group session on the farm to school program at summit so that she could communicate some of the needs of the district to local growers.

The event, while well attended and well received, did little to move our agenda forward in relation to food purchasing. A few weeks following the summit, Amy requested that the rest of us meet without Carol to develop a cohesive plan for the next steps. She felt that the session that Carol led at the summit might have actually been counterproductive. Much of the discussion focused on what she would not buy rather than exploring the local products that could be used in her kitchens. Amy recalled that Carol had not asked any questions of growers, nor had she given a business card or indicated any interest in working further with them. Gregg also expressed frustration, noting that someone commented on a feedback card that the "farm to school people were rude." While there is no indication that this comment was directed at Carol, the overall tone of that particular session was not as positive as the group members had hoped. Amy wanted to go into our next meeting with Carol with a concrete proposal for serving a local product in school lunches before the end of the year.

We knew this was ambitious, particularly since the school year ended in early June, and only a few items are abundantly ready in the early spring in Iowa. We brainstormed several possibilities: radishes, asparagus, peas, lettuce, spinach, strawberries? Radishes seemed like a risky item to serve to young kids and both asparagus and peas are expensive specialty items. Strawberries, even early bearers, would likely not be ready in time. That left us with lettuce and spinach—usually the first items to be found at the markets in the early spring and something that many producers grow. We agreed that a salad of mixed greens and spinach would be a suitable side for the school lunch menu. One of our group members, Neal Jackson, grew microgreens and sprouts; we added this to the list of possible additions to the salads. In addition, the chapter had the initial nine-hundred-dollar grant from IDALS that could be applied to the cost of the lettuce, which we hoped to be able to purchase for $2.50 per pound or less.

We planned to publicize the Spring Greens Day well and thought it would be a good way for the farm to school chapter to conclude its first school year. At this point, however, we had no idea how much mixed lettuce Carol would even require for 6,500 salads, and we did not know what she would expect to pay for it. In addition, we wondered whether the kitchen staff would process the lettuce, or would it have to be delivered to the schools already washed and cut. We did not know whether we should seek out baby greens or mesclun mix, which because of its smaller size would presumably require less chopping, or look for head lettuce. With this plan, which seemed to have as many questions as answers, we considered ourselves prepared for the next meeting with Carol.

Amy opened our next meeting, explaining the goals that we had come up with the day before. She described the Spring Greens Day and stated that we hoped to have a mix of lettuces and spinach and possibly sprouts. "No sprouts," Carol interrupted, shaking her head emphatically, "we don't do sprouts." Sprouts are designated a potentially hazardous food by the U.S. Food and Drug Administration because they provide optimal conditions for bacteria growth when held at temperatures higher than forty-one degrees Fahrenheit. Thus, they are usually avoided in food service kitchens, especially as additions to a salad bar where temperatures are not precisely controlled.

Amy continued, discussing promotion and explaining that we would have press releases and promotional materials in the cafeterias as well. Carol provided the group with the quantities she would need: the last time she served a lettuce salad, she used 365 pounds of washed, bagged, and ready-to-eat lettuce for one day. The lettuce she typically uses comes in twenty-five-pound cases, each case holding five 5-pound bags. The staff only has to open the bag and pour it into a tray; the students serve themselves as they go through the line. Carol's cost for the lettuce was $473 for all 365 pounds, which worked out to $1.30 per pound.

At this point, Amy brought up the nine-hundred-dollar grant from IDALS, which we planned to use to offset any extra cost and allow us to pay farmers around $2.50 per pound for the salad. Carol responded, "technically, we've already spent the grant, we bought apples in the fall." This statement was met with stunned silence around the table. Amy quickly recovered and pointed out that the apples were purchased in early September, before the chapter was established and the grant money materialized. Thus, the grant money should still be available. Next, Carol said, "my guess is that we're not going to find local lettuce for a dollar a pound." She also pointed out that we could not build a sustainable purchasing system by relying on grants. Further, she argued, even if producers gave us a break on cost, "we can't get a one-time 75 percent discount [on the lettuce] and let the public assume that now we'll always have local lettuce."

Although Carol was not opposed to using the grant money from IDALS, she was understandably concerned about public perception and the development of a long-term local procurement system. Paying more for the lettuce, as the grant would allow us to do, could become problematic if parents assumed that local lettuce would suddenly become standard. But it was equally unreasonable to assume that producers would be willing to meet her typical price point, even for a one-time event. Amy responded that we could also use this event as a way to contribute to public awareness about the cost of food.

Our next question for Carol was about the ready-to-eat designation; will the kitchen staff be able to do any preparation? She reminded us that she pays more than eleven dollars per hour for labor and that the kitchen workers already prepare four fruit and vegetable choices each day. If it were possible to get the lettuce at a reasonable cost, she might be able to have her staff prepare it, but she would prefer to have it ready to eat.

We left that meeting with Carol's permission to contact growers for bids. We roughly targeted a mid to late May date for serving, hoping that growers would have lettuce by that time. In addition, Carol indicated that it would be fun to visit farms that might supply the product. Finally, she wanted the producers to fill out a grower checklist for food safety, developed by Iowa State University, to keep in her files. These all seemed like straightforward, manageable requests, and so we began the process of requesting bids and setting up farm visits.

I was asked to put together a bid letter to email to producers, which we sent out to eight growers and one local distributor in March 2011. Three producers did not respond at all to the email; the distributor requested more information about the bid deadline but did not have product available and two growers indicated that their CSA businesses were too busy at that time of year. Three growers responded with interest, though one quoted a price of $5.50 per pound, well out of our price range. The last two growers indicated interest and flexibility on price, our target being between $2.00 and $2.50 per pound to fit within the constraints of the IDALS grant. We were somewhat disappointed with the low response to the bid request, although conversations with other food service directors suggest that this is not unusual. One food service director from a small district in northeast Iowa reported to me that she sent out forty bid requests and received only two responses.

The two growers, David Evans and Rob Duncan, both felt they could meet our price constraints, though David noted that he probably wouldn't make any money. David also pointed out that he would appreciate the publicity that his farm would receive from the project and that he was generally supportive of getting local foods into schools. Rob was more interested in having the business and was excited to have the opportunity to sell to the school district. Because the farm to school group was still unsure whether the school kitchens would be able to cut head lettuce and, if not, whether baby greens that would not require chopping could be used, we indicated an interest in both products. Both growers have CSAs and sell to an area cooperative grocery store. Both were also used to selling their lettuce by the head rather than by the pound. Our request for a price per pound was slightly problematic for both of them, as they would have to estimate the final weight of their head lettuce to ensure that we ended up with enough useable lettuce. In addition, our timeframe might be too early. David pointed out that if the unpredictable Iowa spring weather was warm, he would have plenty of lettuce to sell by mid-May. If, however, we had a cold, wet spring, as in years past, it might be very difficult to have the lettuce ready. Rob, who was growing most of the lettuce in high tunnels, was less concerned about the date. His mobile plastic hoop structures cover multiple rows of produce and can significantly increase production in the early spring and late fall by warming the air and soil around the plants. With this information in mind and still no set price from the producers, we scheduled farm visits with both of them.

In April, Carol, Amy, and I traveled to visit David Evans at Century Farms to get a look at our potential lettuce. It was a rare spring day, sunny and warm with none of the typical Iowa wind. When we arrived, David was fixing his water-wheel planter and hoping to get seed potatoes in the ground by the end of the day. David first took us through the packing shed, where in the summer months his crew would fill CSA boxes and prepare products for wholesale delivery. When we saw it, however, it was used for storing his tractor, potting soil, and several pallets. He warned us to watch our steps as we picked our way through the equipment. I asked him to describe his process for washing mixed baby greens, which I knew he sold at the farmers' market in the spring. He uses a product called Tsunami 100, which is a sanitizer approved for use in organic production. David told us that he would prefer not to use it, as it is harsh and corrosive. Nevertheless, he reasoned, it is much less dangerous than the chemicals used by large-scale conventional growers. After harvest, the mixed greens are first submerged in cold water to quickly cool the leaves and maintain their freshness. They are then put into a solution of Tsunami 100 and water, and finally rinsed for a third time in clean water. David then spins the greens dry in a washing machine before packing them. He also described plans to purchase a new salad harvester that would go on the back of the tractor. A band-saw blade would cut the leaves off just above soil level, and they would be pushed into a basket. David noted that baby greens are incredibly labor intensive, particularly when harvested by hand. He was hopeful that the new harvester would improve his profitability on a product that is often, for him, a loss leader. He grows it because his customers are happy with the early spring salads, but he is still unable to charge enough to make a profit on it, even at the farmers' market where he asks for $3.50 per pound.

David took us out to his fields, where tiny lettuce plants were just beginning to emerge. He cautioned us again about the weather challenges that could make our mid-May date impossible. He also pointed out that he was growing head lettuce, which he could also sell to us at our projected price. As we walked back to the car, we passed David's wife, Jessica, who was cutting seed potatoes for planting with three crew members. Jessica indicated that she had some concerns about the ISU grower checklist, which I sent to her in advance of our visit. She also pointed out that the bid request specified ready-to-eat lettuce and she reminded us that they are not licensed for processing. Thus, none of their products should be considered ready to eat—it should all be washed before consumption.

Jessica had not filled out the grower checklist and was not comfortable with several of the questions. She noted that many of the questions were vague, and some important considerations, such as liability insurance, were not addressed at all. For example, "are storage and packing facilities located away from growing facilities?" Jessica wondered how far is far enough? Additionally, "are wells protected from contamination?" was problematic for her. She said, "well, I hope so," but wondered what, exactly, they should be protected from and what kind of protection was being suggested in the question—a fence, distance from livestock areas, a basic cap? Jessica wanted more information from Carol about her criteria for purchasing from a farm. Carol indicated that she would like to see temperature records for the walk-in cooler—a standard procedure for food service personnel. Such records are not maintained at Century Farms.

Carol noted that, based on David's explanation of the farm, she could see that they have put considerable thought into their postharvest handling procedures. She liked that the produce came in on one side of the packing shed and was loaded out on the other side, minimizing the risk of clean product coming into contact with dirty product. Carol also liked David's description of the salad harvesting process because it would be done by machine, without significant handling. To this, Jessica responded that every item on the farm was harvested by hand, using a knife, without gloves. She leaned forward and raised a hand to emphasize her point. To her, the handling of the produce was a benefit to her customers because they knew each item was handled with care rather than impersonally run through a machine. Carol's food safety perspective led her to appreciate the mechanization of larger scale agriculture, in which food was handled less and was, presumably, cleaner. For Jessica, whose CSA shareholders and co-op customers desired food with a face on it, the handling of produce signified the careful attention that set local food systems apart from industrialized agriculture.

Two days later, Carol, Amy, Gregg, and I drove north to visit Rob Duncan. The day was grey and cold, with a wind that immediately caused chapped fingers and runny noses. Rob is a well-known farmer in the area, rangy and perpetually tanned, with waist-length dreadlocks that he often wraps high in a stocking hat, adding to his already considerable height. Despite his unconventional appearance, his blue-eyed gaze is direct and friendly. Rob was fixing equipment when we arrived, and he told us that he has two main jobs: "growing stuff and breaking stuff." Before starting the farm, Rob and a business partner had operated an organic vegetarian restaurant. He also has a business that serves smoothies and wraps at local festivals.

Rob told us that he planted extra lettuce as soon as he heard about the Spring Greens event and also said that he had been thinking about processing possibilities. Like David Evans, he is not licensed to process, so his greens would not be ready to eat. But, he suggested, if we had access to a commercial kitchen, perhaps at a hotel, we could get the product to meet the specifications. Rob recommended that we purchase head lettuce rather than baby greens or mesclun mix. Although he sells a lot of small salad mix to restaurants, he has mixed feelings about it. He noted that the mesclun is bourgie (bourgeois) and that head lettuce is easier and more sustainable for him to grow, particularly from a labor standpoint. Additionally, he pointed out that chopped head lettuce might be more familiar to the elementary school kids, which would hopefully increase their consumption.

We walked through the fields first, where garlic, onions, and peas were already sprouting. Rob had also put up six high tunnels. In one tunnel, he had lettuce, bok choy, spinach, and kale, some of which had been planted in the fall and overwintered in the tunnel. I commented on how pretty the alternating rows of red lettuce and bok choy were. Rob grinned and responded, "I know, that's why I wanted to show you guys." In the packing area, Rob showed us his new walk-in cooler. He pointed out the stainless steel racks that keep product off the floor. Carol asked whether he kept temperature records; he did not but was happy to keep them for her. He asked how often she would like them recorded and suggested that he could do it as often as hourly. Carol responded that her staff writes them three times a day, once in the morning, once at midday, and before leaving in the afternoon. Carol also asked about hygiene standards for his employees. He noted that there is a flush toilet available, and he has demonstrated proper handwashing procedure and nailbrush use. He also told us that he currently does not have any smokers on staff, which is helpful because he does not have to explain to them why they are required to wash their hands after a smoke break.

Carol had mixed feelings about both farm visits. The lack of processing licensure on the farms made purchasing a ready-to-eat product impossible, and she was concerned that there were no current well-water tests available for either farm. In addition, she was uncomfortable with the use of the washing machine to dry lettuce at Century Farms. Storing equipment in the packing shed at Century Farms was also a concern. "I assume that it's clean and free of farm equipment during the summer, but I would like to see it being used." She noted that it would be scary to buy from Century Farms right now. "Well, not 'scary,'" she corrected herself, "but I would have concerns."

Thus, our next step was to figure out a way to get the lettuce ready to eat. Neal Jackson's greenhouse was licensed for processing because his microgreens are sold packaged and are officially designated as ready to eat. He offered us the use of his space, even though we would not be purchasing any of his product for the event. As we left Rob's farm, Carol commented that the critical step would be talking to Neal and learning more about his processing practices. While we worked to secure a date to visit Neal's facility, however, Carol made an inquiry to the county department of public health. Her contact questioned whether either of the farmers we visited could be considered an approved vendor by the health department for the school district. In addition, in an email to the group and to the state farm to school representatives at IDALS, Carol reiterated her concerns about the farms:

> Lack of documentation for walk-in cooler temperatures, date of application of manure; lack of well water testing certificate; and [the fact that] neither farmer can meet the bid request which was ready-to-eat cut mixed greens since neither is a licensed processor. . . . The other issue is whether or not the USDA requirement of trying to obtain 3 competitive bids is being met. At this time it appears there are only two growers with capacity to supply enough product, yet it is my sense pricing/cost is still somewhat unclear. Until all these concerns can be addressed, I am hesitant to move forth with a Field Green menu day in June.

The email led Amy to assume that our project had reached a dead end, but despite her concerns, Carol was still willing to visit Neal's greenhouse and discuss processing. We planned to meet there the following week so Neal could give her a tour. By this time, I had been helping out at the greenhouse for a few weeks (more on this in chapter 8). I knew that Neal was nervous about Carol's visit, and when I arrived early that morning, he had cleaned up the workspace considerably. He had also put some thought into the purchasing process for Spring Greens Day. Because his business would be processing the lettuce, he had decided that he should purchase it from David and Rob, and then sell it to the school. Thus, the school district would buy the lettuce from Neal rather than directly from the farm.

When Carol arrived, he explained this to her, and she agreed. He would take ownership of the product, ultimately making his business liable should there be any problems with it. Neal showed Carol the harvest area, and he went over his licensure. He is inspected by the Iowa Department of Inspections and Appeals; the certification was posted above one of the refrigerators. Neal explained how the salads would be cut on the long stainless steel harvest table and sanitized in a diluted solution of Tsunami 100, then rinsed again in clean water. Neal explained that the volunteers would be trained in the same way that he trains his employees. He uses what he calls a no hands policy, meaning that workers are always wearing gloves when they handle the product and long hair will always be tied back.

Carol did not have any questions about the process—she nodded a lot as Neal explained the process, and when he was finished, she said, "that should all work fine." She did inquire about his liability insurance. His policy carries one million dollars in liability, and he offered to fax her a copy of it. She indicated that would not be necessary and required no paperwork from him at all. For the rest of the group, this was remarkably anticlimactic, particularly considering the tone of some of the emails exchanged before we met. Neal's licensure ultimately erased the on-farm concerns, a process that Amy later referred to as magic, and allowed us to move forward with the project. As Amy pointed out, the farms still lacked walk-in cooler temperature records and well-water tests, two of Carol's major concerns. Neal's washing procedure was nearly identical to David's: both rinsed the greens in three separate water baths, using the exact same sanitizing product. The only significant procedural difference involved drying the lettuce: David used a washing machine, while Neal had two industrial, food-grade salad spinners (which looked remarkably like washing machines). Neal also carried the documented blessing of the Iowa Department of Inspections and Appeals, which, from Carol's perspective, provided her with the institutional security of an officially inspected facility. Conducting the transaction with Neal's business rather than directly from the farms also provided a buffer between the school district and the site of production. Neal would ultimately be liable for any problems with the product.

Now that the project finally had the official green light, our next steps were to confirm that David and Rob would have the salad we would need and figure out the logistics of getting it washed, chopped, packaged, and delivered. Both growers suggested that a later date would be wise, so we agreed to serve the salads on June 1, the day before the last day of school. We would cut and wash the lettuce the day before, and Neal would deliver it to the school's food service warehouse. Carol requested 275 pounds of lettuce (washed and ready to eat) to fulfill her menu requirements for one day. We, in consultation with the two growers, estimated that we would need about 330 pounds of uncut head lettuce to meet that requirement. At the end of April, David agreed to provide 210 pounds of head lettuce at between $2.00 and $2.50 per pound and Rob would provide 120 pounds at $2.00 per pound. Neal made arrangements to pick up the lettuce from each of them a few days before we planned to process it.

We had a total of six volunteers recruited to help process the lettuce at Neal's greenhouse. I arrived early to start setting up our assembly line. On the harvest table, I could fit a cutting board and four tubs, which would be filled with water and Tsunami 100 sanitizer. We planned to have two lines, with one chopper, one person to move the lettuce from tub to tub, and one person to operate the spinners that would spin the lettuce dry before packaging it. Each spinner had two baskets, so that you could spin one while the other was being filled with product, thus, when the first basket was finished, the second would be full and ready to spin. My experience working on the harvest for Great Greens, which I discuss in detail in later chapters, led me to believe that we would be able to fill one spinner basket in the ten to fifteen minutes that it took to run the spinner. Ideally, we would have the spinners, with about ten pounds of lettuce in each one, running constantly. Neal and I both estimated that, if we started at 9 A.M., we would be finished by about 2 P.M.

By nine, all of our volunteers had arrived and we began working. We started with David's lettuce. I had learned just that morning that he was only able to provide 110 pounds of lettuce, 100 pounds less than planned. Fortunately, Neal had made contact with Rob, who was able to supply an extra hundred pounds so that we would have enough. David's lettuce, which had been grown outside in the cool spring weather, was small and very dirty from a recent rain that had muddied the fields. We decided that it would be beneficial to add an extra prewashing step to deal with some of the dirt. We filled Neal's sink with water, removed the root base of each head, and dropped the leaves into the water for a quick soak. The bottom of the sink was immediately covered with a muddy sludge and the leaves were only marginally improved.

Carol had sent Neal an email indicating how the lettuce was to be cut and what the size of the pieces should be. I had not seen the email, so I called Neal (who was getting the refrigerated truck fixed) to ask him about it. Unfortunately, the document that Carol sent was unreadable. I called the district office to ask. Cindy, Carol's assistant said it should be like the romaine. This information did not help me at all, so I asked for dimensions, and she estimated one to one-and-a-half inches square. Amy had recently attended a food service demonstration at a local high school and gave us a quick tutorial on cutting the lettuce. A quick lengthwise cut along the stacked leaves, followed by several crosswise cuts should result in fairly even squares of lettuce. The first time I looked at the clock, it was already 10 A.M., and we did not even have our first spinner basket half full. At that point, I knew that my earlier optimism about finishing in a few hours was far from realistic. The cutting was incredibly slow, in part because we were concerned about providing small, even pieces of lettuce. Gregg commented that "we should be really picky about it," knowing that Carol's standards were high.

As we slowly moved through David's lettuce, I began to be concerned about quantity. He was supposed to have delivered 110 pounds of lettuce heads, which we anticipated would give us about ninety pounds of finished, chopped lettuce. When we got through with his lettuce, however, it was nearly noon, and we had only sixty pounds of chopped lettuce. David had not provided Neal with an invoice, so we did not have any record of the quantity he provided us. Neal called Rob right away to see whether he could provide more—Rob said he could deliver extra lettuce, but he would have to pick it first. As we started to work with Rob's lettuce, we were happy to discover that the heads were larger and much cleaner than David's. Rob had grown his under the cover of a high tunnel, which kept the spring rains from turning the soil into mud around the plants and protected the plants from the chilly spring, allowing them to grow faster.

Now that we were starting with cleaner lettuce, we did not need to prewash it, so one more person was freed up to chop. With three people chopping, two moving the cut lettuce through the washtubs, and me alternating between spinning, bagging, and removing the cores (to make the chopping more efficient), the process seemed to move a little faster. At 4:30 (seven and a half hours after we started), we finally closed the last box. We finished up with 280 pounds of cut, ready-to-eat lettuce, five pounds more than Carol requested. We had no leftover lettuce heads, so Rob's last-minute delivery had been critical. Neal was able to use the refrigerated truck, which a repairman had fixed at the greenhouse while we worked, to deliver the lettuce to the district offices.

Our experience led Amy to quip at a statewide farm to school meeting that we would never again attempt to serve local salads to the entire school district. After all of our work, the product was fortunately well received by the students. On the day the salads were served, Amy recruited and mobilized volunteers to attend lunch in all of the district's elementary schools to post signs and talk to students about the lettuce. The volunteers reported that many students had several servings of salad and responded positively. I visited two elementary schools and noticed that our lettuce was competing with fresh watermelon, canned peaches, and hash browns shaped like smiley faces as the other three fruit and vegetable offerings. We later learned that just over half of the lettuce we delivered was consumed and that the district disposed of the rest. Since it was served during the last week of school, there was no time to use the leftovers. Carol assured us that, had it been delivered a week or so earlier, she could have used the rest of it in subsequent menus.

The simple salad proved to be one of the most challenging meal additions we could have chosen. Concerns about the weather and supply, difficulties estimating final quantities, ensuring adequate payment for the farmers, and the labor involved in processing all coalesced into a stressful project for a small group of rookie volunteers. The experience also served, however, to solidify the farm to school program as a legitimate organization in the district. The positive press that came from Spring Greens Day, in addition to the well-received farmer fairs and increasing school garden endeavors, made the farm to school chapter popular in the district's progressive university-town setting. Despite the workload and intensity of the project, Carol was positive about moving forward with other activities. Over the years, the district's constituents had criticized the content, quality, quantity, serving procedure, and length of the lunch periods at MCSD. Much of the past criticism was, frankly, unfair. While working with Carol, I found her to be extremely concerned about the health of the students she was serving. But school lunches and, by association, the food service personnel who manage and serve them are often on the firing lines of public perception. Carol's involvement in farm to school was a very public way for her to show her commitment to the community and to student health.

As Amy suggested, MCSD has never again tried to source local lettuce as part of their farm to school programming. The next step for the chapter, and our committee, was to find items that would work more easily into the school kitchen's existing systems. Early in the summer following the lettuce experiment, Carol expressed interest in local melons. For one menu day, she typically required sixty-six 20-pound watermelons. The whole melons arrive in the five production kitchens, where they are sprayed and sliced before serving. Thus, purchasing melons would not require extra labor for processing from either volunteers or the food service staff, who usually cut them anyway. The region south and east of MCSD has sandy soil perfect for growing watermelons and cantaloupes, and several growers distribute melons statewide. Carol was hopeful that we could find a grower in the area who already produced melons for retail or wholesale markets. Through Mark Schultz, the grocery manager in our group, we started by contacting the grower who supplies a local grocery store.

The grower, Roger Daniels, was happy to have us come out for a visit, so on a blazing July afternoon, Carol, Amy, Gregg, Mark, and I drove south to his property. Roger farms eighty acres, twenty of which are devoted to produce each year. Watermelon and cantaloupe are the primary food crops, but he also grows tomatoes, peppers, peas, and some squash. He rotates the twenty acres of produce with corn and soybeans. An experienced farmer, Roger has grown melons for twenty years, which he called "about seventeen too many." When we visited he had four acres devoted to watermelons and estimated a yield of about fifteen thousand 20-pound melons.

Roger already had a delivery schedule, which included a daily drive as far as Des Moines, just over two hours away. His crew of six or seven high school students harvests in the morning and delivers the same day. The melons are packed in large bulk crates and loaded into the back of a pickup. Roger tries to deliver as early as possible to minimize the time the fruit spend exposed to the summer heat in the back of the truck. Roger explained that, for him, "the biggest thing is the risk." When we visited him, he had already spent about twenty-five thousand dollars on his produce but had yet to realize any income from sales. He pointed out that there is no cushion for him if the crop fails. The only crop loss program he is eligible for will reimburse the cost of 20 percent of the crop if he experiences a 60 percent loss. This is inadequate. Roger noted that if he loses 25 percent or more, he would not be able to break even.

As we left Roger's farm, Carol commented that it was interesting to see a farmer growing both commodity crops and produce. She said she has been surprised to learn how little support there is for real-food farmers, as opposed to corn and soybean producers. In the end, Carol purchased sixty-six melons from Roger in August. His price was $3.75 per melon. Carol paid $9.89 to her regular distributor for watermelons that year, so the savings from Roger's produce was significant. The only challenges were related to delivery and packaging; Carol usually received the melons boxed so that there were a few melons per crate. Roger, however, delivered in a large bulk crate. The warehouse employees had to count and sort the melons before they were delivered to the individual kitchens. Despite this minor challenge, Roger's watermelons and cantaloupe have become regular menu items during August and September. Unlike the lettuce, the melons hit the sweet spot of being simultaneously low cost and very high quality. Even though the warehouse workers have to sort them, the kitchen labor is not affected by purchasing a local, whole product. Local food is rarely able to claim both superior quality and a lower price, but in this case it does, at least for a short time at the beginning of the school year.

At the end of the chapter's second year, Carol retired. She has remained active with other food service directors and teaches an annual course about fresh food preparation in school food service kitchens. I have been a guest speaker in that course, sharing our lettuce experience with other food service personnel who are interested in local purchasing. At MCSD, the new food service director, Deborah, arrived enthusiastic about the prospects of the program. She has continued to purchase melons from Roger, even going so far as to take samples to the school board meetings to show how well students at MCSD are eating.

The Healthy, Hunger-Free Kids Act requires that schools serve a diverse selection of vegetables to students throughout each week. The act categorizes vegetables into subgroups based on color, such as dark green and orange, to be consistent with the 2010 *Dietary Guidelines for Americans*. The first project that the farm to school team tackled for Deborah involved fulfilling the orange vegetable requirement by sourcing local sweet potatoes. Her only sweet potato option from the regular distributor was a sweet potato puff that arrived frozen and resembled a tater tot. Instead, Deborah planned to purchase whole sweet potatoes, cut them in half, and top each with cinnamon and butter. She requested 275 pounds of sweet potatoes, each weighing about eight ounces. Cut in half, each would provide two four-ounce servings.

I contacted Neal Jackson, our lettuce project savior. In addition to a greenhouse, he has five acres of land for produce. He grows only three crops, an acre each of sweet potatoes, asparagus, and cabbage. The sweet potatoes and cabbage are rotated each year, the asparagus, a perennial crop, stays in the same plot. These items concentrate the labor in the spring and late fall, outside the summer season. Neal primarily markets his asparagus to restaurants and sells the cabbage and sweet potatoes to area grocery stores. Another advantage of sweet potatoes is their storage life. When Neal built his greenhouse, he included a root storage facility. His acre of sweet potatoes yields about forty thousand pounds. He can store and sell these throughout the winter months, contributing to year around cash flow for his business.

When I contacted him in November 2012 about selling to the schools, he had plenty available at about a dollar per pound. The only challenge would be the size restriction. It had been a good year for sweet potatoes, and many of his were well over two pounds. Deborah thought they could manage anything up to about a pound and a half. Neal was willing to select the smallest possible, and he delivered potatoes that ranged from about twelve to twenty ounces. Delivered in forty-pound cases, the potatoes were easy for the warehouse staff to sort so they could deliver the necessary amounts to each production kitchen. The farm to school chapter printed signs advertising the sweet potatoes, complete with pictures of Neal. Topped with cinnamon, the potatoes were well received with all age groups across the district.

Not long after we started buying sweet potatoes from Neal, I had a conversation with a beginning farmer at a statewide local food meeting.

She had started a CSA and was interested in selling to the school district. I told her that we had been buying sweet potatoes with much success. She asked about price, and I told her that the school had paid about a dollar per pound. She visibly stiffened at the price and told me that her farmers' market price for sweet potatoes was much higher than that. The implication was that the schools, as she suspected, were undercutting local farmers because of their expectations for cheap food imported from other states. What she didn't take into account was that Neal's scale made those dollar-per-pound sweet potatoes profitable for him. A farmer who digs her sweet potatoes with a pitchfork for fewer than fifty CSA shares will have to capture a higher margin to pay for that hand labor. Neal, who plants and harvests with a tractor rather than manually, will turn a profit even with his lower price.

The MCSD farm to school group learned a few significant lessons during those first years. While there is much enthusiasm around the ideas of local sourcing in institutions, the reality is quite complicated. The local food movement emphasizes the development of relationships between individual farmers and consumers. In this model, as discussed earlier in chapter 3, producers are often in the position to educate their customers about how their produce is grown. The lack of uniformity of local food at a farmers' market or in a CSA share is a point of pride for some growers, who want their customers to understand what real food really looks like. An institutional kitchen is much less forgiving. Items that are not uniform cause problems with calculating serving sizes, and a rustic, dirt-encrusted potato just increases labor costs.

For MCSD, the success of the farm to school chapter ultimately came down to finding growers who looked less like small CSAs and a bit more like commodity producers in that they specialized in a few crops rather than being highly diversified. Neal's acre of sweet potatoes is hardly monoculture, but it provides an economy of scale that allows him to sell to wholesale markets. Likewise, Daryl's four acres designated for melons yields enough produce to remain profitable even at prices much below those of a national distributor.

The farm to school team publicized their origins when the sweet potatoes were served, but this is not always the case. Both Neal and Roger sell their food without a face on it at area grocery stores, even though their product may be identified as local. By producing at a larger scale, these farmers may lose some of their individual identity, but they gain a wider market share and make a larger contribution to Iowa's local food system.

To make that larger contribution, farm labor is another important consideration. In the next two chapters, I take a closer look at how farmers balance labor and profitability.

CHAPTER SEVEN

Herd Management

LABOR IN LOCAL
FOOD PRODUCTION

A s WE HAVE SEEN, producers have a lot of marketing options in Iowa. Though nationally growth in the number of farmers' markets has leveled off somewhat, attendance remains robust and most markets in Iowa are thriving. Operators of CSA farms in eastern Iowa are also generally doing well. The continued demand suggests to some producers that the local food movement is more than just a passing fad and that there is real potential to develop sustainable and profitable local food systems.

These opportunities have significant implications on the farm, where increased demand puts producers in the position of having to decide whether to rapidly scale up their operations, collaborate with other producers, or turn business away. And, as I have shown, some may hesitate to make major changes to satisfy new markets such as school kitchens. One of the major obstacles to growth that producers face is access to reliable, affordable labor. It is difficult for an individual or couple to produce on a large enough scale to fully support themselves with a CSA or market farm. To generate enough income on a local food farm to support a family, outside labor is usually required for production, packaging, or distribution. Paid labor, however, is expensive and changes the landowner from the role of producer to employer, a shift many growers are hesitant to make.

This chapter explores an understudied area of local food: how farmers access and maintain reliable labor sources. As you would expect, farmers have diverse strategies, and each has advantages and disadvantages. Farmers may of course simply hire traditional employees to work on their farms. Those who do so note that labor is a major expense and must be managed very carefully to maintain economic efficiencies. These growers have learned that maintaining a successful crew is based on a good, social working environment in addition to sound accounting and financial management. Producers may also invite volunteers to their farm to work. Much of the popular literature on local food, particularly CSA, promotes volunteer labor as a low-cost strategy for farmers that will also increase consumer knowledge about agricultural practices. While producers acknowledge, and are generally grateful for, the benefits of free labor, there are often challenges when volunteers are on the farm. A third strategy for labor is to hire interns, who are often less expensive than traditional employees because they are provided housing on the farm. Not surprisingly, these shared space arrangements can cause headaches for growers and their families. Finally, a rather creative strategy for finding a new source of labor is to use a learning-based event, such as a workshop or field day, to complete a project on a farm. Like volunteer labor, this can be a very low-cost investment for the producer, but field day participants may not have the skills required to complete the task.

These diverse approaches provide us an opportunity to look beyond interactions between producers and consumers, which tend to be the focus in discussions of local food. The typical emphasis on the point of sale, whether at a farmers' market or CSA drop site, has caused both academics and popular writers to ignore farm labor. This gap is not surprising, considering not only our tendency to privilege the activities of the consumer in any market interaction but also the agrarian bias in favor of the independent farmer. Farms in our collective imagination tend to rely on hardworking individual farmers rather than on the more historically accurate network of owner-operator and farmworker. Further, the uncritical assumption that local food is inherently beneficial for farmers, eaters, and communities leads many to assume that farmworkers in local food, if they are considered at all, must also have lives filled with sunny days and fresh veggies.

In places with more extensive networks of migrant and seasonal farmworkers than in Iowa, some researchers have pointed out that the working lives of local food employees do not match the idealized lifestyle we expect of a family farm.[1] Nationally, farmworkers employed in both alternative and conventional production are subject to low-wage, high-risk jobs.

Those who don't speak English well or who are undocumented are further marginalized and lack much of the workplace security and protections enjoyed by laborers in other sectors. In contrast, the volunteer and paid labor pool for the farmers I worked with is mostly made up of white high school or college students. This group has many more options for employment than immigrant farmworkers. In Iowa the implications of labor in the local food system have more to do with issues of agricultural knowledge, subsidized food through free labor, and local investment than the abuses typical in systems that rely on marginalized populations.

Though part of my purpose is to move away from a consumer emphasis, there are some parallels between typical assumptions about producers' relationships with their consumers and their interactions with their employees. Both scholars and advocates have extolled the benefits that local food can have on communities. The view is that local food is inherently beneficial to consumers, who learn about agriculture through the friendships that develop when they purchase directly from farmers. Their new knowledge makes them more inclined to become engaged in their communities; they may participate more in democratic processes or speak out about environmental issues. Sociologist Thomas Lyson calls this phenomenon "civic agriculture," in which the embedding of the food system in local communities causes a ripple effect of positive actions and behaviors by local citizens.[2]

It is unclear, however, how we might measure the civic engagement of local food consumers. If they are active citizens, is that because of their participation in the food system, or is their participation in the food system a result of their already civically informed and active lifestyles? A recent study suggests that local food economies tend to develop in communities with high levels of income and education and where institutions of higher education are present. This may indicate that the investment in local food comes from an already engaged population, with the time and resources to devote to activism, rather than the other way around.[3] In reality, the only concrete measure of consumers' participation in the food system is to add up how much they purchase. This brings us full circle because we ultimately wind up evaluating noneconomic social engagement and knowledge by counting dollars that consumers spend.

As a result, the local food discussion remains squarely in the difficult realm of the so-called conscientious consumer. Given the enormous capacity of Americans to spend money on consumer goods and the considerable free time we spend shopping, it has become second nature to relate our shopping habits to our ethics and values. Consumers regularly get the message that their spending habits are meaningful and have the ability to change the world. Michael Pollan reinforces this belief when he tells people to vote with their fork in support of a new food system.[4] While I do a fair amount of voting with my own fork, this drive to create social change through consumption, whether of hybrid cars or kale, is unsatisfactory. The concept of civic agriculture attempts to emphasize knowledge and civic engagement over economics, but it falls short by focusing only on what consumers will learn and do, instead of thinking beyond that producer-consumer relationship. Anthropologist Laura DeLind sums up the problem concisely: "They (and we) are still relating to each other as one-dimensional abstractions—as producers or consumers, as buyers or sellers—no matter how pleasant our smiles or conscientious our purchases."[5]

When I talked with farmers, I found some parallels between how they interact with their employees and their customers. In both cases, there can be tension between economic gain and personal relationships. As I noted previously with the example of Faye Jefferson and her greens, farmers balance the economic benefits of growing an efficient crop with the challenges of slowly convincing farmers' market customers to buy them. Likewise, as we will see, farmers think very carefully about how labor affects their margins, sometimes down to pennies a minute, while also recognizing that taking extra time to work alongside employees to teach them how to do a basic task will eventually pay off.

In addition, the prevalence—or at least the ideal—of volunteer and intern labor may show how local food systems can enhance agricultural knowledge, reinforce environmental ideals, and create new social ties. The driving force behind Lyson's civic agriculture is that it increases the agricultural knowledge base of the community. This ideal is in contrast to the dominant, centralized food system about which the average person knows very little. Most consumers are physically distanced from sites of agricultural production and processing, both of which are strategically made opaque to avoid public commentary or criticism. Thus, we often lament that people don't know where their food comes from anymore.

Even among farmers, agricultural knowledge is no longer a community resource. Instead, it remains mostly in the hands of an elite few in universities and corporations. Farmers are simply recipients of new information that trickles down from universities and corporate research and development departments, rather than being expert practitioners who learn from and teach their peers and consumers. By using volunteer labor, especially intern labor, farmers are positioned as leaders and experts guiding the next generation of farmers and enhancing the community's knowledge as customers work for their own vegetables.

Much of the local food movement is based on the potential for community development, knowledge enhancement, and relationship building. These are the processes that have excited and mobilized critics of the centralized food system, which allows for little participation. But the presumption that the key value in local food is noneconomic undermines the very reasonable assertion that farmers, farmworkers, processors, and distributors should make a fair living. Just as there is tension between low-income food access and farmers' ability to charge enough for their products to make a living, there is tension between civic ideals of volunteer labor and the ability of local food to provide economic benefits to a community. Food farmers often point out that when consumers purchase their products, which are not directly supported by federal subsidies, they pay the real cost of food. But if those farmers rely on volunteer labor, the consumer still does not pay the real cost of food.

In her work among organic farmers in California, Julie Guthman has explored the tension between organic farming as an environmental and social justice movement and as a profitable enterprise. Labor concerns were largely considered an externality and secondary to agronomic practices during the development of California organic standards. Guthman argues, however, that if organic growers see themselves as part of an integrated social movement, they should logically pursue "labor strategies that secure worker commitment, more year-round and permanent employment, and improved remuneration all the way around."[6] Instead, growers continue to regularly use labor contractors and compensation remains well below a living wage, even when growers recognize and lament the low pay. Thus, while many have touted the potential of alternative (i.e., sustainable, organic, or local) food production to improve both communities and the environment, the concerns of agricultural workers remain overlooked.

Local food farmers experience dilemmas similar to Guthman's organic producers, despite being worlds away in terms of production scale. It is easy to write off large-scale organic production as simply another branch of industrialized agriculture, but there are many parallels between Guthman's producers and the small-scale food growers I spoke with in Iowa. Many want to pay higher wages and recognize the importance of consistent work, even when they cannot provide it. They may use alternative strategies that purport to develop community engagement and agricultural literacy, such as volunteers or interns, but find that these are inefficient. Finally, given the economic constraints of paying workers a permanent living wage, producers' labor pool primarily consists of individuals who have adequate time and resources to work seasonally or on a volunteer basis. Farmers have a number of options when it comes to finding a good source of labor, and their economic efficiencies vary. But each strategy does have some social or civic benefit, according to the farmers I spoke with, regardless of whether it involves a financial transaction.

Team Carrot

During the 2011 annual meeting of the Midwest Organic Sustainable Education Service, several farmers' presentations focused on their labor strategies. In particular, the presenters stressed the importance of procedural protocols and economic efficiencies. Producers also suggested that to be an effective employer, you have to like people and enjoy working with them, especially groups of young people. They claimed that good employee management is participatory; an employer should be prepared to work alongside employees as much as possible. Paul and Sandy Arnold, who gave a detailed description of their upstate New York market farm at a farm conference, suggested that a market farmer's biggest challenge "isn't learning how to grow carrots," it is learning how to become an effective employer. After all, one does not manage people, one manages finances. People must be led, asserted the couple.

Iowa vegetable grower Frank Erikson agrees:

I feel that it's true that you must really like to manage people if you have a sizeable crew, or at least be very efficient at doing it. It does take a lot of management to do it, especially in an agricultural situation where you're showing people how to do things on a regular basis. You have to like working with people and try to develop some efficient skills at doing it. If you're a person that just likes . . . to get away from things and just work at a good speed by yourself, it's going to be a little more challenging for you than if you're used to managing people.

David Evans, whose crew now sports T-shirts emblazoned with the Century Farm logo and Team Carrot on the back, expressed surprise at the extent to which he enjoys his management role. When he began his farm, he expected employee management to be a burden. But one winter, he mused to me: "I miss having them around. I'll see things happening on the farm, like a hawk circling or something, and I wish that the crew was here so I could show them."

Frank Erikson suggested in a presentation for Practical Farmers of Iowa that it is important to spend as much time with employees as possible and work alongside them in the field: "I also try to work with them as much as I can. That sometimes has been difficult, but I think it's important so employees know I'm not just off eating donuts somewhere, they know I'm not just being lazy or whatever. I try to become a good example for them for good work habits. And it's pretty important, I've found, that I come in to work early and that I always stay later than the employees do." The Arnolds agree, noting that group harvesting is a good strategy because it can be lonely and demoralizing to work in the field all alone. The social aspect of group harvesting improves morale and helps to develop leadership among some individuals in the group, who can then help train newer workers. Erikson adds that the group strategy is helpful even when employees are not in the field: "I try to spend as much downtime with employees—what I mean by downtime is, like when we're at break or over lunch. I try to spend time with them and get to know them a little better. I try not to feel like I'm just a boss that shows up and tells them what to do all the time." The best management or leadership strategies according to these producers are participatory and hands-on. According to another farm manager from northern Illinois, the best way to teach employees is to show them and work with them; "you can't learn farming from a book," he says. Especially given that the local food labor pool in the Midwest consists mostly of high school or college students, using a participatory and social approach can soften the difficult aspects of farm labor.

As producers know very well, the work of growing food is hot and physically demanding, so farmers also point out the importance of being attentive to their employees' individual needs and comfort. They know from experience that the physical exertion of farmwork in the heat of a midwestern summer can be unpleasant. The northern Illinois farmer suggests starting employees at half time so they can acclimate to the hard work. Many farmers make a point of harvesting during the early morning hours, noting that plants harvested in hot weather can suffer as much as the harvester. In this regard, both the business and the employees benefit from avoiding working during the hottest part of the day.

Growers also often point out that farms are businesses and profitability is key. According to Erikson, "labor is a great asset but it can be a really serious problem" because of the expense. Farmers who manage crews often calculate profitability down to the penny. Paul Arnold, for example, expects his employees to harvest forty dollars worth of produce per hour. He notes that the average picker can harvest, wash, and pack twenty-five pounds of green beans per hour. The Arnolds sell green beans for $3.50 per pound, so the total value is $87.50 per hour of work, which makes beans profitable. David Evans occasionally times his employees to see how fast they harvest. He can strip a bunch of kale from the plant and bundle it with a twist tie in seven seconds. As the fastest harvester, David encourages his employees to match his pace.

Paul Arnold also points out that transitioning between crops is a significant time waster. "Six people standing and waiting for ten minutes wastes one hour of time." He uses stackable crates and golf carts in the field to move products efficiently back to the washing station and moves employ-

Employees at Century Farms harvest tomatoes.

ees from one field to the next without losing critical time. Frank Erikson adds that employee punctuality is also extremely important: "If you have a crew that you want to send to work, and you're missing two people because they're late to work, that's really holding you up in the field and really decreasing your efficiencies." Because having individuals waiting around is inefficient, Frank emphasizes organization and flexibility. He credits his greenhouse as a way to keep people busy: "I try to plan ahead—at least a day ahead or even a week ahead if at all possible. It's difficult on a farm operation because the weather can really wreak havoc with those plans. I also try to maintain flexibility because of that weather problem. That's one nice thing about having a greenhouse. If the weather gets bad outdoors, we generally can find something to do in the greenhouse that we've maybe neglected during good weather. So we can get some work done there. That has been a benefit." David Evans notes that most employees expect to be working nearly full time, and maintaining consistent work hours helps to keep them motivated. Given these expectations and the role of the weather in determining of day-to-day work, it is important to have rainy-day activities planned. On Evans's farm, he often has employees work in the packing shed or one of two hoop houses during rainy spells.

These producers try to find a balance between social and economic measures when overseeing employees. While they all emphasize the social skills inherent in good leadership, they also point out the basic necessity of economic efficiency. This process exemplifies what sociologists would call embeddedness, in which successful economic transactions are predicated on social relationships.[7] Producers who hire laborers assert that their employees would not be as effective if the working environment was less attentive to their desire for a socially oriented and supportive workplace. Group harvesting, care for employee comfort, and social time spent with workers are key components of economic success. Thus, social and economic processes are inextricably tied and embedded.

Herd Management: Volunteers on the Farm

While conducting fieldwork during the summer of 2008, I worked on several CSA farms in eastern Iowa. Sorensen Family Farm, operated by Jean Sorensen, was at the time one of the oldest and largest CSAs in the state. Jean was surprised by my research approach, noting that while she had been interviewed many times by both researchers and journalists, none had ever offered to provide free labor in return for her time. The first morning I worked at the farm, Jean asked me to pick cherry tomatoes. This particular year, the area had experienced record flooding and cooler than normal conditions, resulting in a late and rather paltry tomato crop. Jean explained that I should pick even those tomatoes that did not appear fully ripe; those that were about half orange were sufficient, because they would continue to ripen and finish for the shareholders over the course of the week. Additionally, it was very important to remove all the stems from the tomatoes; even one stem left on could pierce another tomato in the bucket, causing them all to spoil if left too long.

I set off, five-gallon bucket in hand, and began at the end of a long row of tomatoes, working to my right. When I was about a quarter of the way down the row, Jean came over to check my progress and ask more about my project. She started to my left about five feet away from me, in an area of the row that I had already picked. I started explaining my project to her and answering her questions. She interrupted me suddenly, saying, "You must have done this before." I was not entirely sure of her meaning but replied that I had picked tomatoes before. She explained that usually when a new volunteer came to work at the farm, she would have to go over all the work they had done to ensure that it was done correctly. In the case of the tomatoes, people often left ripe tomatoes on the vine because they are surprisingly difficult to see among the dense green foliage. It occurred to me that volunteer labor, often an important component in community-supported agriculture, might not be as beneficial as it would seem. Even free labor ceases to be worthwhile if the business owner has to redo all the work.

Of course, a farmer may be lucky to have that source of free labor in the first place, even if the quality of work is not perfect. Much of the CSA promotional literature promotes member volunteers as an ideal source of labor. Activist Elizabeth Henderson and Robyn Van En suggest that member-based labor provides an "exceptional opportunity to get help from a new source."[8] Many social scientists working with local food farmers have pointed out, however, that finding CSA members willing to work is actually quite difficult.[9] As anthropologist E. Paul Durrenberger wryly points out, "members do not really care much about participating in CSAs in any way except getting their food."[10] CSA grower Frances Baumgartner agrees that most shareholders are not interested in coming out to work on the farm, noting, "Once in a while people will say 'do you have people come out there and work?' . . . Most people don't want that though."

Those farmers who do have a willing pool of volunteers have mixed opinions as to the benefits of free labor. David Evans's farm is a busy place. The fifth generation of Evanses to farm, he operates a 250-member CSA, direct markets grass-fed beef and pastured poultry, sells at three farmers' markets each week, and sells his vegetables wholesale to multiple grocery stores throughout the state. The entire farm is certified organic and has become a well-known presence in local food production in Iowa. While the scale of David's operation requires him to hire a crew of seasonal workers—with whom, as noted earlier, he has strong social ties—he also welcomes shareholders to the farm to work and occasionally hosts student groups from a nearby private high school to work for on-farm educational activities.

At a winter farmers' market in 2009, I asked David whether he had any onions for sale. He shook his head and said that one problem was that the year had been a bit too wet for onions; weeding is difficult on wet ground and the resulting weed pressure decreased yields. In addition, he had invited a school group to help transplant onion seedlings, called sets, in the field; they had planted the sets too deep, further slowing the progress of the crop. He indicated that while he feels that hosting school groups supports his philosophy that young people should be given the opportunity to understand where their food comes from, errors like these make a difference in his seasonal returns.

Likewise, when shareholders come to volunteer at the farm, David reports that it often actually slows productivity. When someone comes out for the first time, he gives the person a tour of the farm. When they work, he usually stays close by in case they run into problems. But David is the fastest harvester in the field and nearly the fastest weeder (he reports that one employee has much more stamina than he does for all-day weeding). Thus, when he is giving a tour and helping a new volunteer, he is not in the field, and the day's efficiency suffers. In addition, his presence in the field among his crew tends to speed the work overall because they all strive to meet his speed. When he is absent, the crew naturally lags somewhat from their typical pace.

These changes in the work pace in an environment in which profit margins are slim and share boxes must be packed and delivered several times a week led David to wonder whether volunteer labor on the farm has any benefits at all. Even so, he noted that during the 2010 season he asked CSA shareholders to help at farmers' markets. This strategy has been quite successful because he only has to pay one employee to be at a market, and shareholders have proven to be energetic supporters of the farm. He had to gently tell some that they could only help at one market per season because so many people were interested.

Alan and Brenda Marshall, whose story of flooding I told in the first chapter, preferred to keep their CSA small; they had only nineteen share-holders in 2008. Even this small group was interested in seeing the farm and learning more about how a CSA operates. Alan was always willing to let customers come out and see the farm but did not generally encourage them to work. He found that it was difficult to manage a group of volunteers and said that it was "easier for me to just go out and do it." Another issue was that members who worked regular office hours often want to come out on the weekends. Alan and Brenda preferred to keep their weekends free. For customers, a trip to the farm is a nice weekend outing, but for the farmers, it becomes another day on the job.

Advocates of local food, such as Henderson and Van En, look to volunteer labor as a way to enhance the food system. But what do we actually know about the effects on communities or benefits for individual volunteers? Because researchers have mostly looked at volunteerism in older adults, it is difficult to extrapolate how volunteerism in agriculture may be comparable. In eastern Iowa, most farm volunteers and interns tend to be young; often they are college students who volunteer or intern during their summer breaks. Those who have examined volunteerism among young people suggest that membership in volunteer organizations in adolescence increases later engagement in civic and political activities, with potential impacts on a very broad scale in areas such as human or civil rights, animal welfare, and environmental preservation.[11] Although these findings do not directly address agriculture, they may suggest an association between farm volunteers and civic engagement. If volunteerism tends to lead to political activism, then those who volunteer on farms may become more engaged in the broader debates around agriculture. Thus, volunteerism on farms may develop a more civically engaged and informed population of consumers and activists who can play various roles in the food system.

Taking a broad perspective, the idea that local food can help solidify civic engagement and political activism in the long term is encouraging. Unfortunately, it is difficult to point to any specific benefits that this type of volunteerism has directly on the agricultural community in which it occurs. In eastern Iowa, many of the volunteers come from nearby colleges. They are local to the area only a short time before moving on to the next stage in their careers. Even at David Evans's farm, where students who attend the nearby liberal arts college reside in his small town, the vast majority are from urban areas outside Iowa and their presence is temporary. It is unclear in the more immediate term how rural communities will actually benefit from using volunteer labor.

It is important to note, given our task of addressing economic impacts as well as social engagement, that volunteer labor makes no economic contribution to rural communities other than by allowing farmers to lower their production costs. And, of course, lowering production costs is only possible if the work is done correctly and well. In theory, a farmer who saves money on labor has more to spend in his or her community, but ideally, the entire crew would have added economic resources to distribute. As I will discuss further in the next chapter, one way that advocates can promote local food is by clearly explaining its economic benefits to policymakers. Unfortunately, relying on volunteer labor does not result in measurable economic growth.

The use of volunteer labor also results in subsidized products for consumers. Food activists often remind consumers that they spend a remarkably low percentage of their incomes on food. Those who can should pay more to ensure just treatment of farmers, farmworkers, and processing plant employees. These same groups tend to argue vehemently against the current system of agricultural subsidies, suggesting that we should spend our collective tax dollars on healthy foods rather than storable, tradable commodities. In reality, consumers of local food do benefit from subsidies, just not in the way they might expect. Their CSA share is possibly subsidized by the free labor of a college student or a school group. Although volunteers may contribute to a more knowledgeable or civically engaged population over time, as a result of their work consumers do not pay the real cost of food.

Farmers as Substitute Parents: Interns

Another strategy that several producers in eastern Iowa employ, particularly CSA farms, is hosting interns or apprentices on the farm. Interns are often paid at a lower rate than hourly employees but may be offered room and board as a benefit of their employment. Producers have a variety of opinions on interns. David Evans of Century Farms, for example, generally refuses to hire interns because of his own negative experience of being overworked as a CSA intern in northeastern Iowa. In another presentation at the 2011 MOSES conference, a farm manager from a large midwestern CSA noted that the major disadvantage of interns is that each year brings a new group of people to train. He pointed out that making use of local labor sources not only benefits the community by providing local jobs, but it also increases the likelihood that people will return in consecutive years, reducing overall training time and increasing efficiency. Using interns may, however, support the overall mission of the farm by providing educational opportunities and critical hands-on experience for future farmers.

Jean Sorensen of Sorensen Family Farm has hired interns since 2000 to help on her CSA. For many years, the interns were provided room and board in her home and a small stipend in return for their work. Jean indicated that by 2008, when the youngest of her four children was in high school, they were experiencing considerable burn-out from having interns stay in their home. In addition, that year her accountant suggested that she track the expenses associated with housing interns. Jean calculated that housing four interns during that summer cost her nearly $150 per week. She was beginning to question the financial worth of housing interns, whose skills often were not up to her standard. Of the four she housed in 2008, she stated that only one had really been a good worker. She noted that finding good help is difficult. Although many young people have been reading about local food and want to get the organic farm experience, the reality of the physically demanding work often overwhelms them. She suggests that the overall caliber of workers has changed, that young people are less willing to do hard work and are less interested in farming than they used to be. By 2011, Jean changed her intern program so that she no longer housed them, though she paid them more (starting at eight dollars per hour) than when they lived on her farm.

Renee Johnson-Berry has also housed interns at Earth Hill Farm, which produces vegetables, herbs, and wool for local markets. Unlike Jean, Renee housed her apprentices in a "little, fabulous, and funky travel trailer out back." She says that "they would live here for the summer and they got room and board in trade for working, you know, ten hours a week, or whatever. I don't even remember what it was back then." Despite their not living in her home, Renee also quickly ran out of patience with the interns who lived on her property. "I'd already done my parenting routine and a lot of these apprentices seemed to really have missed some of those—you know, their parents had missed—key lessons in how to grow up." Like Jean, her solution was to no longer house people, but she also added another element to the relationship: "Then I started a system where I said, you can have a garden here, you can do whatever you want with it, you know, you can have a big plot, and you can make money. And that worked really well for a number of years." This arrangement gave the apprentices some ownership over part of the work of the farm, while they also helped Renee with her own specific labor needs.

Additionally, some of the young people she worked with have gone on to farm for themselves. "A couple of them are definitely farming," she reports, "farming almost exactly on this kind of scale, on a scale of a few acres." Herein lies the broader benefit to hosting apprentices: they may take the skills they developed on their intern farm and apply them to their own operations later. Interns may learn what not to do on their future farms, as was the case for David Evans, whose intern experience was not positive. David told me that he strives to do exactly the opposite of what he learned on the farm he interned for, particularly in terms of employee relations.

As with the presumed future civic engagement of volunteers, internships may not result in a long-term investment in the local community. The internship model, however, can do more to enhance the agricultural knowledge base than does using volunteers, who may not have any future goals related to farming. Internships certainly engage a population more critical than consumers: future farmers. Those producers who can manage the frustrations of interns are providing the services typically provided in a classroom by the land-grant university system or by a nonprofit agency. Given the interest in beginning farmer programming and education that I discussed in chapter 3, farmers who take on interns make an important contribution to ensuring the long-term viability of alternative agriculture. This lateral transfer of knowledge, in which farmers teach their peers or beginning farmers, has become a key mechanism for enhancing the kind of agriculture that operates largely outside conventional commodity production. By hosting interns, producers have the ability to affect the future of agricultural production, developing the next generation of alternative farmers.

The Field Day

The nonprofit organization Practical Farmers of Iowa is perhaps most well known for its field days, which are held throughout the summer. PFI members host these participatory events on their farms. During a typical field day, the producer takes the group on a tour of the farm and highlights some of recent successes or failures. Some field days are particularly hands-on; for example, one CSA grower had guests harvest their own sweet corn for the meal that concluded the event. PFI provides support staff to assist with advertising, logistics and, importantly, a shared meal. Topics are diverse and may include grass-fed beef marketing strategies, poultry butchering, crop scheduling, or CSA management. In July 2010, I attended a poultry butchering and rotational grazing field day in central Iowa hosted by Ben and Sharon Bradley. The event underscored the importance of sharing knowledge in the local food and alternative farming community, but it also provided an afternoon's worth of labor on the farm as participants were advised by the PFI staff members to be ready to get dirty.

The Bradleys own and rent a total of five hundred acres, most of which are in pasture. They produce beef, pork, lamb, and poultry and have a variety of marketing strategies. Two steers and two hogs are sold each month to a nearby cooperative, and lambs and chickens are sold directly to consumers at the farm. There were a variety of attendees at the field day. Some were already marketing local poultry or had rotational grazing operations and were there to see whether Ben and Sharon could share any new information with them. There were several young people who were hoping to start rotational grazing or direct meat marketing. Some, like me, were researching local food or farming practices in Iowa.

The first part of the field day involved a tour of the Bradleys' farm.

They have only recently started rotationally grazing their beef cattle and are just learning how to best manage the fencing, paddocks, and pasture health. Discussions during the tour included which fence posts work best (you want something light but sturdy and something brightly colored that will be more visible to the cattle); how best to carry the fence posts as you move fencing (a golf bag works well); and, possibly the biggest challenge with intensive, rotational grazing, how to ensure a reliable water supply for each small pasture. Sharon and Ben not only shared their own learning experience and goals (for example, they have considered building a water containment system at the highest point on their farm that would provide a gravity-fed watering system to the paddocks), they also asked for advice from the participants. Several attendees were also rotational grazers and had advice about pasture health and paddock arrangement.

After lunch, we moved on to the participatory part of the field day, chicken butchering. Ben took us to the pasture where the chickens are kept in covered, low pens with open bottoms. The pens, or tractors, are moved every day to fresh pasture. At night, the family dog is tied nearby to bark and keep coyotes, raccoons, and other predators away. We brought fifteen birds back for the demonstration; these would be sold to Ben's regular customers, who were scheduled to arrive later in the day to pick up their purchases. Ben normally butchers his chickens in batches of about a hundred, employing four to six extra people to assist him. There are usually several new helpers each time, often students from a nearby college, and Ben says that while this might slow the process down somewhat, he thinks it is important to teach people this skill. A regular employee, Rachel, who was helping out during the field day, reported that Ben told her not long after she started working for them, "You can't make any mistakes that we haven't made already." Even though this process is a major part of the family's farm income, there is little concern about inexperienced workers doing harm to the bottom line. Ben's overall philosophy is that his skills are worthwhile to pass along, and he sees this as part of the farm's mission.

Ben butchers his birds in two separate areas. The first is an open pole barn where he kills, plucks, and removes the heads and feet. The second stage is in a metal shed, equipped with a stainless steel sink and cutting space, where the birds are eviscerated; the hearts, livers, and gizzards set aside for those customers who want them; and the carcasses inspected for any remaining pin feathers. The finished birds are cooled in a large water tank before finally being packaged in large, plastic zip-lock bags. Ben first showed us his process for killing and cleaning the birds. He has four kill cones attached to the side of the barn. He starts with two birds and explains that they are best killed by severing the blood vessels in the throat, while leaving the windpipe intact. One has to feel for the windpipe and hold it out of the way while sliding the small knife through the bird's throat. After the birds are dead and have bled out, they are scalded in 145- to 150-degree water, two at a time, then plucked. Ben has posted a clock over the tank where, as he held one bird by the feet in each hand and gently swished them in the hot water, he could scald the birds for exactly ninety seconds. Scalding too much longer will burn them, resulting in a pink skin.

The birds are plucked in a mechanical plucker, made by EZ Plucker, two at a time. The machine resembles a washing machine, with a hose attached to wash out the barrel as the birds are plucked. The process takes only about a minute. The drumlike container of the plucker is lined with soft rubber fingers, and as it spins, the feathers are knocked off and wash out the bottom. Finally, the birds' heads and feet are removed. To remove the heads, Ben had a friend with welding skills design a simple piece of iron, shaped into a V that bolts to the side of the barn wall. The chicken's head fits into the middle of the V and is removed by swiftly pulling the bird by the feet. Pulling the heads from the birds in this way loosens the esophagus and windpipe, making the entrails easier to remove later. Cutting through the neck would cause those vessels to contract, making them difficult to fully remove from the cavity. The feet and lower legs are cut off at the knee joint. Ben's demonstration of his technique with two birds took about ten minutes. After he was finished, he asked for volunteers to do the next two birds.

Two people immediately volunteered, both of whom hoped to start raising pastured broilers for sale in the near future, but neither of them had ever processed a chicken before. The first volunteer, a woman of around thirty, quickly and easily killed her bird by smoothly feeling for the windpipe to hold it out of the way. She scalded and plucked the bird without

Ben demonstrates how to scald birds before plucking.

needing assistance from Ben. It took her two tries to cleanly remove the head, the bird slipping out of the iron bracket the first time, but overall she made the process look remarkably easy for someone doing it the first time. The second individual, however, was less adept. He sloshed much of the water out of the scalding tank as he dunked the birds. Ben stepped in to suggest that he do it more gently. When the volunteer tried to remove the head, the bird slipped from his grasp and slid across the barn floor.

These errors by first-time learners may seem irrelevant and a normal part of a learning-based field day. But these birds were to be sold to Ben's customers and, as we began the processing demonstration, a customer arrived at the farm to pick up his birds. He was earlier than expected—he was driving home from western Iowa and stopped at the farm on the way. So he watched as the two inexperienced volunteers processed, and

A field day participant slaughters a chicken for the first time.

in one case dropped, the birds he was planning to buy. The customer's interaction with Ben made it clear that the two knew each other well and that Ben was not concerned that his client had observed the process. But this underscores the potential risk to the quality of the product and the relationship with the customer when using volunteer labor.

I later encountered the woman who stepped up first to butcher at this field day. She now manages her own flock of broilers, which she butchers at her home. She views Ben's field day as the event that gave her the knowledge to start. Having the opportunity to practice a new skill in a low-risk environment was an important benefit for her as a beginning farmer. The field day has the potential to develop future farmers, educate community members, and supply short-term labor for farmers.

Investing in Local Food Labor

Advocates of local food have tended to emphasize community benefits and at times downplay wage work in favor of volunteerism. But we cannot entirely remove economic prosperity from the equation of local food systems, nor should we try. As one CSA and pastured poultry producer commented,

"I'm making business decisions here, I'm not a charity." Financial success for producers is critical, but it is a productive exercise to look beyond the economic transaction. A closer look at farmers' labor strategies can help us think about the importance of the social aspect—whether we call it civic agriculture or embeddedness—of local food production.

First, even paid labor, with its emphasis on economic efficiency and getting one's money's worth, can support a more civically engaged agriculture. In particular, paid labor on small farms is an inherently embedded economic process. Social engagement cannot be separated from economic success for farmers. They repeatedly emphasize the importance of leadership over management and suggest that employers work collaboratively with their employees as much as possible. In addition, being attentive to individual workers' specific skills, desires, and comfort is a strategy for developing long-term employees who are successful at their jobs, which in turn is more profitable for growers.

Second, alternative labor strategies such as using volunteers can increase agricultural literacy and knowledge, a key component of civic agriculture. Producers regularly report that they wish more people knew where their food came from. Thus, engaging people who are typically only consumers rather than producers in the labor of food production becomes a powerful teaching tool. Despite the initial decrease in economic return because of decreased efficiency or errors, developing knowledge about agricultural practices in a community can be beneficial. Theoretically, a CSA shareholder who has participated in farm operations and is more knowledgeable about the labor involved in food production may become an advocate for paying the real cost of food. This outcome would be consistent with Lyson's idea of civic agriculture, but at this point we do not really know how farm volunteers interact with the community and what impact their farm experiences might have.

Alternative labor strategies can also provide learning experiences for volunteers and, even more significantly, for interns, contributing to alternative structures of knowledge dissemination in agriculture. This lateral dissemination of knowledge is very different from the conventional top-down model of land-grant universities and agribusiness and has become a key part of sustainable agriculture.[12] When applied to intern labor, this knowledge transmission can directly develop the next generation of farmers. The knowledge they gain may be significant and applicable to their own operations, as in Renee Johnson-Berry's case. Additionally, individuals who have interned on a farm may be better candidates for beginning farmer funding. In Iowa, for example, to qualify for some beginning farmer loans, one has to prove farm experience. Their internship experience can then tangibly increase the likelihood that they will be able to farm by opening up new opportunities for start-up funding.

Using volunteers and interns is not all positive, however. While it's true that there are benefits to young people learning about food production, volunteers are often new to farmwork and may require a significant investment of the farmer's time. To further complicate matters, in the case of a CSA the volunteer may be a customer of the farm. In this case, the farmer is then more of a tour guide than an employer and, in the worst cases, the farmer may have to redo the volunteer's work. Interns provide an opportunity to develop the skills of beginning farmers; however, providing room and board is often a deeper commitment than a producer can manage. Volunteers and interns may contribute to better agricultural knowledge more broadly, but they may not contribute economically. Their mistakes can actually damage farmers' economic returns by decreasing yields or slowing harvest times. Additionally, the existence of volunteer labor does nothing to benefit the community economically because the volunteers lack wages that would circulate in the area. Interns, similarly, are often not local. Of the four interns Jean Sorensen hired in 2008, all came from neighboring states. Thus, interns' economic impact on the local community is temporary and the knowledge they gain may be applied elsewhere.

Finally, project-based field days can support beginning farmers by allowing them to practice new skills without the long-term commitment that becoming an employee or an intern would require. In addition, the diverse group of attendees at field days can develop knowledge among community members as well as other farmers. The hands-on approach of a field day allows participants to develop new skills while doing purposeful work. At the end of the day, a farm project may reach completion, providing tangible benefits for the farmer and an important sense of shared work for participants.

Agricultural labor has always taken a backseat to farm owner-operators. Our collective emphasis on independent landowning farmers at times

causes us to forget the hired hands who are as integral to a farm's success as Lurvy was to both the story and the farm in E. B. White's *Charlotte's Web*. When journalists or social scientists do address farm labor, it
is often to expose the abuses typical in large-scale production, in which
workers are marginalized both socially and economically. In Iowa, where
migrant labor is a relatively small portion of the agricultural labor force,
food farmers have turned to young people, most of whom have more enthusiasm than experience or skill. The mixed success of these arrangements can provide some important insights into how farmers balance the
economics and values of local food.

I am optimistic about the long-term potential to develop a more agriculturally literate population of activists in the Midwest and beyond. The
current workforce, however, is a fairly privileged population (largely college students) that can afford to work temporary jobs for low pay. Further,
while using volunteers and interns may increase agricultural knowledge
and develop future farmers, these populations also consist of those who
have flexible time and resources to devote to free and low-paid farmwork.
In this context, agricultural knowledge in local food remains primarily
in the hands of the elite. Developing a truly sustainable food system that
attends to both social and ecological concerns requires that labor in local
food can adequately support all workers, not just those who have other
financial resources to fall back on when the season ends.

Of course, the seasonal and economic realities of farming make it very
difficult for small-scale producers to fairly pay themselves, let alone year-
round employees. If part of the aim of the local food movement is to improve our communities socially as well as economically, the interactions
between the farmers and their employees discussed in this chapter are
encouraging. Most important, focusing on labor reminds us that more
individuals are involved in local food than just farmers and consumers,
although the popular press would have us believe otherwise. In the next
chapter, I look more closely at one local food business that does provide
year-round employment to local residents. As with the growers in this
chapter, employee satisfaction is as much a result of the work environment
as it is the paycheck.

—————— ☀ ——————

CHAPTER EIGHT

Working at Great Greens

WHAT MAKES a job a good job? It is not an easy question to answer, really. For a fresh college graduate, a good job may mostly be one that provides enough income to make their college investment worthwhile. For a mother, a good job may be one that allows her the flexibility to be home with her children when they are sick or to attend school events. Our perspective on good jobs shifts as we age and our goals and situations change. Usually, however, once we move beyond the basics of earning an adequate wage, concepts of a good job become more related to how invested we feel in our work or how much we care about the larger mission of our employer.

Most of the research about rural development attends only to the potential for economic impact, not to the quality of the job or the investment of the employee in the work. This research usually suggests that large-scale industry is the best way to improve rural economies and, by extension, the quality of life for rural people. More recently, some have been critical of this emphasis on large-scale development and have suggested that networks of smaller businesses not only boost local economies but also have civic and social benefits. The local food movement, like other buy local or conscientious consumption approaches, tends to favor the second option, promoting the idea that businesses, employees, and customers should be part of a mutually supportive community with shared values. But what do small food businesses offer their employees, and what do their employees think about the work they do? This question is worth examining to understand whether these businesses are really constructing livelihoods that live up to the expectations of the local food movement. Let us first look at what researchers have to say about relationships between workers and their employers and then focus on the day-to-day operations of one rural local food business, particularly the relationship between a boss and his workers, how employees are treated and how they view their work, and the collaborative processes that are critical to the business's operation.

Researchers usually debate the smaller is better thesis in economic terms by examining the differences in wealth distribution associated with large industry versus a set of small, connected businesses. But many social scientists have also questioned the impact of big business on workers. In particular, by talking with workers and actually working in large industries, some researchers have exposed worker mistreatment and abuse in large-scale industry, especially food processing plants. In these systems, workers generally lack decision-making power and may experience racial and gender discrimination on the job. These are not jobs that foster individual growth, empowerment, or community ties.

My research shows how a collaborative working environment in one local food production and processing business, Great Greens, constitutes a significant benefit for its employees and stands in stark contrast to the working environment of large-scale industry so often promoted by rural development specialists. The structure of the business allows workers flexibility and decision-making power, which leads to further investment and engagement with the goals of the business. This case shows the extent to which the local food movement can — and cannot — make the difference its advocates promote.

Is Bigger Better?

Researchers of the rural United States have not painted a very hopeful picture. Rural areas have long been associated with poverty, lower educational levels, and underemployment.[1] Typical rural development strategies associated with agriculture tend to encourage large corporations to build plants that produce seeds or inputs such as fertilizer and chemicals or manufacture value-added products, such as food processing and ethanol production, as a way to add needed jobs and boost economic activity.[2] But the emphasis on conventional agriculture as a mechanism for rural development is problematic, particularly in the Midwest. Agriculture and other rural industries, such as forestry, are being left behind by service or knowledge-based industries and high value products, as in the technology sector, which are growing much faster than rural industries.[3] Further, although conventional production agriculture remains a highly influential segment of the rural economy, it does not actually create jobs to any meaningful extent. The consolidation of midwestern agriculture over the course of the twentieth century has created a widening gap between production and employment because the enormous increases in output have been accomplished with progressively more machines and fewer people.[4]

However, a food system consists of more than just agricultural production, and Iowa has historically had a robust network of food processing in addition to farming. The state was once the leading canner of sweet corn, for example, and many communities relied heavily on the jobs created by food canneries. In Lake Mills, the Cool Spring Canning Company was the area's largest employer throughout the first half of the twentieth century, until it closed in 1957. In 2004, there were 214 food-processing facilities, with annual sales less than five hundred thousand dollars. These included producers of salsa, jams, and pickles. Small-scale meat lockers remain in the state as well; in 2010 there were 162 state-inspected and custom meat processors that handled beef, pork, and poultry.[5]

The USDA Economic Research Service has identified food processing as the most important manufacturing sector in the rural United States. As a stable and relatively recession-proof industry, meat processing has been specifically identified as providing long-term, consistent employment opportunities in the countryside, particularly those areas with access to livestock production facilities.[6] Iowa fits this profile precisely, and the abundant corn crop feeds a lot of hogs. Generations ago, this meant that an individual farmer grew corn and other grains to feed his own hogs and could independently send them to market. As agriculture became more specialized, and especially as meat packers moved out of urban areas such as Chicago to get closer to the point of production and farther from centers of unionization, the system rapidly scaled up to its current enormous proportions. The large capacity of meat processing leads some economists to make major claims about the potential for economic growth based on the demand for suppliers (including farmers) and specialized labor in rural areas. Even while admitting that the average pay in meatpacking plants tends to be lower than in manufacturing and other industries, proponents assert that the large payroll volume can provide more significant economic benefits than other industries can offer.

Social scientists, journalists, and activists have been critical of such claims. They are not convinced that a high-volume of low-wage jobs will make a positive impact on the broader community. Economists' lack of attention to social context, inequality, and the pressure that new populations of low-wage earners put on community services are of particular concern. In addition, these analyses rarely consider the economic restructuring of the 1980s, which resulted in reduced occupational safety and environmental regulations and undermined the influence of labor unions. This debate is very similar to the one that Walter Goldschmidt sparked about the value of large-scale agriculture for rural communities. While economists have tended to overpromote the financial aspects of large-scale systems regardless of the effect on local decision-making power, social scientists have implicated industry in social deterioration. The economic view is that number of jobs outweighs quality of life, occupational safety, or worker autonomy and decision making. The external costs of pressure on school and health systems or social safety nets that result from a rapidly increasing population are rarely calculated. Such pressures are only exacerbated when local communities provide tax breaks to those very industries that cause a population spike.

Critics of the large industry model, who usually include local food advocates, call for reestablishing the networks of small, locally focused, community-based businesses that existed before the consolidation in both agriculture and industry that occurred during the twentieth century. From an economic point of view, however, it is difficult to make a clear-cut argument that small businesses are more economically beneficial than large ones. One study in Iowa during the 1990s assessed the potential benefits of so-called self-development projects in rural areas. The focus was on small-scale firms and businesses and locally based groups, such as co-ops or nonprofit organizations, that engage in economic development projects. Based on a broad national survey as well as specific case studies of eight self-development projects, the authors asserted that the economic gains of such projects were not particularly significant. They wrote that "we would have to conclude that self-development efforts have produced modest economic results in a small proportion of the rural communities in the U.S." They stressed, however, that these projects can make important noneconomic contributions to a community in that they emphasize democratic decision making and result in "an increased sense of community among residents."[7]

European researchers have taken a slightly different path and have argued in favor of alternative food production strategies because they have the potential to combine social enhancement with economic gain. Diverse businesses that interact both economically and socially can be good for rural communities, even when it may be difficult to identify which benefits are social and which are economic. Because alternative agriculture operates mostly outside the bounds of the conventional system, individuals must creatively develop their own new economic and social systems based on local supply chains. These new interactions have the potential to empower rural people to envision a food system and an economic structure in which they are engaged participants rather than being on the bottom end of a trickle-down scheme. The challenge for the researcher or activist arises in trying to understand the tangible effects of a complex, articulated food system on a rural community. This is a much different approach than simply calculating profits, wages, or input costs. Instead, we have to take a long-term, evolutionary look at communities and identify the points at which interacting with the food system, as a producer, worker, or eater, may enhance a person's social or economic quality of life.[8]

Despite the occasional assertion that policymakers pay attention to the social and community effects, both good and bad, of economic development through food systems, usually the enterprise that adds the most economic value wins the political game. Thus, local food has to make an economic case if it is to succeed. It has taken some time to develop a body of research that adequately addresses the economic impact of local food. Past research has tended to be enterprise specific, focusing only on specialty crops, such as muscadine grapes in Mississippi, aquaculture, or Christmas trees. Researchers have simultaneously lauded these types of crops for their newness and potential to add diversity to a region's agricultural production and criticized them for not making any significant economic impact on a state or regional economy.[9]

Only recently have researchers attended holistically to locally produced specialty crops as an industry in its own right in the United States. The Leopold Center for Sustainable Agriculture has been on the forefront of local food impact research. The center's approach has been to survey farmers and both institutional and individual buyers (such as farmers' market patrons) about their sales and purchasing activity for all types of products statewide. In 2013, the center surveyed 120 farmers who reported just over thirteen million dollars in sales.[10] The survey also included purchasers, and, interestingly, grocery stores came out on top as the number one purchasers of local foods, accounting for 68 percent of the tracked local food purchases in 2013.[11] This is an encouraging statistic, indicating that there is considerable interest in local foods beyond the farmers' market and CSA crowd. Local food advocates have long seen institutional purchasing as an important measure of the health of a local food system. Despite all the attention paid to the individuals who patronize farmers' markets, institutions have major buying power that can support a sustainable local food network.

The purchasing and sales numbers are important, but we still know very little about the actual job-creation potential of local foods. Using data collected from farmers, the Leopold Center's study projected that about 110 people are employed for every million dollars in local food sales; thirty-four percent of these jobs are full time, year round.[12] The researchers note that the farmers they surveyed may be operating at an ideal scale for job creation; the farms are labor intensive and still too small to be highly mechanized.[13] Impact reports such as the Leopold Center's are illuminating, and they provide some weight to the argument that local food could provide a boost to rural economies.

Although the debate about the economic advantages of large industry versus small businesses will likely not be soon resolved, there is little debate about the deplorable working conditions in industrial food processing, particularly in meatpacking plants. The Bureau of Labor Statistics reports that serious injury rates among meatpacking workers are three times higher than in other industries.[14] Typical injuries in these plants include lacerations from handheld knives and cutting machinery, repetitive motion injuries, and strains and sprains, as well as injuries from both live animals and hanging carcasses.[15] In addition, temperatures in plants range from very warm areas in which animals are killed, bled, and, in the case of pork, dehaired, using water as hot as 136°F, to cold work areas that are kept at about forty degrees where meat is cut and packaged for final sale.[16]

In addition to the well-documented hazardous working conditions, social scientists have also pointed out how social environments within plants can be hostile. Anthropologist Deborah Fink conducted undercover ethnographic research in Perry, Iowa, at an Iowa Beef Packers plant, which has since been absorbed by Tyson. She showed that, despite legal protections, women and people of color experienced discrimination. Not only was it harder for them to advance to better jobs, they were poorly treated by managers and company human resources and health care staff. In response, they developed a range of social coping strategies; for instance, women often befriended male plant workers who could protect them from some harassment and, in some cases, recommend them for better jobs within the plant. In other cases, workers were hostile to one another. Fink tells of one employee who, for reasons she could not fathom, regularly attempted to sabotage her attempts to keep lean meat separated from fat by throwing his own fatty meat in with her lean cuts. Tools and materials were often stolen or hidden, and managers would regularly scream at employees to force them to increase their speed or efficiency.[17]

Ultimately, employees who work in these large-scale industries are at a significant disadvantage if they attempt to press for better conditions. Many are recent immigrants, some of whom are possibly undocumented or refugees. Others come from backgrounds with low levels of formal education. These socially marginalized populations lack the resources necessary to hire an attorney to plead their case, even if they are legally protected. Precisely because of their job-creation potential, meatpacking plants can count on remarkable political support, even if the jobs they create are low paying and dangerous. As a result, legislators reward them with tax breaks and further decreased regulation.[18]

Packinghouse workers experience challenges beyond the plant floor as well. Researchers in Guymon, Oklahoma, found that workers' pay was too low to afford local housing. The prevailing rates were too high and workers could not afford the up-front costs of damage deposits. In addition, demand far outstripped supply, leading to overcrowding and long commutes for those unable to find local housing. Further, despite the plant's offering health insurance, employees were ineligible until they had completed six months work. Many employees did not stay employed long enough to qualify. In other cases, those who qualified could only afford to insure themselves, leaving their family members without coverage. The result was, of course, a population largely reliant on emergency services, straining the local health care system.[19]

Great Greens

If large-scale industry emphasizes quantity over quality of jobs, is it inherently true that a small workplace is better for employees? And does it make a difference whether the business is producing and processing local food? During my research, I worked in one business whose employees certainly do have a very different experience than those in large industrial plants and corporations. Great Greens, based in southeast Iowa, is a small business that grows and processes organic sprouts and microgreens as well as garden crops for wholesale. Although the size of the facility means that it does not make a major economic contribution in the region, focusing on the work environment helps us look beyond capital and address working conditions in rural areas. Great Greens employees have a great deal of autonomy, flexibility, and decision-making ability in their work. Although some employees at Great Greens may lack interest in the finished products, they have a strong interest in the success of the business.

Great Greens is owned and operated by area native Neal Jackson, who had made the farm to school salad project feasible (see chapter 6). The business is certified organic, licensed for processing, and includes both an indoor greenhouse and five acres of garden crops (some of these are described in earlier chapters). In the greenhouse, Neal grows a variety of sprouts and wheatgrass. The largest product category is the sprouts, which includes sunflower, pea, radish, carrot, amaranth, basil, and fennel. He sells them to grocery stores, as well as to high-end restaurants, where they

are used as plate garnishes and salad additions. Wheatgrass, the imma-
ture form of the common wheat plant, is the other major product category
in the greenhouse. The seeds germinate and the plants grow for seven to
ten days before harvest. The grass is then put through a juicer, where the
thick, green juice is extracted and frozen in one-ounce plastic containers.
Neal sells the juice to natural food stores throughout eastern Iowa.

I first met Neal in the fall of 2010, when I attended a meeting of the
Regional Food Systems Working Group hosted by the Leopold Center for
Sustainable Agriculture in central Iowa. Although Neal was not a participant, his products were to be used in the lunch provided at the meeting.
The event organizer called me because I was an eastern Iowa resident and
asked whether I could deliver the sprouts to the meeting. Neal dropped
several boxes by my house late one evening for me to drive over the next
day, acting as a volunteer ad hoc distributor. Later, I met Neal again at
the annual conference of Practical Farmers of Iowa. Not long after that
interaction, we met for a formal interview during which I learned about
the history of Great Greens and his background.

When it came time for me to decide where to get hands-on experience
with the kinds of jobs that local food enterprises provide, Neal's business
stood out as an interesting and diverse operation in the area. At Great
Greens I could engage in both farmwork and food processing. In addition, I knew that Neal distributed other growers' produce and that he
hoped to develop further collaborative relationships with other producers.
Ultimately, Great Greens serves as an excellent example of a small-scale
food production and processing business that engages with direct marketing (through farmers' markets) as well as institutional sales. The business exemplifies the kind of diverse, sustainable operation that local food
advocates believe will transform rural communities for the better, both
economically and socially.

Neal grew up on a small acreage in southeastern Iowa. The family did
not farm for a living; Neal's father operated a sawmill for a while and then
started truck driving to provide most of the family's income. According
to Neal, "we didn't have enough land to do a traditional farm, or to actually make money." However, on their six-acre home plot, the family had
a large garden as well as milk goats and dairy cows, which supplied the

majority of their food needs throughout the year. In addition, the family managed an eleven-acre timber parcel.

Neal's parents were Amish, like many of the families in the area; however, they left the church less than a year before Neal was born because they "didn't agree with the rules and regulations." Of the seven children in the family, Neal was the second youngest. He notes that his oldest brother, seven years his senior, has the clearest memory of living Amish. Despite leaving the church, Neal attributes much of the ethos of food production and self-sufficiency to their Amish heritage. Neal grew up "helping plant, weed, harvest, can, and freeze all kinds of fruits and vegetables, butcher chickens, butcher sheep, and cows."

Although the family left the Amish church and way of life, religion continued to be important for the family. After high school, Neal left his home community for Maui, where there was a sister church to the one he attended in Iowa. Neal spent most of the 1980s there working in a variety of grounds maintenance and mechanical jobs.

> Yeah, for the first few years I worked for a grounds maintenance company. The first few weeks I was weeding the flowerbeds, and I knew that wasn't going to last very long. Then I got on the mowing crew—that was better. Then I was the mowing crew supervisor for most of the accounts that we had. We had high-end accounts that we did grounds maintenance on. I also got to trim coconut trees, so that was a fun experience. . . . I got to climb 130-foot coconut trees on the beach and trim them overlooking the ocean.

Soon, Neal was ready for a new endeavor, so he started his own mobile repair business. Along with his groundskeeping duties at the previous job, he was responsible for the maintenance and repair on all the equipment. He used those skills and contracted himself out to various resorts, hotels, and grounds management companies to repair their equipment. Neal says the experiences of gardening as a young person and his work in Maui helped him develop an excellent set of skills. He notes that the work was "a pretty good fit for a while until I got the systems up and running, then the entrepreneur that I am, it drives me nuts to hang around in maintenance mode."

In 1989, Neal returned to Iowa and was hired by his church, a large nondenominational Christian congregation, as the grounds supervisor. In this role he oversaw two hundred acres of "woodlands, prairie restoration, land, several ponds, kind of a big commercial garden, an orchard, roads and parking lots, and athletic fields and lawn areas." The church had a strong emphasis on sustainable food production and sustainable lifestyle, and the expansive grounds produced food that the church used when it hosted meetings of denominational leaders and held events. In the mid-1990s, a group of church members expressed interest in growing wheatgrass:

> So, it started off as kind of a group effort, and everybody shared the work and everybody shared the benefit. Then it turned into a few people share the work and a lot of people share the benefit. That's kind of the way it goes. Anyway, I was involved with growing the wheatgrass, and then at some point there was only a few people doing the work, so that kind of fell apart. I picked it up as kind of a business model. Then I realized really quick that I've gotta expand and target a bigger audience — this is going to fly.

Thus, Great Greens started as a business in March 1998 with wheatgrass juice. Neal quickly expanded into microgreens, including sunflower and buckwheat sprouts, snow pea shoots, and daikon radish sprouts. Neal notes that the small greens contain "a more concentrated nutrition, and they're very digestible. And they're just a nutrient-dense food. And besides that, they're tasty."

Meanwhile, about that time, a local woman obtained grant funds to develop a local food directory. Additionally, she hosted the first of what Neal calls a buyer-food farmer matchmaker meeting, where restaurant buyers and growers gather to exchange information and ideas. At this meeting, he met several chefs as well as the buyer for the student union of a local university. At the time the union had a juice bar "down in the basement, back in a corner." According to Neal, "they would buy my wheatgrass to juice for a while until that fell apart. But then, over time, we'd find more customers and more restaurants opened up. Golly, I mean now, [the area] is pretty saturated with really good restaurants."

The business had humble beginnings. Neal started in a foreclosed mobile home, which he had moved to a small trailer park just off the main highway. He "bought and gutted out the middle of it," and installed a waterproof floor by laying plywood and coating it with epoxy paint. There was no space for a compost pile at the trailer park, so Neal would haul all the waste materials back to his mother's property to compost. He would fill barrels of finished compost and take them back to the trailer to plant the wheatgrass and sprouts. Not surprisingly, the mobile home was a less than ideal space in which to run a business.

After many years of looking, Neal finally found a property that was located near his aging mother's house and was suitable for building a larger greenhouse facility. Unfortunately, the property sits near the English River, which, like most of the watersheds in eastern Iowa, reached record flood levels in both 1993 and 2008. Neal's solution was to build a large greenhouse space over what will eventually be a long-term root crop storage space. The greenhouse and an outer deck are high enough to remain dry during even record floods. Additionally, the walls are engineered to withstand heavy flooding and, Neal notes, if the property were to flood, it would do so in the summer months, when the storage space would be mostly empty. "I just felt like, OK, this is a risk I can take."

Neal moved the business into the new greenhouse in 2008, and he notes that it still feels as though he is in transition. By spring 2011, the root cellar space was still in a planning stage, the large deck outside was not finished, and the components of a walk-in cooler, which he purchased from a grocery store that had closed, were stacked in a corner. Neal had big plans for the space: "There'll be a loading dock out here, and I just plan for a lot of workspace there. Out beyond the roof I'm planning to put a greenhouse, a specialty greenhouse for starter crops and high value crops. And now I'm just realizing that I'll probably be able to use that space for curing onions and garlic or whatever in the fall. So, probably, that will get used for various things." The new building sits on six acres of land, which includes the creek and the flood plain. In early 2011, Neal closed on an additional seven acres, just to the west of the property, where he hopes to do more greenhouse and garden production. His five acres of garden crops are a short drive north of the greenhouse property.

In addition to overseeing these various projects—wheatgrass, growing sprouts, and garden crops—Neal does all the deliveries personally. He also markets and delivers produce for a group of Amish growers:

> They're brothers and cousins that are working together, and they market to other wholesale accounts as well. But you know, in season, I'm going around to a lot of these places anyway. It only makes sense to try to take their product along and try to help them market and deliver their product. The way that works is, I find out what they have available, let my customers know, take the orders. I tell them ahead of time, but on delivery day I pick it up, load it on my truck, and deliver it. It doesn't always happen this way, but I've delivered product to the customer that they've picked that morning. They're out there at five picking cucumbers and zucchini, getting it washed and boxed up, and it's on my truck at eight and delivered by noon.

All this work must dovetail with his family's schedule: his wife has a full-time professional job, and he does the majority of childcare for his two daughters. Neal's business would not be possible without hiring outside labor.

In 2011, Neal had at least seven regular employees, plus a collection of friends and acquaintances he would hire occasionally to help with large jobs. Three women, Sara, Trina, and Becky, do the day-to-day work in the greenhouse. They are assisted occasionally by Jessica, who is Sara's niece. Jim works exclusively in the gardens, managing the produce from seed to harvest. Neal's nephew works one evening per week, the night before harvest, removing the sunflower seed hulls from the sprouts so that they are clean for the harvesters. Finally, Rick attends to plant watering in the greenhouse on the weekends.

I started working at Great Greens in April 2011 as an unpaid volunteer. Neal and the staff were all aware of my research agenda and for a time I was known as the dissertation lady. I spent several days a week at the greenhouse and garden plot through August 2011. During my time there, I primarily helped with harvesting wheatgrass and sprouts. I planted cabbage seeds and sweet potato starts, called slips. Later in the spring, I helped transplant the sweet potatoes and assisted with hand weeding.

I also harvested asparagus. In addition, Neal asked me to help with more administrative tasks, such as obtaining bar codes for his products and doing market research. I also did occasional odd jobs, such as caulking the seams in the greenhouse walls to reduce condensation and sanding the walls of a newly constructed walk-in cooler to prepare for painting.

Neal says the work at his business is not great, in that "it's part time, it's odd hours, you know, it's not consistent, there's no health benefits. I mean, I haven't been able to afford that." In addition to the challenges of the work and workplace, Neal operates in an area known in the state for poverty and drug use. "I had a single mother that I've known for a long time," he recalls, "and she was working for me. She really liked this kind of work. I thought it would work into a full-time thing. Anyway, she got into some drug problems and kind of messed up things for herself." Despite the challenges with the work and his location, he has been able to cultivate a stable staff of people who are invested in their jobs and the business. Noting that as someone who has been primarily self-employed for his adult life, he has little experience as a boss, but "I try to be flexible, I try to be kind, I try to take care of my employees as best I can."

When I spoke with the employees, they told me that the flexibility offered at Great Greens was one of its main benefits. Before working for Neal, Becky worked at a local Pizza Hut restaurant for twelve years. She told me that she hated everything about it: the uniforms, the people, the cooking, and the "corporate bullshit." Ultimately, she found her job at Great Greens thanks to Sara, who knew she was unhappy at her restaurant job. She feels lucky to have the job and wonders where else someone could work in which you can have flexible work hours and call in when you need to. She likes that Neal does not require them to keep specific hours because the greenhouse employees know how to schedule their work time so that all the necessary tasks are completed.

Given the realities of most of their lives, flexibility is clearly critical. As Neal had told me, the daily lives of the staff at Great Greens did seem stressful and overwhelming. Sara had worked for Neal the longest, six years. She came in every day to at least check in on the sprouts as well as manage the harvest on Wednesdays and the wheatgrass juicing on Thursdays or Fridays. She has three children of her own, eighteen-year-old twin boys and a younger daughter; in addition, she has taken custody of her brother's three daughters. Trina had worked for Neal for two years and is the mother of three children, one of whom had serious health problems. Becky, who lives with Sara and had been working at Great Greens for one year, had recently overseen the movement of her grandmother into a nursing home and was taking care of her finances. Becky has eleven siblings, a combination of step-, half-, and full brothers and sisters, scattered around the Midwest. Six siblings were adopted by other families, and several have had encounters with the law. Finally, Jim had been working for Neal for about three years. He was an avid gardener and had worked with Neal on the grounds of the church years before. Jim was deeply religious and had a stable marriage of many years. In 2008, he suffered a heart attack, which, understandably, led him to be cautious about his level of physical work.

Neal was aware of and somewhat shocked by his employees' situations. In an interview, he stated: "They've come from horribly messed up lives. And, you know, numerous times they've made comments like 'oh, it's so refreshing here, we come here to get away from our relatives and our life.' So I don't really know what to make of that other than that I appreciate it. If I'm doing something right, I try to keep doing it." When I began working for Great Greens in the early spring of 2011, Neal was hoping to develop an official employee incentive plan, including a profit-sharing system. He readily admitted that he was not knowledgeable about the best way to establish a plan but felt that it would help his employees become more invested in the success of the business.

Optimistic predictions of rural revitalization through local food rarely take into account the realities of rural poverty, drug use, family dissolution, and the hollowing out the middle phenomenon.[20] Particularly for those leaving the professional world to begin a second career as a farmer, the gap in socioeconomic class and life experience between an employer and employees may be stark. This gap is compounded when a farmer sees food production primarily as a labor of love. The agrarian idea of farming as a higher calling does not consider the position of workers, whose main interest is to take home a steady paycheck. On the one hand, we see financial projections, such as those of the Leopold Center, that portray local food in flat economic terms. On the other hand, in recent memoirs

and popular journalism, local food becomes a mission undertaken by pas-
sionate individuals who see their livelihoods as a way to mend social and
environmental damage wrought by conventional agriculture. At Great
Greens, the situation is more nuanced. For the most part, the employees
care very little about the products they grow. They are not interested in
local or organic agriculture; they do not shop at the farmers' market; and
they are ambivalent about the consumers who purchase their products.
But they are in full support of Great Greens and take significant pride and
ownership of their work.

During my time at Great Greens, I spent much of my time doing day-to-
day tasks with the crew. On most Wednesdays, I helped Sara, Trina, and
Becky harvest and package the microgreens and then juice wheatgrass on
either Thursdays or Fridays. Each process is mostly managed by the employees without a high level of involvement from Neal, with the exception
of the garden crops, with which he still is regularly engaged. I found Neal's
employees to be remarkably concerned about the success of the business,
even though they were not necessarily invested in, or even supportive of,
the specific products or tasks for which they were responsible.

Harvest

Microgreens are the largest sales category for Great Greens, and this is
what Neal says pays the bills on a day-to-day basis. Neal grows sunflower
and snow pea sprouts, along with several varieties of radish sprouts. These
are sold as prewashed salad mixes at several retail outlets in eastern Iowa.
In addition, he grows some specialty items, such as carrot, fennel, and
amaranth that are primarily sold to high-end restaurants, where they
are used as colorful garnishes and salad components. All the sprouts are
grown in the greenhouse on homemade racks made from wood or PVC
pipe. The seeds are planted directly in trays of compost, which is made
on-site from leftover plant residue and unused product. The seeds are watered on a specific schedule, and after germinating the trays are placed
on light racks, where the sprouts grow under lights until they are ready
to harvest. The seeds germinate and grow until they are just a few inches
tall, a process that generally takes one to two weeks. The constant cycle of

planting and harvesting maintains a consistent supply of greens for weekly harvesting.

The sprouts grown at Great Greens are harvested by hand. Snow peas and sunflowers are cut with a knife or scissors; smaller items, such as carrot and fennel sprouts, are harvested with mechanical clippers. After the sprouts are cut, they are soaked in tubs of sanitized water. Like David in chapter 6, Neal uses Tsunami 100, a food-grade sanitizer approved for organic products. The sanitizer is highly concentrated, requiring only about a teaspoon in several gallons of water. After a soak in sanitized water (forty-five seconds is sufficient to kill any pathogens, though the greens often soak for longer), the greens are moved to large industrial salad spinners to dry. When I started helping at the greenhouse, only one spinner was operational. It would hold about fifteen pounds of product and spin for ten to fifteen minutes to dry the greens. In May, Neal purchased a second spinner. After the greens are spun, they are packed by hand into bags, weighed, and sealed. Some of the small specialty items go into clamshell containers that hold only a few ounces. Others, such as sunflower and snow pea sprouts, are packed in bags ranging from five ounces to one pound.

Sara, Trina, and Becky had developed their own rhythm for harvesting, usually beginning between eight and nine. Sara preferred to harvest and Trina preferred to bag and weigh products. Becky preferred to avoid harvest entirely; she would rather plant. But three people were usually required to make the job manageable. Becky would move between harvesting and bagging or would place filled bags into boxes before storing them in the cooler. In addition, Becky was often the one to manage cleanup. She would empty the trays of compost, empty the coolers of old items, and keep the floor tidy. Neal's customers called their orders to him by Monday each week. On Tuesday, Sara, or in some cases her cousin Jessica, would count out the necessary number of bags and plastic clamshells and label them. By Wednesday, the harvesters only had to fill the available containers to arrive at the right number of orders.

The day before I first helped with the harvest, Sara warned me to come prepared to get wet and dirty. The team uses a garden hose to fill the bus tubs, rinse them out before refilling them, and spray out the spinners before each new product is dried. In addition, each tray of compost is dumped into a large barrel after the plants are cut, resulting in numerous spills of dirt. The crew works at a rapid pace; Trina, in particular, liked to try to weigh and fill containers quickly enough to empty one spinner basket (filled with nearly fifteen pounds of product when fully packed) before Sara filled the next basket. They preferred to start with the high-volume items and get those finished early in the day. Trina always wanted to get snow peas out of the way first; these were her least favorite sprouts to pack because the plants tend to stick together, making it difficult to get the right amount in each bag before weighing. With other products, she prided herself on her ability to take the right weight of product and fill the bag correctly the first time.

Neal also appreciated their speed, but for a different reason. He felt that the product improved if it could be chilled quickly after harvest. Thus, he hoped they would move the plants from the trays to the cooler as efficiently as possible. In fact, he hoped that after the installation of the large walk-in cooler, they might even harvest in the cooler. The crew, however, did not like this plan at all. Trina commented that she would have pneumonia in no time. Becky noted, "Neal gets a lot of crazy ideas." Despite Neal's preference for working in a chilled environment, I understood that it would not happen without the approval of the crew.

None of the employees who worked in the greenhouse, with the exception of Jim, were particularly interested in the products they grew. One of the first days I helped harvest the sprouts, Trina asked whether I ate all organic food. She adamantly declared that she never eats organic, though she admitted that there was one salad mix from Great Greens that she liked. Sara, likewise, was not interested in consuming the sprouts, relying instead on a steady intake of Mountain Dew during her workday. All three women were smokers and stopped at least twice during the harvest period to step outside for a cigarette break. There is a tendency to uncritically associate health with anything related to local food. Although from this perspective, organic farms are inherently healthier for people and the environment, and small farms are inherently healthier than big ag, these assumptions eliminate the actual diversity of experience in people who engage in the work of local food production.

Despite their disinterest in the sprouts, the group at Great Greens was extremely concerned about how well they sold. Because there was no walk-in cooler, the sprouts were stored in one three-door seventy-two-cubic-foot refrigerator. One small upright freezer held frozen wheatgrass juice and seeds. Each Wednesday morning before harvest, the coolers had to be cleared out to make space for the freshly cut items. One morning, as Becky cleaned the coolers in preparation for the harvest, Trina arrived and pointed to eight cases of five-ounce bags of mixed greens. "What's that?!" she asked. Becky assumed that it was leftovers from retailers that Neal had picked up and reimbursed them for as well as leftovers from the farmers' market. Trina was irritated and wondered why we had put in the effort to harvest extra product for the farmers' market if it was not going to be sold.

Sara revealed similar feelings to me, recounting a recent error at a co-operative grocery store. The produce manager planned a sale to promote Great Greens' products. Neal agreed to the slightly lower profit margin and had the crew harvest extra for the week. Then, when the sale occurred, the produce manager who planned it was on vacation, so there was no promotion and sales did not rise significantly. Thus, much of the extra product was wasted. In addition, Neal reimburses the store for any unsold produce. Sara is openly critical of this policy, noting that the store will be less motivated to sell the product if they know they will not lose money on anything not sold. Neal has a slightly different take, noting that in the long term, he thinks reimbursing the retailer makes sense. He points out that the store will naturally want to move all the product they can, so they might hold onto older product and try to sell it even if it is past its prime so that they are compensated for it. This hurts him because the orders are inconsistent if retailers are holding and trying to sell older product and not buying fresh from him each week. Additionally, he suggests that there is a risk that the customer will purchase old product and not be happy. For these reasons, he feels it is more beneficial to ensure that the retailers have fresh product every week, even if it means reimbursing them for what does not sell.

Ultimately, despite the employees' complaints about the work and disagreements with Neal about how the process can best be completed, they

all show a marked interest in the success of the business. They are concerned about the level of sales and always willing to harvest extra. But
they are frustrated with both Neal and the vendor if the extra product
goes unsold—even though, as hourly employees, any extra harvest benefits them because it takes longer and results in a higher wage for the day.
Despite earning more, the crew is only satisfied with that extra work if
it results in product sold. Further, they are proud of their efficiency and
attention to detail. Trina often pointed out the speed with which she could
accurately fill the bags and indicated she felt stressed out if there were too
many barrels of sprouts waiting to be bagged.

The dramas and frustrations related to unsold sprouts are invisible to
the patrons who buy them at specialty grocery stores. While the farmers
may be highlighted (in fact, Neal is one of the growers promoted with a
large photo at a nearby high-end grocer), Trina, Becky, and Sara stay well
behind the scenes. They have little interest or belief in the supposed benefits of the certified organic plants they carefully tend and harvest. Instead,
they want to see business growth and steady work. From their perspective,
the chaos of their daily lives bears little resemblance to their perceptions of
their well-heeled customers who enjoy an artsy display of sprouts on their
plates at an expensive restaurant. If local food is to build social cohesion
through education and consumer experience with agriculture, those consumers should experience more than the photo on the grocery store wall.

Wheatgrass

The second major income generator for Great Greens—and the product
Neal first sold—is wheatgrass juice. The juice is sold at retail stores in
eastern Iowa. While the microgreens may serve as a garnish at a high-
end restaurant, the customers for wheatgrass juice are primarily health-
conscious individuals or those suffering from illness. Sara explained to
me that wheatgrass first became popular as a natural remedy for cancer
patients.

The crew juices wheatgrass on Thursday or Friday of each week. The
grass is grown in the same manner as the sprouts: in trays of compost
under grow lights. When space allows, there may be as many as thirty

trays of wheatgrass to harvest, and each is cut by hand with a knife. Trina makes sure that the grass goes into the tubs of sanitizer and into the spinner baskets so that it all faces the same direction. Each handful of harvested grass is carefully placed in the rectangular tubs to form two orderly rows of grass. This can be tricky because the first few bunches will want to float around in the water. Then, the grass is placed around the spinner basket so that the root ends all face the same way. Trina, who prefers to feed the juicer, states that it is easier for her to put the grass through the machine if it is all facing the same direction. When I first saw the wheatgrass juicer, I commented to Sara that it was quite a contraption. She laughed and said that Neal is a master of contraptions, calling him MacGyver and claiming that he once jumped a car battery using a computer battery. The juicer is a heavy stainless steel machine with a motor attached to a spigot. In the spigot is an auger that feeds the grass through while pressing out the juice. The pulp is extruded out the side and the juice comes out the front of the spout.

As with the sprouts, Neal is most concerned about product quality. He wants the juice to be chilled as quickly as possible and to go directly into the freezer to ensure freshness. To start chilling the juice, one end of a food-grade plastic bag is attached to the juicer spigot and the other end sits in a plastic tub in which he has installed a small spout like those found at the bottom of a beverage cooler. Pressing a small lever opens the spout and lets the liquid out. A small hole is cut in the bottom corner of the bag, which is taped around the bottom spout. Then, ice packs are put in the tub to surround the bag. The juice comes out the juicer spigot and fills the bag in the ice packs. Someone then fills disposable one-ounce plastic containers with wheatgrass juice, snaps on the lids, and puts them in a tray for the freezer. After the cups are frozen solidly, they are packed by the dozen into a small cardboard box and labeled with the Great Greens sticker and instructions about how best to consume the juice.

Neal's desire to keep the juice as cold as possible led him to develop a new juicing contraption in the spring of 2011. He acquired some metal tubing used in bars for tap beer, noting that it would cool more quickly than a plastic bag and would more efficiently chill the juice. He also took a medium-sized cooler (about two by three feet) and cut one hole in the lid and one in the side. His plan was to place the juicer on top of the cooler and put the beer tubing inside the cooler with very cold water. The juice would go through the chilled tubing and out a spigot fitted in the hole on the side of the cooler. The cold water would chill the juice more thoroughly than the ice packs in the old system.

One morning in May, Neal had chilled two buckets of water in the freezer and had all of the parts of the system ready. But when I arrived, he felt he was running late and did not want to set up the new juicer. Trina was curious, though somewhat skeptical, about the system. Her main concern was that setting the juicer on top of a cooler would make it too high for her to reach. Despite feeling late, Neal agreed to set up the new juicer at Trina's prodding. He started by attaching a metal tube to the juicer and placing it on top of the cooler. Unfortunately, the top of the cooler had cup holders and ridges that did not allow the juicer to sit flat. I found some Styrofoam squares to place on top of the cooler. Although this allowed the juicer to sit flat, it also made it less stable. When the juicer was on top of the cooler, Neal started to attach a bag to the beer tubing, which was sticking out of the top of the cooler. At this point, I realized that we had not filled the cooler with the cold water. So, we took the juicer down and filled the cooler with the water that was waiting in the freezer. Immediately, the water began to leak out of the cooler's bottom spigot (which Neal had installed). Neal, atypically, muttered, "shit," as he tried to tighten the valve. He got the leak slowed to a drip, and Trina helpfully pointed out that it would need a different kind of seal in the future. Next, we hooked the bag up to the juicer—in this way, the system is the same as the old one—the juice comes from the juicer and goes into a bag, which feeds it into the next stage, in this case, into the chilled tubes. Once the bag was on the tubes, however, two separate bands, one plastic and one metal, were required to seal it. As soon as we had it put together, Trina started juicing. She did have to stand on a stepladder to reach the top of the juicer. Immediately, the bag began leaking where it was attached to the beer tubing. Trina said that she knew that the rings Neal had used would not work. Eventually, however, we realized that the leak came from a hole in the bag, not the seals. We turned off the juicer, dismantled everything, and Sara and Trina attached a new bag.

By the time the new bag was attached, Neal was feeling even more stressed about being late for his deliveries. Sara and Trina pointed out that he was often late, so why worry about it today. Trina started feeding the machine, and I set up the cups to be filled. We knew it would take a few minutes for the juice to get through the tubes, but it seemed to be taking an extremely long time. We wondered whether the tubing was leaking inside the cooler, but a careful peek (we had to lift the lid where the juicer was sitting) showed clear water. Next, Trina put some pressure on the bag to try to force it into the tube. She got some of it moving, but not much, then it stopped completely. Trina tried to siphon some of it through by sucking on the other end of the tube, though this had no effect. Again, she tried pressing on the bag to move some juice through. Unfortunately, she pressed too hard and the bag burst, spilling juice over the top of the cooler.

Thus ended the new juicing system. Sara and I salvaged what we could from the broken bag and set up the old system to finish the job that day. Despite the employees' criticism of the new system and their assumption that it would not work, both Sara and Trina were very involved in trying to make it work. Trina, especially, commented on the seals and tried various strategies to get the juice to flow smoothly and stop the various leaks. While they often chided Neal for his ideas and teased him about his MacGyver tendencies, they also were always willing to work with him to implement a new system, despite their skepticism.

Juicing wheatgrass may be the most disliked job at the greenhouse. Sara has declared she will not juice on Mondays, only on Thursday or Friday, even though that Neal would prefer she and Trina juice twice a week. Before I helped the first time with juicing, Sara commented, "if you like repetitive, boring work, you'll be fine, but if you've got a little ADD in you, it's hard." Each employee has strong opinions about the juicing process. Trina prefers to feed the cut wheatgrass into the juicer and does not like to fill the cups. Sara will fill cups but generally only does it in short segments: she will fill cups for a while, then go occupy herself elsewhere while the bag fills some more before coming back to do more cups. Becky tends to stay in the back of the greenhouse as much as possible, "playing in the dirt," as she says.

The women's work preferences are important for what they tell us about how local food can and cannot change rural society. When local food production is viewed as a labor of love, we ignore the experiences of workers who spend their days doing some tasks they like and others they would prefer to avoid. The employees at Great Greens are simultaneously frustrated by and interested in Neal's new ideas. Their overall desire to work for a successful business that allows them significant flexibility and autonomy encourages them to support many of those ideas, even when they find them questionable.

In addition, the consumers of the wheatgrass juice, more than the sprout buyers, tend to provoke criticism from the crew. Sara indicated that some of their wheatgrass customers like to take the leftover pulp (which is usually composted) and use it as a compress for joint pain. The women went on to tell me that one customer allegedly uses the juice as an enema. This elicited shouts of laughter from the group as they agreed that many of the purchasers of wheatgrass juice were more than a little unbalanced. In some cases, wheatgrass juice drinkers would volunteer to help on juicing days so that they could have access to the pulp. Trina, in particular, found this irritating because they rarely worked as efficiently as she did. In one case, Trina flatly refused to work with a volunteer who worked too slowly and claimed that the process of feeding the grass into the juicer was therapeutic. Trina noted that their time at the greenhouse is work, not therapy. The employees were offended by the suggestion that their income-producing activities were the volunteer's idea of personal self-care.

Like the sprouts, the wheatgrass process again shows the gap between food workers and the consumers who can afford their products. The Great Greens employees find considerable humor in some customers' uses for the juice and its byproducts. They are not amused, however, when their customers come to the greenhouse to volunteer and slow their daily progress or declare the work they do therapeutic. The employees have little patience for those who have the luxury to do their jobs for free. In fact, Sara regularly declared that I should be paid for my time at the greenhouse, noting that Neal was getting a lot of work for free. She only grudgingly accepted my explanation that I was actually getting something from him and the rest of them in return for the work I did there.

Garden Crops

The third major product category at Great Greens consists of the garden crops that come from a five-acre plot of land a few minutes' drive from the greenhouse. On this land, Neal grows asparagus, sweet potatoes, and cabbage, which he sells to grocery stores and restaurants. Sara, Trina, and Becky have no involvement with the garden crops. Instead, Jim does much of the day-to-day work, with Neal helping with major events such as planting days. When I started working at the greenhouse in April 2011, the sweet potatoes and cabbages were in their early stages.

One of my first tasks was to cut sweet potato slips. In the back of the greenhouse, about twenty-five plastic dish tubs sat half-filled with compost. Several mature sweet potatoes had been cut in half and placed cut side down into the compost. With consistent watering, the eyes of the sweet potatoes sprout. These little sprouts are cut and placed in groups of fifty into plastic cups of sand and water, where they will root so that each will become a new sweet potato plant. The mature potatoes will produce unlimited slips as long as they are watered and trimmed regularly. Jim's method of cutting sweet potato slips was patient and methodical. He carefully combed the bins of potatoes with his hands, feeling for slips that were at least four inches long. Neal's goal was to plant ten thousand plants in the acre he designated for sweet potatoes.

In April, we also seeded cabbages, which would later be transplanted into the garden. Just as with the sweet potatoes, Jim was a methodical worker. The cabbages are seeded into trays with seventy-two small, round cells filled with compost. Jim explained to me that he first pokes a small hole in the middle of each cell. Then he goes back and drops a seed in each divot. After all the cells have seeds, he takes a small stick and pushes the seed further into the soil—about one-quarter-inch deep—then fluffs the top of the soil over the seed. After that has been done to all the cells, he goes back through, removes any little sticks that might impede germination, and tamps the soil down with his fingers so that the seed "gets good contact with the medium."

While we worked on these projects together, Jim and I talked about working at Great Greens. His perspective differed from that of Sara and her crew. Jim had been working for Neal about three years. He told me that he liked the work, even though others would find it boring and repetitive. He told me that many people would be overwhelmed with having more than twenty trays of cabbages to seed. "But you just keep at it and pretty soon you're down to the last one." Jim was in his early seventies and, despite having gardened his entire life, he had not lost a sense of awe about the process. He talked to me about how amazing it was that tiny seeds would germinate and poke up through hard, compacted soil. "They really have to work at it," he said, gesturing with his shoulder as though he were pushing up through something. He expressed amazement that a "whole big head of cabbage" will come out of the tiny black seeds, noting, "I guess that's why God's God." In addition to the pleasure he took in working with plants, Jim indicated that he truly enjoyed working for Neal. A heart attack in 2008 required Jim to become more careful about physical exertion, which Neal always takes into account. While planting sweet potatoes, for example, Jim drove the tractor while Neal and I balanced rather precariously on the back of his homemade planter (yet another contraption). During the hottest mornings, Neal asked whether I could harvest asparagus to save Jim the strain. In addition, Neal valued Jim's knowledge of plants and gardening. The two would often talk together about the best way to achieve high yields, and, while Neal's plans were usually implemented, he always took Jim's expertise into account before moving forward.

Employment at Great Greens

Despite the mixed reviews about the products and level of enjoyment of the work at Great Greens, all the employees I spent time with were heavily invested in their jobs. They all hoped to see the business grow, even as they at times expressed irritation with their own customers (such as the wheatgrass consumers) and encountered frustrations (such as unsold products) on the job. In addition, their views about business growth were strategic, and they were very clear that infrastructure must be developed first. Becky wanted more light racks so that she could plant more to ramp up production. Sara wanted to see the business's sales increase in general but was cautious about the current lack of cooler space. In 2010, Neal hired a part-time marketing coordinator (whom I never saw while I was working there). This individual wanted to expand sales by having a permanent booth at a nearby farmers' market. Sara pointed out that the coordinator had never worked at the greenhouse, had never helped with harvest, and knew nothing about the business. She and Becky both expressed frustration at her lack of working knowledge of the day-to-day operations of Great Greens, even as she attempted to boost sales and market the products. Becky and Sara both clarified that they wanted to see the business grow, but that their extensive knowledge of the current infrastructure constraints suggested a more measured and conservative approach to expansion. In addition to their desire to improve the business, the Great Greens employees' camaraderie stands in stark contrast to the hostile, dangerous environments that researchers report in other industries. Although Neal is unable to offer health insurance to his employees, he is quite concerned about their wellbeing, as his attentiveness to Jim shows. Trina also often needed time off to care for her special needs son. Neal never questioned that this was her first priority.

My time at Great Greens made it clear that working for a small business is not necessarily a utopian experience. Both the employees and Neal at times exhibit significant frustration with the process, with their customers, or with each other. Despite the lack of interest in the products among some of the employees, the crew at Great Greens is very committed to the success of the business, and each person is invested in his or her job. For the women in the greenhouse, much of their satisfaction comes from the high level of autonomous decision making they enjoy. Neal does not dictate the hours they work, nor does he interfere excessively with how they complete their jobs. When he changes the equipment or the process, he works it out collaboratively with the crew. Even when the employees are skeptical about the potential for success of a new endeavor, such as the new wheatgrass juicing system, the group is willing to work with Neal to bring the idea to fruition. Jim's investment in his work stems primarily from his interest in and enjoyment of gardening. He appreciates Neal's concern for his health, and Neal, in turn, values Jim's experience.

If local foods are to continue to increase market share, more and more producers will need to hire outside labor. Despite the assertion by some that the relatively small scale of alternative agriculture will never make any significant economic impact on rural economies, there is still good reason to consider the kinds of jobs created by small-scale farms and processors. There is community value in businesses that support workers' abilities to care for their children or aging family members. Sara and Trina have the flexibility to care for their children's medical needs, attend school events, and bring their kids to work as needed. This allows them to engage in their community as parents and at their jobs as productive employees. Likewise, flexible jobs allow workers to maintain strong ties with extended families, such as with Becky's caregiving for her aging grandmother. All of this also contributes to a good quality of life for workers. At Great Greens, the work looks very different from the low-wage jobs typical of the service industry or large-scale processing. Employees at Great Greens lack health benefits, but they avoid the rigid structure of a corporate environment and the well-documented risks found in meat processing jobs.

Nevertheless, my experience at Great Greens suggests that the vision of local food businesses uniting rural residents in a community of shared values is likely overstated. An at times cavernous gap divides food workers from the consumers who purchase their specialty products. Local food is often portrayed as a way for everyday people to learn more about where their food comes from, or, to use Thomas Lyson's term, to increase agricultural literacy. Unfortunately, some of those students may miss the point that food production is work, not therapy.

——————— ☼ ———————

CHAPTER NINE

Good Fences Make Good Neighbors

FARMERS WORK with a number of different people to get their products from farm to table. They rely on employees and volunteers to get the daily work done; they look to inspectors and farm support agencies to answer questions about everything from production to finances; market managers guide their decisions about packaging and displays at the farmers' market; and, yes, farmers respond to their customers' needs. But local food is not only affected by people who are actively involved in the process of growing, selling, marketing, or purchasing it. In Iowa, as I have consistently noted, local food farming occurs alongside an enormously efficient and prolific system of commodity production.

Both researchers and journalists frame the local and conventional systems as contradictory sets of practices. The two are not seen as compatible; rather, they operate as two distinct food streams with oppositional strategies, goals, and outcomes.[1] But this opposition becomes less clear when one spends time talking to and working with farmers and their employees. In Iowa, local food farmers share the landscape with conventional grain operations and large animal confinement facilities. While the two systems appear to be distinct, practitioners of each live next door to one another; they attend the same churches and community events. My conversations with local food producers reveal a more complicated relationship than the public discourse might suggest. Most food farmers are, like Tom Stearns, broadly critical of federal farm policy and agribusiness and their related effects on rural communities. They especially condemn the close relationships between federal policymakers and corporations. They also recognize that local policies, especially those related to suburban sprawl, represent a threat to all farmers. Further, growers do occasionally have conflicts with neighbors that result from differing farming strategies; aerial spraying, in particular, can cause problems for small organic farmers. In other cases, however, local food producers take advantage of the skills, equipment, and strategies of large-scale farmers to make their own operations more efficient or blend elements of both systems on the same farm. Although food growers in Iowa may be ideologically opposed to the current trends in food and agriculture, they still find many opportunities to use the strategies and equipment typical of conventional farming.

Farmers, Policy, and Agribusiness

Food farmers are primarily critical of policy that supports commodity farming and the related agribusiness firms that are often the major beneficiaries. CSA farmer David Evans laments that the federal Farm Bill limits farmers' flexibility and that the emphasis on corn in the state reduces land values for alternative farmers. David is a graduate of Iowa State University and a former Peace Corps volunteer; he is articulate and well versed in agricultural policy and economics. Over the years that I have known him, he has become increasingly critical of large-scale agriculture in the state. "I didn't start doing this to become preachy," he comments, "but more and more I find myself getting preachy." He explains, for example, how land values are most closely tied to corn production. All farmland in Iowa has a corn suitability rating, or CSR, which is tied to the soil composition and the historic yields on the property. The higher the CSR, the higher the land value. Transitioning land out of corn production for a long period could, theoretically, reduce the CSR of the property because the yield data for those years is lost. Thus, according to Evans, anyone inclined to grow less corn in Iowa may have to weigh their decision against the real risk of losing money on a future land sale.

While farm policy and subsidies receive much of producers' ire towards conventional agriculture, agribusiness giant Monsanto holds a special status among many food farmers. Based in St. Louis, Monsanto's signature products are the herbicide Roundup, and its companion seeds, genetically modified to be Roundup Ready. Roundup is a broad-spectrum herbicide, which means it kills any plant it comes into contact with. But Roundup

Ready seeds are engineered to be resistant to Roundup. A farmer can plant Roundup Ready seeds and then, after the corn or soybean plants have emerged along with the usual crop of weeds, spray the field with Roundup. The weeds die, but the corn or soy (or canola or wheat in other regions) remains unharmed.

Thus, Monsanto produces two complementary products so that farmers' seed and weed control needs are met by one company. Roundup's active ingredient, glyphosate, has for many years been considered relatively harmless to people and the rest of the environment. In 2014, however, the World Health Organization reviewed the existing scientific literature on glyphosate and declared it a probable carcinogen. Further, over time, several weed varieties have become resistant to glyphosate. Driving across Iowa in 2014, I saw many fields littered with weeds, including tall, scraggly waterhemp and Palmer amaranth, a particularly vigorous weed that can produce thousands of seeds per plant. As a result, Monsanto and other agribusiness firms have quickly scrambled to develop crops that are resistant to more potent herbicides, such as 2,4–D, best known as an ingredient of Agent Orange.

Even if Iowa's local food producers do not purchase seeds or inputs from Monsanto or from other companies such as Pioneer or Syngenta, they pay close attention to the activities of those companies. The vast majority of crops grown in the state are modified to be resistant to herbicides or some insects. In 2014, 97 percent of the soybean crop and 95 percent of the corn crop was grown from genetically modified seeds. These agribusinesses are not only selling their products to most farmers in the state, they are also deeply embedded in the global agricultural political system. Richard Dresdner, a small-scale pork producer, feels that most people believe that subsidies primarily benefit farmers. But, he points out, that belief ignores the complicated interconnections between policy and agribusiness:

> What people don't understand in this country—they complain about the farmers, especially now, being subsidized still. But the thing of it is, they're not just subsidizing the people in this country. They're subsidizing agriculture around the whole world. . . . We'll pick on Monsanto a little more—you go buy a bag of seed corn from

Monsanto, OK? Say they're selling it to us for three hundred dollars a bag, OK? You go down to South America and go to any other country, and they're selling it for a fraction of that price. So who's subsidizing Monsanto? Who is subsidizing the rest of the world? U.S. citizens, through the U.S. farmer paying the ridiculous price for it.

Dresdner grows all of his own non-GMO feed on 160 acres and strives for a self-sufficient closed system. Although he is proud that he can avoid supporting large corporations by growing his own feed, his strategies do not completely protect him from coming into contact with GMO grains. His neighbors all plant genetically modified seeds, and pollen drift and contamination, especially of corn, is a constant worry: "The corn will cross-pollinate, so I try to put that in the middle of the field so there's less chance of it. But there's almost no way around that, thank you DuPont and Monsanto and all these people. By god, especially with their soybeans, their Roundup, if I plant all non-GMO—but if they come in and find GMO, I can be sued up one side and down the other. But they can cross-pollinate all they want, and that's just fine. It bugs me." According to farmers, not only do agribusiness firms benefit from federal policy, their products are dangerous in rural neighborhoods. In particular, the problem of cross-pollination could put Richard in danger of a lawsuit from a powerful company, even though it is their product encroaching on his crops through pollen drift.

Environmental and health concerns about glyphosate (Roundup) are common among Iowa food farmers. David Evans predicts that when the final patents run out on Roundup Ready seeds and more corporations start genetically modifying seed to resist glyphosate, Monsanto will quietly stop producing the product altogether. He points to research that implicates glyphosate in the overall reduction of nutrients in animal feed crops and, by association, the food system. Dresdner makes a similar argument:

They say, you know, Roundup . . . won't let the corn and the soybeans absorb the vitamins and minerals that it used to be able to absorb. So that makes your corn and soybeans deficient in vitamins and minerals, so, naturally, it keeps going up the food chain. They're figuring like Alzheimer's disease and cancers and especially the stuff that little kids get, you look at the last ten years that Roundup's been around now, probably a good ten years going on fifteen and how our health is going down. And they're linking all that back to Roundup.

It is likely that Evans's and Dresdner's references to reduced micronutrients in food come from a study published in 2009 indicating that genetically modified soy had lower levels (12–14 percent) of clinically relevant phytoestrogens.[2]

Overall, the body of research on GMOs is contradictory and confusing. It is especially difficult to find published research that does not have a tie to either agribusiness (sometimes through university funding) or anti-GMO activism. The bodies of both livestock and humans are complex, making it challenging to identify a health outcome in either that could be reliably linked to the consumption of a genetically modified product. In addition, the research of the effects of GMOs on health has not been undertaken in a systematic way. Studies use various measures and parameters, different subjects and models, and they report their results differently.[3] Scientific reviews frequently note that there is a lack of consistent data and that even if several studies declare a genetically modified product safe, there are always others that express concern and recommend further research.[4]

Regardless of the scientific merit of GMO research or the actual health effects on livestock or people, genetic modification is one of the hot topics in food that often drives consumers to seek out organic or locally grown products. Thus, regardless of whether growers have strong opinions about GMOs, they certainly recognize that many consumers see their organic products as superior to conventionally produced foods. As a result, they may become part of the anti-GMO crusade by association. What is most interesting in the preceding comments are the ways that producers very astutely note how federal policy acts to constrain alternative production and primarily benefits agribusiness rather than farmers.

Concerns about the industrial system have been, in some cases, the impetus for alternative producers to develop their particular strategies in the first place. One grower, an Iowa native who sells certified organic fruits and vegetables at a large farmers' market in the area, states that as a child she was puzzled by the immense quantities of corn and soybeans near her home. She wondered, *Who eats all this corn?*, assuming that a nearby corn syrup plant must single-handedly meet the global demand for corn syrup. She laughed and noted that she was only thinking about the Karo corn syrup found in the grocery store and assumed the local factory supplied the whole world with little bottles of corn syrup. At the time, she had no idea how Iowa's corn was used and that most of it was not for human consumption. The oddities she observed as a child stayed with her when she began her own small farm: "I went in thinking I want to do the opposite of what other farmers are doing — I'm going to grow food."

Rural Relationships

Other growers lament the changes in rural culture that have come with large-scale agriculture. Renee Johnson-Berry, a vegetable grower and fiber producer, says that she is deeply saddened and distraught about the changes in rural culture with the changes in agricultural production:

> You know, working cooperatively with your neighbors, personal re-
> sponsibility, . . . and learning how to make do with what you've got, if
> you can't afford to go to town and buy it. Really resourceful, personal
> responsibility, you know, self resourcing issues that just are like drifting
> off somewhere in the wind because we really are, at least here in Iowa,
> we're really losing true rural culture. . . . Yes, rural existence does still go
> on — but a self-reliant, personal responsibility, rural culture is waning
> — to put it mildly.

From her perspective, the changes in modern farming have undermined the commitment to hard work and personal responsibility so often attributed to farmers.

Fifth-generation farmer Richard Dresdner also expresses concerns about changes in his immediate neighborhood:

> Our family's always been in agriculture. My grandpa — my mom's father
> — is just a couple miles from here. And up there, there's a big John
> Deere store, and my grandfather originally started that store. . . .

Agriculture sixty years ago was a lot different than it is today. You go over here a mile away, and I don't even know who my neighbors are. When I was a kid, there'd be any car that went up and down the road or anybody that lived within a ten-mile radius, you knew who they were. Nowadays you don't know who anybody is. Everybody is getting so removed.

Johnson-Berry specifically relates the change in rural culture to the "huge, huge shift in farming styles" over the past few decades. The comments from these producers are consistent with the suggestion of Walter Gold-schmidt and other social scientists that large-scale agriculture disrupts community relationships and cohesion. Both Dresdner and Johnson-Berry advocate for closed-system farming practices, in which there is little waste and few outside inputs. Farming practices that make good use of on-farm resources indicate both thrift and self-sufficiency, qualities that are hall-marks of rural culture and the agrarian ideal.

Renee Johnson-Berry suggests that her parents' farming practices, which embodied a closed-system approach, taught her a lot about respon-sible methods:

> Things were a much more closed system back then where you grew the hay, you grew the grain to feed the cattle. So, it was a way to turn those crops, which really in the mainstream commodities market aren't worth a lot—it was a value-added system. And, I mean, every-body's farm used to run that way, so I learned that.
>
> [But] nobody wants to work, because most people don't farm or-ganically or have a relatively closed system—it's just harder work . . . people don't want to work that hard. People don't want to make a commitment to livestock.

Richard Dresdner sees his closed-system approach, in which he uses his own grain for feed, roasting and extracting his own soybean oil for its fat content, as a way to contribute to his community: "I won't buy my seed corn from Pioneer (that's a DuPont product) or any of the big companies. . . . I always buy my stuff from small, family-owned seed companies. Be-cause, just like what I'm doing, I want to keep the money I make in my community. So, why do I want to do the opposite with what I'm buying?" By keeping money in the community, agriculture and its related businesses can enhance rural areas rather than diminishing them. In addition, the closed-system approach supports Dresdner's own profit motive. It is frugal and makes good use of his entire farm:

> The way I raise hogs now . . . like all these cornstalk bales—I don't know how many I've got, probably a hundred bales. Plus with the corn and soybean meal and all. We can take that and we can change that into, basically, all our feed needs next year. So it's one complete cycle all the time—and I have very little outside, I don't have to go out and get anything. It's a closed system and that's what I want. And if people can't see past the end of their nose to see that's the way you make money, then that's too bad!

These farmers see alternative practices as a way to reinforce rural values of thrift and self-sufficiency while also improving relationships within the agricultural community. Neal Jackson comments on the inherent tension between competition and solidarity among farmers. Jackson not only grows for his own company, he distributes other farmers' products. I asked him whether it was difficult to balance cooperation and competition:

> I think you have to keep the big picture in mind, number one. Number two, you have to treat people properly and there needs to be an atmosphere of trust. . . . You have to accept that you don't just step on people's toes. You have to respect other people's markets and what's established. Doesn't mean you can't grow what they're growing if you decide to do that. But I think it requires a healthy respect for one another. And I think you can still have competition, and by no means do I intend to squash competition or eliminate competition, because I think it's really important. You know, it's like a fundamental principle —it's important. Competition really is important.
>
> But I think it can have a really ugly side to it that's destructive. And I would like to eliminate the destructive side of competition without hindering the positive side of competition. And the other thing that I firmly believe is that if food production, if that's going to

be viable, we have to start working together. You know, I'm not a big history buff, so I'm just kind of repeating what I've been told about the breakdown for our agricultural system. It took a major diversion, I think it was like in the forties, when collectively the farmers decided to let go of control of marketing the product. So farmers just wanted to be farmers and let somebody else market it. Well, it's turned into now the farmers have no control, and they're at the whim of the marketers and the middle agents between the farmer and the customer. It doesn't take anything to realize the truth in that.

In this view, the changes in contemporary agriculture have led to a loss of power for farmers. One way to regain control over products and markets is through aggregation and cooperative endeavors among producers. Fred Kirschenmann, agricultural analyst and former director of the Leopold Center for Sustainable Agriculture, agrees and suggests that aggregation among farmers may be the most effective strategy to rebuild the agriculture of the middle and fill the gap between large-scale commodity sales on one end of the spectrum and very small-scale direct market sales on the other. At the 2011 annual meeting of the Practical Farmers of Iowa, Kirschenmann stated that farmers should "have a set of relationships, not supply chains, but value chains so that people function together as partners rather than competitors."

This tension between a supply chain and a value chain represents one of the key challenges of local food. Is local food a profitable marketing strategy, or is it a set of social connections? Can it be both? Neal Jackson suggests that there are ways to bring a better set of relationships into the typical interactions of capitalism. Competition is good, but only when it is based on trust and respect. For him, the ideal local food system results in empowered farmers who have more control over their products from seed to sale. This requires that farmers take more responsibility in the system and move beyond just being farmers.

Given the current demand for local food in Iowa, we rarely see the ugly side of competition that Neal referenced. Farmers I interviewed would occasionally comment on other growers' strategies. Jean Sorensen wondered aloud more than once why David Evans would pack his own CSA share boxes rather than have customers pack them—a procedure she sees as much more efficient. Occasionally, a grower who sold to the cooperative grocery store in Iowa City would mention a farmer known to compare product prices and then attempt to undersell other growers. Others would comment on farmers who sold their products at a low price, one noting that "nothing hurts local food more than the little old lady down the road selling her eggs for fifty cents a dozen." Faye Jefferson's experience being labeled a fly-by-nighter by more experienced growers also suggests that, at least at some markets, vendors are territorial and sensitive to competition.

Certainly the farmers I worked with had opinions about the activities of other farmers, but they often saved their most direct criticism for policy and agribusiness. Of course, embedded in those comments are implicit criticisms of the conventional farmers who engage in these practices. Renee Johnson-Berry's statements about the hard work required to be organic subtly suggest that industrial farmers are not hard workers. Richard Dresdner's comments about the environmental and economic advantages of a closed system suggest that industrial farmers are not economically rational. Neal Jackson's assertion that industrial farming has eliminated farmers' ability to manage their own economic destinies implies that those who engage in alternative practices are better able to take control of their own businesses. David Evans also argues that there is a large disconnect between conventional growers and small-scale organic producers. He suggests that each method requires significant differences in knowledge and skill. Evans's broad knowledge of vegetable varieties and organic methods is quite different from the knowledge required to produce commodity crops, a process he refers to as "point and click agriculture." In his view of conventional growers, "all they can do is drive bigger tractors than me."

City versus Country

In addition to their criticisms of conventional farming practices and federal policies, food farmers also express frustration at local zoning codes that negatively affect all kinds of agriculture. The increasing suburbanization of farmland in Iowa is a significant concern for both food and commodity farmers. A central Iowa farmer explains: "You have people coming out . . . then the farmers who've been there forever. The people who are coming out don't understand the culture of rural life and that things aren't going to be just like they were in the city." Johnson-Berry's farm is less than ten miles from a growing urban area, and she is often wary of her new neighbors as housing subdivisions have been steadily built around her farm.

> Everybody that ever moved in over there, I went over: "Hello, I'm Renee Johnson-Berry, I'm your neighbor across the road. I don't know if you know this or not, but this is a functioning organic farm. There are a couple things we need to talk about so we can get off on the right foot. One, I love dogs—your dog at your house and my dog at my house—that's how I love dogs. You need to know that I have every legal right to shoot your dog if it's worrying my livestock. And if you spray and it drifts on me, I will sue your fucking ass to kingdom come." I don't say it like that, but, you know.

In addition, she argues, the increase in suburban development has strained county resources as new residents advocate for faster snow removal and require new water and sewer infrastructure in the area. Johnson-Berry points out that the zoning and development policies enacted by the county supervisors do not take into account the environmental impact of chemicals applied to suburban lawns or the economic strain that results from the demand for extra services.

County zoning policies that support residential, as opposed to agricultural, zoning also impede small-scale agricultural businesses. One potential farmer recently inherited forty acres from his grandparents. The acreage is a smaller parcel of the original farm and has no buildings or infrastructure. As it is, with no dwelling, the property is zoned agricultural, and he pays approximately six hundred dollars in taxes each year. If he were to build a house on the property, it would automatically be zoned as residential property, and the taxes would increase tenfold. Even if he engaged in agricultural production, which is his intent, the zoning would remain residential. Although in theory the zoning policies are meant to discourage wealthy people from buying parcels of land and benefiting from agricultural zoning when they are not farming the property, alternative farmers point out that the policy is simply a short-sighted approach created by individuals who have little knowledge of the diversity of agriculture in the state. The county zoning ordinance only recognizes as a farm one that is larger than forty acres and engaged in commodity production.

Urban sprawl may ultimately lead to some solidarity between alternative and conventional producers. New rural residents who are unfamiliar with driving on country roads or navigating around farm equipment can pose a danger. "I feel so sorry for my large farming neighbors," says Johnson-Berry. "They're driving down the road with their tractors, and these buttheads cannot wait to get around them, so they pass inappropriately. I've almost had head-on collisions because these buttheads are passing a tractor with a wagon on the crest of the hill." The subdivision that sits across the road from her property has also interrupted the typical procedures of the area farmers. She goes on:

> For years, we had a neighbor who would run his cattle up the road and into our pasture. But when they built fucking vinylville over there, they tore out all the goddamned fences, so now, if cows ran through all their fucking pristine little chem-lawn lawns, they'd be livid.
>
> And when it was just farmland, you'd throw Gene's cows out the north side and you get somebody with a truck to follow them, and you get one person to stand at each driveway to keep them from turning in the driveway, then you steer them into my driveway and they run. You can't do that anymore. So it limits possibilities for farmers when this kind of sprawl happens.

Although the issue of county zoning and urban sprawl is one of many concerns that may initially seem unrelated to agriculture, farmland preservation and increasing urbanization is an ongoing issue throughout Iowa. Thus, despite their criticisms of industrial practices, alternative producers may find common ground with conventional producers who are also negatively affected by the encroachment of vinylville.

Consumers and Wild Carrots

In addition to its effects on farming practices and rural culture, many local food producers blame the conventional system for eliminating consumer knowledge as well. I assisted David Evans at one of his regular farmers' market stalls one Saturday morning in late September 2010. The table was piled high with fall crops, including beets, kale, cabbages, and a large bin of bright orange carrots. The carrots had caused several shoppers to stop in their tracks and come to the booth. Not only were they bright and eye-catching, their twisted, irregular shapes would never be found in a grocery store among the ruler-straight rods that typically pass for carrots. A young boy of about ten approached with his father. The boy was astonished by the carrots and picked several up, turning them over in his hands to get a good look. The father explained that they had come straight from the farm. The boy looked thoughtful and asked, "so, are they . . . 'wild' carrots?" His comment caused his father and David and me to chuckle, but it reinforced the challenges faced by food farmers whose products often look very different from the produce found in a conventional grocery store. Consumers who are used to seeing their identical carrots neatly wrapped in plastic may be hard pressed to even categorize David's, which in comparison appear undomesticated, atypical, and wild.

Local food farmers often argue that the mainstream food system has disenfranchised consumers, which causes difficulties for those who rely on direct markets for their living. CSA farmer Jean Sorenson views every share delivery, which she personally oversees, as a way to talk to her customers and remind them about seasonality and the realities of food production. She also employs strategies such as purposely bagging together potatoes that are of vastly different sizes. She says, "I don't want people to think that potatoes come out of the ground all the same size, like they do in the grocery store." CSA shares often include weekly newsletters describing growing practices, challenges, and recipes to address the knowledge gap. In particular, CSA farmers often mention needing to explain why particular crops have been successful or not. If, for example, a year is bad for tomatoes, it is important to explain to shareholders why. For many eaters who are accustomed to purchasing tomatoes whenever they choose, scarcity in a poor crop year is a new experience.

Thus, seasonality and availability are some of the more difficult concepts for consumers to understand. Faye Jefferson, during her years vending at farmers' markets, was surprised at the lack of knowledge about seasonality among farmers' market shoppers.

> People, even fairly sophisticated people, would expect you to produce spinach in July, and you'd have to explain that that's a crop that doesn't tolerate heat at all, and the season for spinach is May and April and it's done. Then you get a little in the fall again. So the seasonal thing was the biggest—because if you've only gotten food from a grocery store all your life and you've gotten stuff from all over the world, you think that everything's in season all the time. And that amazes me, because people that grow up in Iowa know that there's a season for soybeans and that there's a season for field corn, and everybody's real aware of what that is. But vegetables—not so much!

She attributes the lack of seasonal knowledge to the typical reliance on grocery stores, which sell fruits and vegetables year round, regardless of whether they are in season. The lack of awareness is not limited to seasonal availability. Some market customers may not even be aware of what products can or cannot be grown in Iowa. David Evans laughed as he recalled a request for avocados while selling his produce at a small-town market.

The differences in cost between local food and standard fare are also problematic for producers. Many farmers suggest that their customers' lack of knowledge about the realities of food production, coupled with a sense of entitlement to cheap food, undermines their own profitability. Renee Johnson-Berry states: "That's just insane the way people don't understand where their food came from. One of my favorite things is, if people think beef is expensive—well, when it's a hundred and three, I want you to ride on a hayrack, schleppin' eighty pound bales, that are coming at you, coming out of that baler every, you know, every sixty seconds or whatever, and throw those fuckers three feet over your head, and then tell me, then *discuss* with me, how expensive beef is." Many farmers lament the current system of subsidized agriculture and cheap food because it makes it difficult to justify their prices to consumers. Neal Jackson notes that it is difficult for him to compete with large-scale vegetable growers in California who benefit from state policies subsidizing water and federal immigration policies that support unfair labor practices. Consumers' lack of knowledge and desire for cheap food, according to food farmers, is also a result of the industrialization of food, which values quantity over quality. As a result, farmers like Jean Sorensen must add consumer education to their job descriptions to ensure that their customers are willing to pay the higher price for mismatched potatoes and wild carrots.

Being Neighborly

In Iowa the conventional system is more than just abstract federal policies or the marketing and distribution strategies of distant corporations. Food farmers regularly have direct interactions with conventional farmers. The relationship between alternative and industrial producers can be contentious. The close proximity of food and commodity farming at times causes friction between friends and acquaintances. One CSA grower notes that the idea of organics sometimes makes conventional farmers she knows bristle. She says, "we're not a threat to them, really, we just do things in a different way." David Evans says of conventional growers, "for every one who's supportive, there are six who think you're crazy."

Growers also suggest that they are outliers in the community and face some social repercussions for their alternative practices. One grower, whose large family manages 160 acres of organic soybeans, grass-fed beef and pork, and vegetables, says, "most people around here think we're about a bubble off." He goes on to say: "There's a circle of neighbors around here, and they don't have a lot to do, so they talk about us. They drive by and see our cow out in the road, and they run into town and tell the other guys in that circle." Other producers' neighborhood reputations, however, may benefit them. The Murphy family's goat cheese business regularly benefited from others' unwanted livestock. One daughter explained: "We're kind of old MacDonald's farm; people just give us stuff. We get kittens, we get goats, we get dogs." As described in chapter 4, the family's initiation into goat cheese production came when they were given a goat by friends who operated a commercial goat dairy. The goat was blind and therefore not a good fit in the large operation. The family also keeps a milk cow, and the first they owned was a lame Holstein that also came from a large-scale dairy. Another daughter laughed: "That's when we had the 'disabled dairy.' We had a three-legged cow and a blind goat!"

While alternative farmers' status as community outliers may affect how their conventional neighbors relate to them, the realities of conventional farming practices can have direct negative consequences on organic farms. One early July morning in central Iowa, David Evans and his employees were picking broccoli and turnips for Century Farms. The group heard the drone of a small plane approaching and watched as it dove low over the neighboring field of seed corn. The plane was spraying fungicide, a standard ingredient in the chemical cocktails that coat Iowa's monoculture of corn and soy. Driving along I-80 in midsummer, one is often treated to the daredevil shows of tiny planes dramatically swooping over roads and under power lines to eject chemicals onto the endless acres of corn and soybeans.

As the plane made its first pass, the pilot did not turn off the spray soon enough. David and his crew watched as a cloud of toxic spray drifted over his buffer of trees and into his hayfield. The hay was to be certified organic during the following year, but if any of it was contaminated, those parts of the field would have to wait out another three years for certification. David, outraged, first contacted the landowner, his neighbor. The field in question, however, was a plot contracted by Monsanto. Because Iowa law prohibits corporations from owning farmland for commercial production, seed companies contract with farmers to produce their products. In these arrangements, farmers are usually compensated per acre. They generally are responsible for soil preparation and possibly some early nitrogen application, but the company does the majority of the planting, chemical application, and harvest. In this case, the landowner had prepared the soil in the spring but was not involved in any chemical applications during the rest of the season. David's next step was to contact the local Monsanto field office. The pilot of the plane was contracted by Monsanto, and was not an employee of the company; therefore Monsanto denied any responsibility for application errors. David's farm is listed on the state Sensitive Crop Registry, which is supposed to be reviewed by aerial applicators and local farmers before they spray, however, as David drily notes: "They rarely do." In fact, fungicides are exempt from these processes, further complicating the situation for Evans.

The local Monsanto representative later wrote, "as sometimes happens between neighbors, we had an unfortunate issue arise." Indeed, neighborly disputes in agricultural communities are not unheard of, as individuals often negotiate the realities of shared boundaries and unpredictable pollen drift or livestock. There are often fences to mend, both literally and figuratively. It was jarring for David, however, to realize that his neighbor's property was ultimately controlled by a large corporation whose resources and power far outstripped his own. In the end, about two acres of the field were contaminated and could not be certified on schedule. Though the landowner was sympathetic to David's situation, he was powerless to do anything, given the contract with Monsanto. David said that the two are friendly with each other, despite the competing needs of their crops.

Beekeepers may face the greatest risk from chemical overspray. Nationally, and in Iowa, declining bee populations have received a fair amount of attention. The White House created an interagency task force that issued recommendations in May 2015 that would reduce honey bee losses, increase the population of monarch butterflies (another important pollinator species), and restore or enhance pollinator habitat on both public and private lands. Time will tell how well the strategies protect bees in Iowa, where the needs of the corn and soy crop tend to take precedence over most everything else.

At a field day for Practical Farmers of Iowa in the summer of 2011, a local farmer and beekeeper lamented that he had spent the day with a bunch of dead bees. They had been exposed to insecticide spray, aimed at eradicating Japanese beetles from a nearby soybean field. Despite his having been notified by the sprayer and confining the bees to the three hives for thirty-six hours, one hive died completely and another was mostly eliminated. As in the situation with David Evans, the neighboring landowner had little control over the spraying. Crop dusters are contractors and keep their own hours. The Iowa Department of Agriculture and Land Stewardship maintains a pesticide bureau that will investigate any claim of spray on a sensitive crop. When asked what happens when a farmer calls the bureau, however, a local CSA grower responded, "honestly, not much." A representative will come out to investigate and agree that you've been sprayed, then sends the sprayer a warning letter. According to the grower, a sprayer who receives three letters is subject to a fifty-dollar fine.

A local honey producer notes that sprayers are required to notify bee-keepers before spraying and are not supposed to spray anywhere between six and eight A.M., when bees are most commonly out of the hive. But the state law "doesn't really have any teeth." Although the best strategy from the perspective of the honey producer is to move the hives, this is not al-ways possible with hives weighing between two hundred and four hundred pounds and on short notice.

Growers are understandably frustrated when the industrial system en-croaches directly on their operations. Renee Johnson-Berry again relates this to new agricultural systems and the lack of personal responsibility that has accompanied them: "If you say anymore to someone 'good fences make good neighbors,' they're not going to know what the hell you're talking about. . . . It means you keep your shit in—it means you have a responsibility." Unfortunately, pesticides and pollen move with no regard whatsoever for fences, literal or figurative. Aerial sprayers are not neigh-bors, and pesticide regulations are inadequate for organic growers and beekeepers. Thus, even when a conflict arises that would have been nego-tiated between neighbors in the past, the looming presence of agribusiness changes those relationships.

Despite these potentially contentious situations, some producers have developed cooperative relationships with their conventional neighbors. One of these, Kelly Lange, is a CSA grower in east central Iowa who also produces open-pollinated corn, which she sells primarily to organic dairy farmers who use it to grow their own feed. Before the development of hybrid—and later, genetically modified—seeds, all corn was open pol-linated. A monoecious plant, corn has both male and female flowers on the same plant. The tassel at the top of the stalk is the male flower that produces pollen; the silk at the end of each ear is the female flower that receives the pollen. The wind blows pollen from the tassel onto the silk of other plants, pollinating the plant so it can produce seeds (the corn ker-nels). A plot of open-pollinated corn will be genetically diverse, with traits from genes of many other corn plants nearby. In contrast, hybrid seeds are created from plants that have been made to pollinate themselves; two lines of inbred seeds are then crossed, or hybridized. Developed for commercial use in the 1930s, the process creates genetically uniform plants that are vigorous and reliable. The hybrids grow and mature at the same rate and are all the same size, making them ideal for mechanical harvesting. But hybrids are also genetically identical, which means that if one plant is susceptible to a pest or disease, the rest of the crop is too. Open pollination provides a traditional method for growers to maintain biodiversity and cultivate natural resistance in their corn crop.

Hybrids dominate the industry, and open-pollinated corn is practically unheard of nationwide. In Iowa it seems especially remarkable that a grower could successfully produce it on seventy-two acres when surrounded by thousands of acres of GMO corn. Lange admits that her corn is probably contaminated by GMO pollen. She could have her corn tested in a lab using procedures that have become more affordable and reliable over time. But, she points out, "it's another expense, and there is nothing I can do about it even if my population does contain some GMO genes." Her strategy is to maintain a good distance from her conventional neighbors' farms. Lange keeps her corn in the middle of her property, which gives her about a distance of one-quarter to one-half mile from her neighbors' fields. She points out that she could try to time her planting so that her corn is pollinating well before or after the neighboring farms, but because she takes advantage of a neighbor's larger combine and has him harvest her open-pollinated corn in the fall, her corn-growing schedule needs to coincide with his combining schedule.

The neighbor harvests Lange's corn right after he finishes his soybeans and before he does his own corn. Lange points out that if the combine is not completely clean, she can easily sort out a stray soybean. But if the neighbor had recently harvested corn, she would not be able to distinguish his grains of corn from her own. This tight schedule requires her to have her corn ready as soon as the soybeans have been harvested, in early October each year. Before the adoption of Roundup Ready soybeans, which mature earlier, she had more time, usually until the end of October.

In addition to harvesting, she has her neighbors do the primary tillage each year in her gardens. With only ten to twelve acres in vegetable production, it is not cost effective for her to keep large equipment that is rarely used. She notes that her neighbors spend "about ten minutes" tilling the gardens when they drive by her farm and that they do a better job with their "massive equipment" than she could do with hers. This relation-ship shows the flexibility of Iowa farmers, both alternative and industrial. Although it would not be cost effective for them to own the equipment themselves, small producers benefit from the large equipment that large-scale grain operations require.

Merging the Two

While some small producers may have an antagonistic relationship with their conventional neighbors, or at least the sprayers they contract, other producers individually develop creative strategies that involve merging the industrial and the alternative systems on the same farm. Alan and Brenda Marshall moved back to his family's small farm in 2005 to help care for his aging mother. Alan manages the farm while Brenda works in town. In 2008, Alan had forty acres in corn and soybean rotations, for which he received direct subsidy payments. His long-term goal had always been to start an organic farm when he retired. When he took over the farm from his mother, he implemented organic practices as much as possible but was financially unable to entirely move away from his family's established conventional production. He had read about community-supported agri-culture and knew several CSA producers, so he thought that might be a good niche for his operation. Because of federal restrictions before 2008 on vegetable production for growers receiving subsidy payments, Alan could only grow three acres of vegetables for sale to continue receiving subsidies. His solution was to continue growing conventional corn and soybeans but to also add a very small CSA to the operation. Thus, while his grains went to the local co-op and out into the commodity market, he also personally delivered nineteen vegetable shares each Friday during the summer.

Larry Robbins has also creatively merged the industrial and alternative systems on his farm. He has farmed 470 acres of grains organically since 1989. He uses long rotations of corn, soybeans, small grains (peas and bar-ley), and alfalfa to maintain soil fertility and interrupt pest cycles. He sells his soybeans to Silk for use in their soy milk, and much of his corn crop is sold to a nearby grain and feed company. The remainder of his grain crop is feed for his beef cattle herd. Even with long rotations that include nitrogen-fixing plants such as soybeans, peas, and alfalfa, his farm lacked adequate nitrogen. This is a perennial problem for organic farmers, who are prohibited from using the inexpensive and widely available synthetic nitrogen fertilizers on their farms. He initially solved this problem by raising hogs. He used the manure for fertilizer and sold his hogs at one of the many independent buying stations that used to dot the landscape. But, he says, "we just about went broke in the nineties," as did many other Iowa hog farmers.

In 2008, Larry added a new enterprise to his farm and contracted with Sara Lee to finish forty-four thousand turkeys. Sara Lee provided the specifications for the enormous barn that stands on his property. He purchased it and provides all the labor. Sara Lee delivers the birds at three weeks of age. He feeds them to about twenty weeks, at which point they are more than forty pounds each, and the company returns to pick them up. Contract farming arrangements have been widely criticized because of the power imbalance between the corporation and the farmer. Larry's contract with Sara Lee is hundreds of pages of detailed instructions, and it regulates areas of the farm well beyond the turkey barn. For example, because the turkeys are genetically very similar, they are extremely delicate, and any pathogen could quickly kill the entire flock. The Robbins family has to be vigilant about hygiene, and they cannot even have a parakeet in their house for fear that it might infect the turkeys with a strain of avian influenza. Indeed, the 2015 outbreak of highly pathogenic avian influenza H5 only heightened attention to biosecurity among livestock producers. Most producers with confinement barns implement detailed protocols for entering and leaving barns; workers may need to shower before entering the facility and maintain separate clothes that do not come into contact with outside contaminants.

Larry was, however, able to negotiate with Sara Lee about the bedding typically used in the barns. The contract initially specified the exact poultry litter Larry should use, but he argued that a different type, one that included humates (a coal byproduct that stimulates and encourages the growth microorganisms in the soil) would be equally suitable for the turkeys and more beneficial for his crops. Larry was pleased with his small

A sign posted to keep people away
from Larry Robbins's turkey barn.
Photograph by Roshan Malik.

victory and noted that it has improved his soil nutrient balance. In addition, the turkey barn adds another income stream for the farm, which he hopes will encourage his adult son to consider taking part in the operation.

The Murphy family's goat cheese operation also blends small-scale food production with conventional farming. The bulk of their 220 acres is in corn and soybeans as well as a herd of beef cattle that ranges from sixty to a hundred head. The Murphys are moving toward grass-fed beef production; however, they currently sell most of their calves at the local sale barn by the time they reach about five hundred pounds. This strategy ensures better cash flow and a quicker return than finishing the steers on grass, a process that can take from eighteen months to two years.

The Murphys take advantage of both local and worldwide markets for their cheese, beef, and grains, and their family's employment reveals a rather unconventional pairing. Both husband and wife are engaged in the farmwork, the wife and oldest daughters overseeing the goat cheese. The husband manages the grain and beef cattle and works off the farm as a site coordinator for Monsanto. Kerry Murphy comments: "'Mon-Satan!' we're kind of a weird dichotomy here!" She goes on to say: "You know the interesting thing, he's not the only 'natural' guy, or person, there. . . . We know the inside of Monsanto. It's not as horrid as it's made out to be." While the family questions the current focus on monocropping systems, Kerry argues that the current criticism of GMOs may not be entirely valid. Although she agrees that there is a lot of false propaganda in favor of genetic modification and expressed concern about the unknown future effects, she also states: "Now as far as Roundup and those kind of things, the pesticides and the herbicides that are used now—they are far more safe than what we were using twenty years ago. They're fewer, there's less environmental damage going on because of those pesticides and herbicides that they're using now. But that also has to do with the GMO crops that they use now, because they're resistant to the disease and the bugs."

In contrast to Richard Dresdner, Kerry argues for one of the advertised benefits of GMO seeds: they result in lower chemical applications on fields. As with much of the rest of GMO research, the results are somewhat mixed depending on the specific crop and chemical. The use of Roundup Ready seeds has certainly reduced the variety of chemicals applied to crops. Glyphosate will reliably kill any plant it comes into contact with, so farmers can use one herbicide on all their Roundup Ready fields. But this strategy has also resulted in a huge increase in glyphosate application. The USDA's chemical application reports show in 1996, corn growers applied less than ten million pounds of glyphosate nationwide; in 2014, that number had increased to almost thirty million pounds.[5] Soybean applications are even more dramatic. About ten million pounds in 1996 increased to nearly 110 million pounds in 2012.[6] There is little doubt that this increase is responsible for the weed resistance that farmers are experiencing.

Insecticide use has also changed as a result of GMO production. Pests such as the European corn borer and the corn rootworm, sworn enemies of a corn grower, have been typically annihilated using classes of insecticides such as organophosphates and pyrethroids. Organophosphates, in particular, are one of the most common causes of poisoning worldwide and have been repeatedly implicated in rural suicides, particularly in developing countries. The genetically modified solution involves inserting *Bacillus thuringiensis* (Bt), a naturally occurring soil bacterium, into corn. Bt is toxic to caterpillars, including the corn borer and rootworm, but not other classes of insects, so it does not affect adult pollinators. Thus, Bt corn has been used as a more targeted pest control mechanism. The numbers are encouraging: between 1995 and 2009 insecticide application on corn declined by about 80 percent.[7] As with glyphosate, however, the targeted pest started becoming resistant to Bt. Now insecticide use, particularly in Bt corn and Bt cotton, is again on the rise. Ultimately, Kerry Murphy notes, "it's not a perfect world."

The examples in this chapter suggest that the relationship between the alternative and industrial systems are more complex than they might initially seem. Although we often think of them as oppositional, in some cases the systems are complementary. Commodity crops and CSA or organic grains and conventional turkey barns can exist on the same farm. This creative strategy stretches our vision of what a diverse farm might look like.

Although the broad media and academic discourse may portray alternative and conventional farming systems as entirely incompatible, the actual behavior of local food farmers suggests a more nuanced reality. Further, promoting only the industrial or the alternative system, with the intent of eliminating one or the other, may even be entirely unnecessary in Iowa. According to the Leopold Center for Sustainable Agriculture, it would require only 10,548 crop acres to meet statewide demand for twenty-eight fruits and vegetables currently not typically produced in Iowa.[8] Considering that nearly twenty-three million acres are devoted to corn and soybeans, 10,548 represents only a tiny percentage of available cropland. Spreading that acreage over Iowa's ninety-nine counties would result in 106 acres of vegetable production in each county to meet demand.

In many cases the actions of alternative farmers who attempt to meet the demand for local fruits and vegetables suggest, as does the Leopold Center, that two seemingly opposing systems may be compatible. In some cases, the industrial system interrupts the typical relationships between neighbors, as corporations manage the land they use to develop their products. In other cases, small-scale producers point out the discomfort that their strategies cause their conventional neighbors, even as they find solidarity in the face of increasing urbanization. Still others take advantage of the large equipment or skills of their conventional neighbors or even merge the two systems in creative ways to make a profitable and unconventionally diverse farm. Thus, it is rash to simply declare alternative systems and local marketing strategies as blanket opposition to the dominant system. Instead, in Iowa, combining alternative and industrial systems may provide a range of possible strategies for individual growers.

CHAPTER TEN

Looking Downstream

THE HEIGHTENED popular attention to local food in recent years has bolstered attendance at farmers' markets, increased CSA memberships, and supported the development of farm to school programs nationwide. The consumers, activists, and academics interested in local food, however, have not always understood the concerns of the farmers who grow what they buy, eat, and study. This sudden popularity has also made local food the darling of the new agrarians. In their conception, local food has the ability to revitalize rural areas by empowering self-sufficient farmers. Because food farmers operate largely outside the federal commodity support programs, they are presumed to be less reliant on public assistance to move their crops from field to market.

This view is compelling, but it ignores a few key realities. One of the most problematic tendencies of agrarianism is the belief that farmers are, or should be, wholly self-sufficient. A thorough reading of history reminds us that farming in Iowa would not be possible if not for the early federal investments in drainage as part of the Swamp Land Act of 1850. Further rural infrastructure investments in roads, irrigation, and the postal service supported emerging prairie communities. These investments continue not only with direct support from the federal farm program but also with current attention devoted to enhancing modern services such as rural broadband access throughout the state. It is difficult to buy the argument that any kind of farming is, or has ever been, truly self-sufficient.

Further, the local food producers I spoke with in Iowa, by and large, argue that they would benefit from more public investment in their activities, not less. They look to the enormous benefits enjoyed by their conventional neighbors and their vegetable-growing colleagues in California, and they dream about how even a fraction of that investment could enhance their style of farming. Food farmers would like to make better use of publicly funded agricultural resources such as extension services, conservation programs, tax credits, and land-use incentives. Their distance from these programs stems from shortcomings in the programs, not because of farmers' unwillingness to interact with them.

The farmer-centric view of rural communities enshrined in agrarian thought is mirrored in the local food movement as a whole. The Know Your Farmer campaigns and the farmer photos one finds in any upscale cooperative or supermarket are some of the key marketing strategies of organizations that support local food. While I would not have written a book about farmers if I did not agree that they are central actors in local food systems, they are not the only ones involved. I look forward to seeing an artistic photo of the workers in a local meat locker or cannery that processes food from my region for area retailers. Better yet, let us represent the truck driver or distribution hub that moves food from farmers to nearby retailers. Somehow, these critical components have not captured the imagination of activists or marketing teams. Erasing them paints an incomplete picture of the food system and effectively inhibits the consumer knowledge that local food is supposed to enhance.

In addition to promoting distribution chains, let us also invest in training new participants. The current energy among young people to get involved in local food is very strong. Unfortunately, they often struggle to find their place. They tend to idolize producers and desire to become farmers themselves; however, access to land and knowledge is a significant barrier. Many lean toward environmental studies majors in college and may ignore useful business classes. If butchers and truck drivers were portrayed as attractive and fundamental to local food as are farmers, perhaps more young people would gravitate toward those jobs.

The other privileged identity in local food is, of course, the consumer. Again, largely because of the assumption that local food happens without public investment, we look to the consumer to do the heavy lifting: attend the farmers' market, learn to prepare the unfamiliar items in your CSA share, volunteer at your local school to support farm to school programming. Emphasizing producers and consumers at the final point of sale skews our ideas about how local food systems function. The farmers' market transaction is actually the culmination of a significant amount of work on the part of farmers, their employees (or volunteers or interns), the media who promote and write about local food, the inspector who assesses the cheesemaker's pasteurization equipment, the market manager who assures that the scale is accurate, the butcher who cut the meat, or the conservation agent who advised on a sustainable pasture management system.

Ultimately, by focusing so heavily on farmers and consumers, we have ignored other relationships that support local food. I have illuminated some of those interactions in these pages and suggest that attending to them is critical if we want to enhance local food. I also hope to have shown how local food interacts with the global, industrial system that dominates Iowa. Rather than pitting local in direct opposition to global, I suggest that local systems are informed and sometimes enhanced by their relationships with commodity systems. Local food producers are simultaneously embedded in and separate from commodity agriculture. It is true that local food producers face a number of challenges not experienced by commodity farmers. For example, in addition to managing the planting and harvesting of their crops, local farmers are responsible for marketing and selling their products. Local food producers require reliable sources of labor and must develop social and economic relationships with diverse individuals and organizations. Nonetheless, local food farmers are embedded in the larger industrial food system. They must constantly interact with the conventional system and experience similar challenges, such as access to land, as those that commodity farmers face.

Unlike commodity producers, direct market farmers spend considerable time packaging and delivering their products. Growers selling at farmers' markets may spend years perfecting their strategies for bringing produce to market and displaying it in efficient, appealing ways. CSA share boxes are typically individually packaged; growers who opt to have shareholders assemble their own shares must have someone from the farm to oversee the process. Growers often deliberately present their produce in ways that show the seasonality and nonuniformity of whole, unprocessed foods. In so doing, they see themselves as having a role in educating the public about agriculture and food production.

Another agrarian blind spot is the need for farm labor and the resultant relationships that develop from these arrangements. Access to reliable labor is perhaps the most pressing challenge for local food growers who want to expand their operations. Unlike highly mechanized corn and soy production in Iowa, diversified vegetable or livestock farms are very labor intensive. Producers may use a variety of strategies to obtain labor, including hiring hourly employees, using volunteers and interns, or taking advantage of a field day to complete a project. Each of these has advantages and disadvantages. Producers invest significant time and social energy as well as money in hourly workers. Although interns and volunteers are less costly, they are often inexperienced and may slow overall production. Field days may provide a group of people to assist with one project but are not viable long-term solutions for labor.

Hired labor not only provides an economic benefit to communities, it provides an opportunity for creating new social relationships within the food chain. Small-scale diversified production, in addition to being labor-intensive, is seasonal and somewhat irregular. As a result, farmers spend considerable time planning so that employees' time is well spent and as consistent as possible. Further, growers who cannot afford to provide traditional benefits, such as retirement plans or health insurance, attempt to compensate by creating positive working environments and developing strong social relationships with their employees. Some employers provide flexible work hours and give workers considerable decision-making authority. Others note that group harvesting and collaborative work maintain employees' motivation and energy. These traditional employer-employee relationships provide some insight into embedded economic transactions. The farmers I spoke with point out that without this thoughtful attention to the social elements of the workplace, they would have less economic success.

The use of volunteers or interns on farms can be problematic not only because of the potential economic loss in the case of inexperienced workers but also for loss of wages that would otherwise circulate within the local community. The promotion of volunteer and intern labor as a strategy to enhance local food does not support an equitable system. Those who have the opportunity to increase their agricultural literacy through working as volunteers or interns tend to be those who have other resources to support themselves while they work for little or no pay. In addition, volunteers who declare that the work is therapeutic or serves some higher purpose are at odds with employees who base their living on such work. Finally, consumers are not paying the true cost of food if it is produced with volunteer labor.

Despite the many issues specific to local food producers, the alternative system is not entirely separate from conventional agriculture and the global food system. There is much overlap between the two food streams that is not ordinarily considered in popular and scholarly discourse.[1] Both alternative and conventional farmers operate within the constraints of government policies and local land tenure systems. Current trends in land rentals affect local food farmers, just as they do aspiring grain producers. Farming support organizations—state-funded and private nonprofit— attempt to assist both conventional and alternative farmers. This dual role can be challenging for the organizations and for the farmers. Some local farmers are suspicious of extension service personnel and their historic ties to chemical-intensive practices.

Farmers' economic strategies may combine elements of conventional and alternative production. The rhetoric of the Farm Bureau, decrying criticisms of conventional agriculture, ignores the creative diversification of farmers who engage with both conventional and local systems. Farmers such as Larry Robbins and the Murphys merge industrial practices and alternative techniques on their farms. Larry Robbins's combination of organic grains with conventional turkey farming shows how the two agricultural systems can complement one another rather than compete. Those farmers who have adopted some elements of conventional production provide a potential model for moving forward. Neal Jackson and Roger Daniels show that a willingness to specialize can provide financial returns on even very small acreages. Neal's one acre of sweet potatoes is profitable and makes his food accessible to the public school system. Farmers whose sweet potatoes contribute only to their small CSAs do not make nearly as large an impact on food access. Further, Neal's distribution business aggregates produce from a number of growers so that they can sell throughout the region. Instead of insisting on direct market relationships, those growers have employed Neal as a middleman (a category that local food advocates largely dismiss) to increase the reach of their food. In some cases, grant-supported food hubs have developed to fill this gap as well. Of course, those projects last only as long as their funding continues.

While support for local food remains strong, the friendly markets, such as farmers' markets and CSA, are limited. Growers face long waiting lists for the most popular farmers' markets. Even with an overall increase in the number of CSAs in the past years, the turnover in both shareholders and farms remains high. These factors make operations such as Neal's and Roger's even more critical. The middleman is not inherently problematic; in fact, a distribution system can provide another opportunity for meaningful rural work. The infrastructure between farm and table is important even in local systems. This is an area in which local food needs to look a bit more like the conventional system with reliable, structured distribution networks that efficiently move foods between farmer, processor, and consumer.

Although local food might benefit by looking more like the conventional food system, the two systems do not always easily coexist. The risk of aerial overspray is a constant concern for organic producers and beekeepers. Some growers of local food are critical of the production and marketing strategies of corporations, which reduce consumers' knowledge about the economic and health consequences of conventional agriculture. These farmers' desire to educate their customers may cause problems when they attempt to sell their products to institutions. David Evans takes pride in his crooked and oddly shaped wild carrots, and Jean Sorenson makes sure to package her potatoes so that customers receive different sizes and shapes. For food service directors who want to purchase local carrots or potatoes, however, uniform products make processing less difficult and serving sizes easy to calculate.

Because local food farmers in Iowa are simultaneously separate from and embedded in the industrial system, they must draw knowledge from a variety of sources that include extension agents, equipment dealers, and university scientists. Farmers often especially emphasize the benefits of learning from other growers. Their peers can help them with finding and using the equipment needed in small-scale vegetable production and provide tips about how to maintain a committed workforce. Beginning farmers, in particular, value the advice of more experienced producers. To facilitate this process, Practical Farmers of Iowa and Midwest Organic Sustainable Education Service have created mentorship programs for new and aspiring farmers. Such programs are important because local food farmers lack access to some services provided by state and federal governments, such as the disaster insurance provided by Farm Services Agency.

Iowa State University Extension and Outreach continues to develop programming for local food. Although growers are cautiously optimistic about the ability of extension personnel to better support local food production in the state, they note that such programming often closely resembles that which is provided to conventional farmers. As Neal Jackson observes, his local extension agent often replies to his inquiries by noting that "you're the expert." Other farmers, particularly meat and dairy producers, rely on processors, equipment dealers, and inspectors to navigate their heavily regulated direct sales. Statewide farm to school efforts also provide expert advice for farmers. Food safety researchers, in particular, have offered guidance on postharvest handling and packaging that helps farmers comply with the needs of institutions.

While local food farmers may prefer to learn from other growers, the increasing engagement of extension personnel and regulatory agencies in direct marketing also benefits local food by legitimizing it. The ever-expanding networks of knowledge surrounding sustainable agriculture, particularly mainstream scientific research, support the development of sustainable agriculture by including it in the broader—and well-accepted—discourse of scientific agriculture.[2] Local food producers who are able to effectively engage with both professional experts and colleagues may be best positioned to further expand their farms and local food systems overall.

Future Challenges and Opportunities for Local Food

The research in *Making Local Food Work* has largely examined how local food producers are addressing current challenges. Many of these are related to lack of appropriate political support structures, infrastructure, and the learning curve inherent in a new endeavor. But some of the overall challenges on the horizon for agriculture will also affect local food producers, including such issues as climate change, the end of cheap energy, global population increase, and the continuing depletion of natural resources.

Some argue that local food is a solution to addressing these problems, and a way to feed a growing population. Tom Stearns, whose fiery speech opened the first chapter of this book, would agree. If food insecurity is one cause of global unrest, localizing food systems so that communities have control over their own food production and distribution may be one way to alleviate instability. Likewise, those who argue that conventional agriculture is a driving force behind climate change and poor water quality may look to local food as a solution. In contrast to conventional farms, local food farms tend to be more biodiverse and protective of soil and water resources, and may be better positioned to continue production even in the face of major environmental challenges. But farmers who operate without the political and financial support systems and who bear the full cost of marketing and distribution for their businesses may also be less able to weather increasing fuel prices, costs of environmental remediation, or additional infrastructure that could become a reality in the context of a changing climate. As I have pointed out, direct marketing means that the producers control their product from seed to final sale, but they also have to pay for the fuel to get products to market. Because local food is currently more a collection of individuals than an integrated system, it does not benefit from the economies of scale that the conventional food system enjoys. In short, the risk local food farmers face from an environmental, political, or economic downturn is higher than that faced by a conventional farmer who enjoys steady political support, subsidies, and an integrated commodity system.

One solution to this lack of connection is to develop integrated regional systems. Most of the farmers I worked with distributed their food within about a ninety-mile radius of their farms. This hyperlocal approach is satisfying to the locavores, but it does not encourage (or require) the producer to engage with a system of distribution that could absorb some of the work and cost associated with direct marketing. Just as I suggest that a farmer who specializes is better able to serve institutional markets, this same approach to production makes that farmer better able to take advantage of a regional distribution system that would allow farmers to focus on farming and let others do the work of distribution and marketing.

I am not the first to suggest that regional systems could hit the sweet spot by encouraging sustainable, biodiverse farming practices, reducing carbon footprints associated with the conventional food system, and using economies of scale to the best advantage.[3] This approach is another trick of the conventional trade that local food could effectively adopt. As I have noted, such measures require that we cease focusing only on farmers as the most important workers in the food system. Local governments can change zoning and regulations to encourage food farming, but these do very little good if there is not an integrated distribution system available.

Given the typically diverse production strategies associated with direct market agriculture, local food farms may be better able to respond to the environmental pressures that we know are on the horizon. But without a supportive political and economic structure to help buffer other challenges out of their control, it will become more difficult to get the food off the farm and to the consumer.

Future Directions in Research and Advocacy

There are many opportunities for further research on local food production, including studies that emphasize the role of producers. For example, despite the assumption that local food production is more environmentally sustainable than commodity production, there is little data on the biodiversity of local food farms. More information about the varieties of crops and livestock that local food farmers produce would improve our knowledge about the potential for local food farming to enhance biodiversity and preserve rare seeds and animal breeds. Research about labor and the potential for local food farming to economically enhance rural areas is sorely needed. While many studies predict the job growth potential of local food systems, there is little data about the quality or compensation of these jobs. More information about the number of local people that farmers employ would help us understand the extent to which direct market agriculture actually benefits the local community. Finally, a holistic picture of local food systems must also include such often invisible intermediaries as small distributors and processors. Meat processing, for example, is a critical component of a healthy local food system, but the number of small-scale meat lockers has been in steady decline. An assessment of the needs and experiences of butchers and their role in small communities would be a useful addition to our understanding of local food.

Initial developments in the local food movement largely occurred without the support of state and federal governments or agricultural science. Instead, individual communities slowly developed their own systems of production, distribution, and markets. In eastern Iowa, where farmers' markets have long been a part of even small communities, farmers have continuously diversified their sales strategies. Now, thanks in part to steady demand, many growers simultaneously sell at farmers' markets, operate a CSA, and serve institutions. The success of these grassroots activities has captured the attention of policymakers and researchers, who are now attempting to provide support and develop new ways to further enhance local food systems.

The increasing popularity of local food has created many opportunities for beginning and small-scale farmers as well as conventional growers looking to diversify their farms. Recent investments that state agencies, legislative bodies, and universities have made in policy and research suggest that there is real support for making local food a permanent sector of Iowa's agricultural economy. Farmers now have many sources from which they obtain knowledge and support. Producers have done their part as well by continuously investigating new marketing opportunities, sharing knowledge with other growers, and increasing the scale of their operations. There is a clear sense of optimism among growers and food activists that local food systems will continue to become more accessible for consumers. Growers still face challenges, particularly in sourcing labor, but they also have better access to systems of support thanks to the investments in local food made by consumers, policymakers, researchers, and other farmers.

Like many anthropologists, I find myself often saying, "It's not that simple!" We cannot accurately capture local food in one farmer-consumer interaction or Know Your Farmer campaign. We also cannot assume that local food is inherently more pure, just, or sustainable than any other system. Instead, local food systems are only as ecologically and socially beneficial as their participants make them. Looking critically at the entire network can show the potential for local food to enhance rural communities, but we have to take off our direct market relationship blinders to see them.

There are numerous opportunities to develop policies that will support alternative food systems. As I have pointed out, many alternative farmers interact with and use the strategies of the conventional system. Given this overlap, let us start supporting alternative farming using mechanisms similar to those that conventional farmers enjoy. Currently, much of the support for alternative agriculture is in the form of grant programs and incentives, including farm to school grants, conservation incentives, and specialty crop and marketing grants. Although these programs do inject funding into alternative agriculture, the coverage is spotty and unequal. Anyone who has ever attempted to complete a USDA grant application knows that it requires a significant investment of time, the ability to formulate grant-specific language, and the patience to navigate the notoriously unfriendly online Grants.gov submission process. The available programs are most accessible to initiatives with experienced grant writers and can be out of reach for an individual farmer or community group. Subsidizing agriculture is hardly a new phenomenon, and it works to drive production, as we clearly see from our acres of corn and soy in Iowa. If there is political value in local food, then policymakers should direct consistent and equally accessible funding toward it.

Policymakers could do more to support small-scale processing through tax credits and zoning regulations that are friendly to small rural businesses. Such policies should recognize even small farms as agriculturally viable and encourage economic activity rather than discourage small farm-based businesses. Local governments should also pay close attention to how those changes interact with state and federal policies at the farm level. They need to recognize the vast incentives that drive commodity production and understand that county-level policies will do very little to shift production practices in Iowa. County boards could make a more meaningful impact by investing in processing and distribution, improving infrastructure for existing local food farmers. City councils should think about where farmers' markets are located and support the development of markets outside affluent neighborhoods. School boards would be well served by investing in dedicated farm to school personnel.

Those who may not have access to a farm but want to be involved in food production should look for opportunities in processing and distribution. New business start-ups are never easy, but farming has some extra barriers. It has taken Robert Tomanek several years of investment of time and energy, as well as self-financing improvements on his rented land, to become established enough in the community that neighbors will alert him to land opportunities. Support for beginning farmers is strong; the efforts of extension services, PFI, and other organizations are commendable, and they should continue. Nevertheless, there is a need to better support other elements of the food system. Rather than funding temporary food hubs, aggregation sites, or farm to school projects using short-term grant money, let us encourage entrepreneurial young people to make more permanent investments in food infrastructure. Food system advocates, including retailers, should do their part by promoting not just farmers but all elements of the supply chain. Business schools could provide tangible examples of processing start-ups and distribution endeavors.

Farmers can do their part by scaling up and specializing, at least just a bit. I am not advocating for thousands of acres of monoculture, but a few acres of a high-value product can be profitable and build a local food inventory for institutional markets. Although individual producers experience the specific constraints of their own land base, even very small farms can produce for institutional markets if they develop their businesses with a perspective of scale and efficiency. Institutions can make an impact by contracting with growers for future crops. The relation of scale and institutional purchasing is a circular conundrum: institutions see small farms as risky because they may not have the necessary supply; farmers are hesitant to scale up and specialize because they do not trust institutions to follow through. It will take some movement on the part of both farmers and institutional buyers to make local food a consistent part of school, hospital, and care facility menus.

Finally, careful consideration should be given to farmwork if we are to build a new system of labor-intensive agriculture. Farmers cannot simultaneously take advantage of volunteer labor and claim that their consumers pay the true cost of food. Although volunteer labor may reduce immediate costs for a farmer, it can be economically detrimental if volunteer labor is unskilled. More important, agricultural labor should not be reserved for those privileged enough to do it for free or those marginal enough to be exploited. If local food farms are to make an impact on social justice, they should pay a fair wage. Operations such as Neal Jackson's have an advantage in that they provide year-round employment, but even seasonal work can benefit a local economy. In the long term, cultivating a returning staff of experienced workers is to the farmers' advantage, as new employee training is reduced.

The ability of local food to resist larger systems of agribusiness or globalization is not as important as its potential to create opportunities for more rural residents to make a living. Approaching local food as an articulated system rather than focusing on one actor or one relationship illuminates some of those opportunities. The challenges and barriers associated with local food production that I have pointed out also represent prospects for making these systems stronger. There is plenty of work to go around for those willing to invest the necessary energy and capital. That work includes promoting diversity among farms as well as growth in distribution and processing. There is a place for small CSAs or market farms, but if the goal is to develop a sustainable and economically viable food system, some farmers need to move toward larger marketing outlets. Local food should not be presented as having only one face on it. To build the most resilient food system, we should acknowledge all the faces that are too often hidden in even the shortest food chains.

ETHNOGRAPHIC RESEARCH is a long-term investment in a field site. Researchers sometimes spend decades working with the same population or in the same place. But at some point researchers step away to write up their findings, and things change. Since I finished the bulk of my research in 2012, life on the farm did, indeed, go on. Some of the farmers I worked with are still in business. Century Farms remains one of the largest CSAs in the state, although their shareholder numbers have not increased much in the past five years. They have constructed a large new packing facility, complete with loading docks and a larger walk-in cooler. David and Jessica have always taken a creative approach to their business, and in 2015 they offered a lifetime share to their current members. For five thousand dollars, a shareholder would receive a spring, summer, and winter CSA share as long as the farm is in operation. If they go out of business within five years of the lifetime share purchase, the shareholder will be reimbursed a prorated amount. Given their success, I am optimistic that those who purchased a lifetime share will enjoy many years of good food. Great Greens also continues to thrive; Neal still operates the greenhouse, sells sweet potatoes to the school district, and works with Amish growers to get their produce to market. He has turned over much of the greenhouse sales work to Sara, who now responds to customers and manages the logistics of filling orders each week. Rob Duncan's business also remains successful; he continues to sell to the school district, at several markets, and through a CSA. Likewise, Richard Dresdner's specialty pork is still in high demand, and Frances Baumgartner has kept Walnut Acres small and manageable.

Several others have transitioned out of farming. Jean Sorensen transferred ownership of her farm and business in 2015 to a young farmer who grew up in the area. Alan and Brenda Marshall ended their CSA but started a very successful cheese operation soon after. Their cheese was so popular that they soon felt the pressure to scale up, which would have required them to take on debt. Their desire to remain debt-free, in combination with the enormous workload of the dairy, led them to end their business in 2014. They have since retired to a small farm farther north. The Murphys have not resumed their goat cheese sales after putting production on hold in 2012, and Faye Jefferson ended her CSA not long after having major knee surgery in the year following my interview with her. Renee Johnson-Berry and her husband sold their farm to move closer to their son on the West Coast.

As some farmers moved on, others moved in. Of the sixteen farms listed in the Local Foods Connection 2015 CSA guide, nine started after 2012. The organization continued to host the CSA fair through spring 2016. That year, attendance by both farmers and potential shareholders was too low to justify continuing the event. LFC board and staff members speculated that the high visibility of CSAs and local food in general made the fair obsolete for most consumers. In an attempt to diversify their income, LFC asked farmers to contribute twenty-five dollars to the cost of the event, but many were unwilling to do so. LFC continues to link low-income families with local food and has added a farm stand model to their programming. Using grant funding, they contract with a local grower (Rob Duncan in the first year) who provides fresh produce at wholesale prices. The farm stand is set up in a low-income area at a neighborhood center frequented by families who live nearby. The produce is priced to be affordable for local residents.

The farm to school chapter I helped start continues to succeed. After the first year, I served as president of the nonprofit overseeing the program as well as serving as the farm to school coordinator. In 2013, all the wiser for the lettuce experience, I was able to purchase more than nine thousand dollars in local food for the school lunch program. By 2015, under new, paid leadership, the chapter spent more than twelve thousand dollars on local food. The program continues to be well received in the community, and the relationship between the chapter and the school district has remained very strong.

The biggest organizational change in Iowa's local food landscape involves the ISU extension service. Much of the statewide local food programming previously managed by the Leopold Center for Sustainable Agriculture has been transferred to the extension service. This process included moving eight staff members from the Leopold Center and hiring another eight. Although they are only a few years into this new model, the resources that the extension service has injected into local food support and advocacy have been meaningful. Their programming is only partially devoted to farming; they also have community-level resources for food systems planners, food businesses, and consumers. As one of the initial readers of *Making Local Food Work* noted, the ISU extension service will continue to focus its programming on the agriculture that has the most economic impact: commodity production. But the recent management change suggests that the service sees real value in the future of local food.

Local food has not taken over Iowa's agricultural economy since I started this research, but it has more than held its ground. Perhaps most encouraging is the growing presence of alternative agriculture in spaces usually reserved for the old-guard commodity producers. In 2016 I attended the Ag Leaders banquet, hosted by Iowa's secretary of agriculture. I sat in an enormous banquet hall on the Iowa State Fairgrounds and was served a full plate that included *both* beef and pork with several sides. The room was packed with representatives from the major commodity groups, the Farm Bureau, agribusiness and input dealer representatives, and legislators. High school agriculture students enrolled in FFA (generally known as Future Farmers of America) were seated throughout the room, standing out in their signature blue jackets with yellow stitching. This was my second time at the event, which is a fascinating study in the social networks of Iowa agriculture as agribusiness and commodity group representatives talk to the FFA students about their home farms and presumed future studies at Iowa State University. Cards are passed and offers of internships discussed.

I caught the eye of a young woman I had met recently at a farm safety event; she sank into a chair next to me, grateful to see someone she knew. Slightly built, with dreadlocks to her waist, she helps manage the farm at the Maharishi School of Management in eastern Iowa. Known for their organic food and transcendental meditation, the school falls well outside the typical model of agricultural production. She quietly requested a meat-free plate and after some puzzled conversations among the staff, was presented a meal of cheesy party potatoes, salad, and a roll. We talked about organic farming, compost, and garden systems as others around us commiserated about the predicted low commodity prices and hoped for a successful ISU football season. Later, the legislator at our table, from a rural south central Iowa county, was curious about composting and asked several insightful questions about the Maharishi University's process, drawing the rest of the table into the conversation. I left that banquet feeling optimistic that there will continue to be more dreadlocks among the blue FFA jackets in years to come. As ISU, the commodity groups, and the Farm Bureau continue to recognize local food farming as part of the agricultural landscape, rural county legislators and others will ask about composting and alternative practices. When the Iowa Ag Leaders dinner is as diverse as a midsummer CSA share, we will know we have made progress.

Notes

PREFACE

1. R. Manning, "The Trouble with Iowa: Corn, Corruption, and the Presidential Caucuses," *Harper's Magazine*, July 20, 2016, 23–30.

CHAPTER ONE

1. M. Pollan, *The Omnivore's Dilemma: A Natural History of Four Meals* (New York: Penguin, 2006); B. Kingsolver, *Animal, Vegetable, Miracle: A Year of Food Life* (New York: HarperCollins, 2007).

2. "Oxford Word of the Year 2007: Locavore," http://blog.oup.com/2007/11/locavore/.

3. http://www.ers.usda.gov/data-products/chart-gallery/detail.aspx?chartId=48561&ref=collection&embed=True.

4. http://www.farmtoschool.org/about/what-is-farm-to-school.

5. H. McIlvaine-Newsad, C. D. Merrett, and Patrick McLaughlin, "Direct from Farm to Table: Community Supported Agriculture in Western Illinois," *Culture and Agriculture* 26, no. 1–2 (2004): 149–163, 160. The phrase "malaise of modernity" comes from the title of Charles Taylor's 1991 CBC Massey Lectures, published in book form by House of Anansi Press, p. 160.

6. C. C. Hinrichs, "Embeddedness and Local Food Systems: Notes on Two Types of Direct Agricultural Market," *Journal of Rural Studies* 16 (2000): 295–303, 301.

7. T. A. Lyson, *Civic Agriculture: Reconnecting Farm, Food, and Community* (Lebanon, NH: Tufts University Press, 2004).

8. Jeffrey K. O'Hara, *Market Forces: Creating Jobs through Public Investment in Local and Regional Food Systems* (Cambridge, MA: Union of Concerned Scientists, 2011); D. Swenson, *Exploring Small-Scale Meat Processing Expansions in Iowa* (Ames, IA: The Leopold Center for Sustainable Agriculture, 2011).

9. A. Enderton and C. Bregendahl, *2013 Economic Impacts of Iowa's Regional Food Systems Working Group* (Ames, IA: The Leopold Center for Sustainable Agriculture, 2014).

10. M. R. Drabenstott, "Beyond Agriculture: New Policies for Rural America—A Conference Summary," *Proceedings: Rural and Agricultural Conferences* (October 2000): 1–5, 42.

11. W. Goldschmidt, "Conclusion: The Urbanization of Rural America," in *Pigs, Profits, and Rural Communities*, ed. K. M. Thu and E. Durrenberger, 183–198, 183 (Albany: State University of New York Press, 1998).

12. https://www.nass.usda.gov/Quick_Stats/Ag_Overview/stateOverview.php?state=IOWA.

13. https://www.nass.usda.gov/Quick_Stats/Ag_Overview/stateOverview.php?state=IOWA.

14. https://www.nass.usda.gov/Statistics_by_State/Iowa/Publications/Annual_Statistical_Bulletin/2014/10_14.pdf.

15. https://www.agcensus.usda.gov/Publications/2012/Online_Resources/Typology/typology13_ia.pdf.

CHAPTER TWO

1. Cacao is a major cash crop in Belize. The entire crop is certified organic, allowing the country to enjoy the highest price per pound in the world. For more information see E. Stanley, "Monilia (*Moniliophtora roreri*) and the Post-Development of Belizean Cacao," *Culture, Agriculture, Food, and Environment* 38, no. 1 (2016): 27–36.

2. M. Pollan, "Naturally," *New York Times Magazine*, May 13, 2001.

3. P. B. Thompson, "The Agrarian Vision: Sustainability and Environmental Ethics," in *Culture of the Land: A Series in the New Agrarianism*, ed. N. Wirzba, 3 (Lexington: University Press of Kentucky, 2010).

4. K. M. Dudley, *Debt and Dispossession: Farm Loss in America's Heartland* (Chicago: University of Chicago Press, 2000), 6 (quoting Leo Marx).

5. W. Berry, *The Unsettling of America: Culture and Agriculture*, 3rd ed. (San Francisco: Sierra Club Books, 1996).

6. L. Marx, *The Machine in the Garden: Technology and the Pastoral Ideal in America* (New York: Oxford University Press, 1964); Dudley, *Debt and Dispossession*, 6.

7. W. Goldschmidt, *As You Sow: Three Studies in the Social Consequences of Agribusiness* (Montclair, NJ: Allanheld, Osmun, 1978).

8. Ibid., 185.

9. W. Goldschmidt, "Large-Scale Farming and the Rural Social Structure," *Rural Sociology* 43, no. 3 (1978): 362–366, 365.

10. M. N. Hayes and A. L. Olmstead, "Farm Size and Community Quality: Arvin and Dinuba Revisited," *American Journal of Agricultural Economics* 66, no. 4 (1984): 430–436, 430.

11. C. K. Harris and J. Gilbert, "Large-Scale Farming, Rural Income, and Goldschmidt's Agrarian Thesis," *Rural Sociology* 47, no. 3 (1982): 449–458, 455.

12. L. M. Lobao, M. D. Schulman, and L. E. Swanson, "Still Going: Recent Debates on the Goldschmidt Hypothesis," *Rural Sociology* 58, no. 2 (1993): 277–288.

13. Hayes and Olmstead, "Farm Size and Community Quality," 431–433.

14. For further discussion of corporate interests in agriculture, see R. Manning, *Against the Grain: How Agriculture Has Hijacked Civilization* (New York: North Point, 2004); M. Pollan, *The Omnivore's Dilemma: A Natural History of Four Meals* (New York: Penguin, 2006; M. Nestle, *Food Politics: How the Food Industry Influences Nutrition and Health* (Berkeley: University of California Press, 2007).

15. Thompson, "The Agrarian Vision," 5.

16. E. T. Freyfogle, "Introduction: A Durable Scale," in *The New Agrarianism: Land, Culture, and the Community of Life*, ed. E. T. Freyfogle, xiii–xli (Washington, DC: Island Press: 2001).

17. Ibid., xxvii.

18. See M. M. Bell, *Farming for Us All: Practical Agriculture and the Cultivation of Sustainability*, Rural Studies Series (University Park: Pennsylvania State University Press, 2004); N. Hassanein, *Changing the Way America Farms: Knowledge and Comunity in the Sustainable Agriculture Movement* (Lincoln: University of Nebraska Press, 1999).

19. Lyson, *Civic Agriculture*.

20. Ibid.; T. A. Lyson, "Civic Agriculture and Community Problem Solving," *Culture and Agriculture* 27, no. 2 (2005): 92–98.

21. E. P. Durrenberger, "Community Supported Agriculture in Central Pennsylvania," *Culture and Agriculture* 24, no. 2 (2002): 42–51, 42.

22. B. Wells, S. Gradwell, and R. Yoder, "Growing Food, Growing Community: Community Supported Agriculture in Rural Iowa," *Community Development Journal* 34, no. 1 (1999): 38–46, 45.

23. C. Goland, "Community Supported Agriculture, Food Consumption Patterns, and Member Commitment," *Culture and Agriculture* 24, no. 1 (2002): 14–25, 22.

24. G. Gillespie, D. L. Hilchey, C. C. Hinrichs, and G. Feenstra, "Farmers' Markets as Keystones in Rebuilding Local and Regional Food Systems," in *Remaking the North American Food System: Strategies for Sustainability*, ed. C. C. Hinrichs and T. A. Lyson, 65–83 (Lincoln: University of Nebraska Press, 2007).

25. C. Brown and S. Miller, "The Impacts of Local Markets: A Review of Research on Farmers Markets and Community Supported Agriculture (CSA)," *American Journal of Agricultural Economics* 90, no. 5 (2008): 1296–1302; A. Trauger, C. Sachs, M. Barbercheck, K. Brasier, and N. E. Kiernan, "'Our Market Is Our Community': Women Farmers and Civic Agriculture in Pennsylvania, USA,"

Agriculture and Human Values 27, no. 1 (2009): 43–55; J. R. Farmer, C. Chancellor, A. Gooding, D. Shubowitz, and A. Bryan, "A Tale of Four Farmers Markets: Recreation and Leisure as a Catalyst for Sustainability," *Journal of Park and Recreation Administration* 29, no. 3 (2011): 11–23.

26. For more on shareholder turnover, see Goland, "Community Supported Agriculture, Food Consumption Patterns, and Member Commitment"; D. J. Kane and L. Lohr, *Maximizing Shareholder Retention in Southeastern CSAs: A Step Toward Long Term Stability* (Santa Cruz, CA: Organic Farming Research Foundation, 1997); L. Oberholtzer, *Community Supported Agriculture in the Mid-Atlantic Region: Results of a Shareholder Survey and Farmer Interviews* (Stevensville, MD: Small Farm Success Project, Future Harvest CSA, 2004).

27. Durrenberger, "Community Supported Agriculture in Central Pennsylvania," 42.

28. L. B. DeLind, "Considerably More than Vegetables, a Lot Less than Community: The Dilemma of Community Supported Agriculture," in *Fighting for the Farm: Rural America Transformed*, ed. J. Adams, 192–206 (Philadelphia: University of Pennsylvania Press, 2003); L. M. Stanford, "The Role of Ideology in New Mexico's CSA Organizations: Conflicting Visions between Growers and Members," in *Fast Food / Slow Food: The Cultural Economy of the Global Food System*, ed. R. R. Wilk, 181–200 (Lanham, MD: Alta Mira Press, 2006).

29. Å. Svenfelt and A. Carlsson-Kanyama, "Farmers' Markets—Linking Food Consumption and the Ecology of Food Production?" *Local Environment* 15, no. 5 (2010): 453–465, 458.

30. J. Guthman, A. W. Morris, and P. Allen, "Squaring Farm Security and Food Security in Two Types of Alternative Food Institution," *Rural Sociology* 71, no. 4 (2006): 662–684, 662.

31. J. Guthman, "'If They Only Knew': Color Blindness and Universalism in California Alternative Food Institutions," *Professional Geographer* 60, no. 3 (2008): 387–397.

32. K. Lambert-Pennington and K. Hicks, "Class Conscious, Color-Blind: Examining the Dynamics of Food Access and the Justice Potential of Farmers Markets," *Culture, Agriculture, Food and Environment* 36, no. 1 (2016): 56–65, 62.

33. E. M. DuPuis, D. Goodman, and J. Harrison, "Just Values or Just Value? Remaking the Local in Agro-Food Studies," in *Between the Local and the Global: Confronting Complexity in the Contemporary Agri-Food Sector*, ed. T. Marsden and J. Murdoch, 245–247 (London: Elsevier, 2006); J. L. Harrison, "Neoliberal Environmental Justice: Mainstream Ideas of Justice in Political Conflict over Agricultural Pesticides in the United States," *Environmental Politics* 23, no. 4 (2014): 650–669.

34. E. M. DuPuis and D. Goodman, "Should We Go 'Home' to Eat?: Toward a Reflexive Politics of Localism," *Journal of Rural Studies* 21, no. 3 (2005): 359–371, 364.

35. S. Connelly, S. Markey, and M. Roseland, "Bridging Sustainability and the Social Economy: Achieving Community Transformation through Local Food Initiatives," *Critical Social Policy* 31, no. 2 (2011): 308–324.

36. R. P. King, M. S. Hand, G. DiGiacomo, K. Clancy, M. I. Gomez, S. D. Hardesty, L. Lev, and E. W. McLaughlin, *Comparing the Structure, Size, and Performance of Local and Mainstream Food Supply Chains* (Washington, DC: USDA Economic Research Service, 2010), v.

37. See, for instance, S. Martinez, M. S. Hand, M. Da Pra, Susan Pollack, K. Ralston, T. Smith, S. Vogel, S. Clark, L. Lohr, S. A. Low, and C. Newman, *Local Food Systems: Concepts, Impacts, and Issues* (Washington, DC: USDA Economic Research Service, 2010), 42.

38. Brown and Miller, "The Impacts of Local Markets," 1296.

39. P. Cantrell, D. Conner, G. Erickcek, and M. Hamm, *Eat Fresh and Grow Jobs, Michigan* (Traverse City: Michigan Land Use Institute, 2006), 2.

40. A. Myles and K. Hood, *Economic Impact of Farmers Markets in Mississippi* (Starkville: Mississippi State Extension Service, Mississippi State University, 2010), 3 (on seasonality), 4 (on popularity).

41. O'Hara, *Market Forces*, 31.

42. Ibid., 31.

43. F. Thicke, *A New Vision for Iowa Food and Agriculture: Sustainable Agriculture for the 21st Century* (Fairfield, IA: Mulberry Knoll Books, 2010), 145.

44. http://www.iowaagriculture.gov/Horticulture_and_FarmersMarkets /pdfs/FarmersMarketEIS2009.pdf, 3–4.

45. D. Swenson, *The Economic Impacts of Increased Fruit and Vegetable Production and Consumption in Iowa: Phase II* (Ames: Leopold Center for Sustainable Agriculture, Iowa State University, 2006), 22.

46. D. Swenson, *Investigating the Potential Economic Impacts of Local Foods for Southeast Iowa* (Ames: Leopold Center for Sustainable Agriculture, Iowa State University, 2009).

47. A. Starr, "Local Food: A Social Movement?," *Cultural Studies—Critical Methodologies* 10, no. 6 (2010): 479–490, 486.

CHAPTER THREE

1. W. G. Murray, "Struggle for Land Ownership," in *A Century of Farming in Iowa: 1846–1946* (Ames: Iowa State College Press, 1946), 11.

2. B. L. Gardiner, *American Agriculture in the Twentieth Century: How It Flourished and What It Cost* (Cambridge, MA: Harvard University Press, 2002), 180–186.

3. P. Burnett, "Academic Freedom or Political Maneuvers: Theodore W. Schultz and the Oleomargarine Controversy Revisited," *Agricultural History* 85, no. 3 (2011): 373–397.

4. See, for example, J. Hightower, "Hard Tomatoes, Hard Times: The Failure of the Land Grant College Complex," in *Radical Agriculture*, ed. R. Merril (New York: New York University Press, 1976), 87–110; J. Todd, "A Modest Proposal: Science for the People," in *Radical Agriculture*, 259–283.

5. Food and Water Watch, *Public Research, Private Gain: Corporate Influence over University Agricultural Research* (Washington, DC: Food and Water Watch, 2012), 8.

6. M. Duffy and D. Smith, *Farmland Ownership and Tenure in Iowa, 2007* (Ames: Iowa State University Extension, 2008), 11.

7. Michael Duffy and Ann Johanns, *Farmland Ownership and Tenure in Iowa 2012* (Ames: Iowa State University Extension, 2014).

8. https://www.agcensus.usda.gov/Publications/2007/Online_Highlights/Fact_Sheets/Farm_Numbers/farm_numbers.pdf; https://www.agcensus.usda.gov/Publications/2012/Preliminary_Report/Highlights.pdf.

9. "About the Leopold Center," www.leopold.iastate.edu/about/leopold-center.

10. http://www.practicalfarmers.org/about/mission-vision-values/.

11. Duffy and Smith, *Farmland Ownership and Tenure in Iowa, 2007*, 9.

12. Ibid., 10.

13. www.practicalfarmers.org.

14. M. Duffy, D. Smith, W. Edwards, and B. Johnson, *Survey of Iowa Leasing Practices, 2007* (Ames: Iowa State University Extension and Outreach, 2007), 4; M. Duffy, W. Edwards, A. Johanns, *Survey of Iowa Leasing Practices, 2012* (Ames: Iowa State University Extension and Outreach, 2012).

15. Duffy, Smith, Edwards, and Johnson, *2007 Survey*, 3; Duffy, Edwards, Johanns, *2012 Survey*, 4.

16. Ibid.

17. Duffy, Smith, Edwards, and Johnson, *2007 Survey*, 3; Duffy, Edwards, Johanns, *2012 Survey*, 3.

18. J. G. Arbuckle, *Rented Land in Iowa: Social and Environmental Dimensions* (Ames: Iowa State University Extension, 2010), 9.

19. Ibid., 16–17.

20. Ibid., 17.

21. Ibid., 9.

22. Ibid.

23. Ibid., 10.

24. Ibid.

25. Ibid.

26. Ibid., 12.

CHAPTER FOUR

Portions of this chapter previously appeared in B. Janssen, "Local Food, Local Engagement: Community Supported Agriculture in Eastern Iowa," *Culture and Agriculture* 32, no. 1 (2010): 4–16.

1. C. A. Cone and A. Kakaliouras, "Community Supported Agriculture: Building Moral Community or an Alternative Consumer Choice?," *Culture and Agriculture* 51/52 (1995): 28–31.

2. USDA, *2012 Census of Agriculture* (Washington, DC.: United States Department of Agriculture, 2014).

3. S. Gradwell, "Community Supported Agriculture Takes Root in Iowa," in *CSA Farm Network* (Stilwater, NY: CSA Farm Network, 1998), 32.

4. The CSA listings are available at https://www.ams.usda.gov/local-food-directories/csas. The annual fair has been discontinued (see epilogue).

5. http://www.ers.usda.gov/data-products/chart-gallery/detail.aspx?chartId=48561&ref=collection&embed=True.

6. For number of farmers' markets, see https://www.idalsdata.org/fmnp/index.cfm?fuseaction=main.formFarmersMarketDirectory (number of farmers' markets); for per capita ranking, see D. Otto, *Consumers, Vendors, and the Economic Importance of Iowa Farmers Markets: An Economic Impact Survey Analysis* (Des Moines: Iowa Department of Agriculture and Land Stewardship, 2010).

7. Otto, *Consumers, Vendors, and the Economic Importance of Iowa Farmers Markets.*

8. Swenson, *Exploring Small-Scale Meat Processing Expansions in Iowa*, 2.

9. Ibid., 6.

10. R. J. Johnson, D. L. Marti, L. Gwin, Slaughter and Processing Options and Issues for Locally Sourced Meat, USDA report 2012, 11, http://www.ers.usda.gov/media/820188/ldpm216-01.pdf .

11. E. M. DuPuis, *Nature's Perfect Food: How Milk Became America's Drink* (New York: New York University Press, 2002).

CHAPTER FIVE

1. R. A. Vogt and L. L. Kaiser, *"Still* a Time to Act: A Review of Institutional Marketing of Regionally-Grown Food," *Agriculture and Human Values* 25, no. 2 (2007): 241–255.

2. C. Simpson, "Why Farm to School Will Save Our Food System," December 10, 2013, www.huffingtonpost.com/maria-rodale/why-farm-to-school-will-s_b_4418 448.html.

3. J. Poppendieck, *Free for All: Fixing School Food in America* (Berkeley: University of California Press, 2010).

4. For more on the history of the National School Lunch Program, see Ann Cooper and Lisa M. Holmes, *Lunch Lessons: Changing the Way We Feed Our Children* (New York: Harper Collins, 2006); Susan Levine, *School Lunch Politics: The Surprising History of America's Favorite Welfare Program* (Princeton, NJ: Princeton University Press, 2008).

5. M. Kalb and M. Lott, "2011 National Farm to School Network: Legislative History and Movement Building," USDA webinar, April 12, 2012.

6. J. M. Bagdonis, C. C. Hinrichs, and K. A. Schafft, "The Emergence and Framing of Farm-to-School Initiatives: Civic Engagement, Health and Local Agriculture," *Agriculture and Human Values* 26, nos. 1–2 (2008): 107–119.

7. E. Serrano, A. Kowaleska, K. Fuller, L. Fellin, and V. Wigand, "Status and Goals of Local Food Wellness Policies in Virginia: A Response to the Child Nutrition and WIC Reauthorization Act of 2004," *Journal of Nutrition Education and Behavior* 39, no. 2 (2007): 95–100.

8. Bagdonis, Hinrichs, and Schafft, "The Emergence and Framing of Farm-to-School Initiatives,"108.

9. M. Story, M. S. Nanney, and M. B. Schwartz, "Schools and Obesity Prevention: Creating School Environments and Policies to Promote Healthy Eating and Physical Activity," *Milbank Quarterly* 87, no. 1 (2009): 71–100.

10. M. W. Hamm, "Linking Sustainable Agriculture and Public Health: Opportunities for Realizing Multiple Goals," *Journal of Hunger and Environmental Nutrition* 3, nos. 2–3 (2008): 169–185.

11. A. A. Joshi, M. Azuma, and G. Feenstra, "Do Farm-to-School Programs Make a Difference? Findings and Future Research Needs," *Journal of Hunger and Environmental Nutrition* 3, no. 3 (2008): 229–246.

12. J. Kloppenburg Jr. and N. Hassanein, "From Old School to Reform School?," *Agriculture and Human Values* 23 (2006): 417–421.

13. Poppendieck, *Free For All*.

14. P. Allen and J. Guthman, "From 'Old School' to 'Farm-to-School': Neoliberalization from the Ground Up," *Agriculture and Human Values* 23, no. 4 (2006): 401–415.

15. Joshi, Azuma, and Feenstra, "Do Farm-to-School Programs Make a Difference?"

16. B. T. Izumi, K. Alaimo, and M. W. Hamm, "Farm-to-School Programs:

Perspectives of School Food Service Professionals," *Journal of Nutrition Education and Behavior* 42, no. 2 (2010): 83–91.

17. A. Leyda, "From Farm to School through the Statehouse: The Importance of State Legislation for Iowa's Farm to School Program," *Drake Journal of Agricultural Law* 16, no. 1 (2011): 168–182.

CHAPTER SIX

Portions of this chapter previously appeared in B. Janssen, "Bridging the Gap between Farmers and Food Service Directors: The Social Challenges in Farm to School Purchasing," *Journal of Agriculture, Food Systems, and Community Development* 5, no. 1 (2014): 129–143.

1. http://fieldtofamily.org/programs/farm-to-school/.

CHAPTER SEVEN

Portions of this chapter previously appeared in B. Janssen, "Herd Management: Labor Strategies in Local Food Production," *Anthropology of Work Review* 34, no. 2 (2013): 68–79.

1. M. Gray, *Labor and the Locavore: The Making of a Comprehensive Food Ethic* (Berkeley: University of California Press, 2014).

2. Lyson, *Civic Agriculture*.

3. I. B. Vasi, S. Rynes, C. Li, and J. Nielsen, "The Resurgence of the Locavore: The Growth of Multi-Motive Local Food Markets in the United States," paper presented at the American Sociological Association Annual Meeting, Chicago, August 22–25, 2015.

4. M. Pollan, http://pollan.blogs.nytimes.com/2006/05/07/voting-with-your-fork/?_r=0.

5. L. B. DeLind, "Place, Work, and Civic Agriculture: Common Fields for Cultivation," *Agriculture and Human Values* 19 (2002): 217–224.

6. J. Guthman, *Agrarian Dreams: The Paradox of Organic Farming in California*, 2nd ed. (Oakland: University of California Press, 2014), 51.

7. M. Winter, "Embeddedness, the New Food Economy and Defensive Localism," *Journal of Rural Studies* 19 (2003): 23–32.

8. E. Henderson and R. Van En, *Sharing the Harvest: A Citizen's Guide to Community Supported Agriculture* (White River Junction, VT.: Chelsea Green, 2007).

9. DeLind, "Considerably More than Vegetables"; C. A. Cone and A. Kakaliouras, "Community Supported Agriculture: Building Moral Community or and Alternative Consumer Choice?," *Culture and Agriculture* 51/52 (1995): 28–31;

C. A. Cone and A. Kakaliouras, "The Quest for Purity, Stewardship of the Land, and Nostalgia for Sociability: Resocializing Commodities through Community Supported Agriculture," in *CSA Farm Network*, vol. 2 (Stillwater, NY: CSA Farm Network, 1998), 26–29; Stanford, "The Role of Ideology in New Mexico's CSA Organizations."

10. Durrenberger, "Community Supported Agriculture in Central Pennsylvania."

11. M. Kirlin, "Civic Skill Building: The Missing Component in Service Programs?," *Political Science and Politics* 25, no. 3 (2002): 571–575; L. S. Tossutti, "Does Volunteerism Increase the Political Engagement of Young Newcomers? Assessing the Potential of Individual and Group-Based Forms of Unpaid Service," *Canadian Ethnic Studies* 35, no. 3 (2003), 70–84; A. M. Omoto, M. Snyder, and J. D. Hackette, "Personality and Motivational Antecedents of Activism and Civic Engagement," *Journal of Personality* 78, no. 6 (2010): 1703–1734.

12. J. Kloppenburg Jr., "Social Theory and the De/reconstruction of Agricultural Science: Local Knowledge for an Alternative Agriculture," *Rural Sociology* 56, no. 4 (1991): 519–548; Hassanein, "Changing the Way America Farms"; Bell, *Farming for Us All*; M. S. Carolan, "Social Change and the Adoption and Adaptation of Knowledge Claims: Whose Truth Do You Trust in Regard to Sustainable Agriculture?," *Agriculture and Human Values* 23, no. 3 (2006): 325–339.

CHAPTER EIGHT

1. T. A. Lyson and W. W. Falk, "Forgotten Places: Poor Rural Regions in the United States," in *Forgotten Places: Uneven Development in Rural America*, ed. T. A. Lyson and W. W. Falk, 1–6 (Lawrence: University Press of Kansas: 1993).

2. D. D. Stull and M. J. Broadway, "Killing Them Softly: Work in Meatpacking Plants and What It Does to Workers," in *Any Way You Cut It: Meat Processing and Small-Town America*, ed. D. D. Stull, M. J. Broadway, and D. Griffith (Lawrence: University Press of Kansas, 1995), 61–84; M. S. Henry, M. R. Drabenstott, and K. Mitchell, "Meat Processing in Rural America: Economic Powerhouse or Problem?," in *Communities of Work: Rural Restructuring in Local and Global Contexts*, ed. W. W. Falk, M. D. Schulman, and A. R. Tickamyer (Athens: Ohio University Press, 2003), 55–78.

3. Drabenstott, "Beyond Agriculture."

4. W. A. Galston, "Rural America in the 1990s: Trends and Choices," *Policy Studies Journal* 12, no. 20 (1992): 202–211.

5. L. Krouse and T. Galluzzo, *Iowa's Local Food System: A Place to Grow* (Mount Vernon: Iowa Policy Project, 2007).

6. M. S. Henry, M. R. Drabenstott, and K. Mitchell, "Meat Processing in Rural America: Economic Powerhouse or Problem?" in *Communities of Work: Rural Restructuring in Local and Global Contexts*, ed. W. W. Falk, M. D. Schulman, and A. R. Tickamyer (Athens: Ohio University Press, 2003), 55–78.

7. J. L. Flora, G. P. Green, E. A. Gale, F. E. Schmidt, and C. B. Flora, "Self-Development: A Viable Rural Development Option?," *Policy Studies Journal* 20, no. 2 (1992): 276–288, 285.

8. See H. Renting, T. K. Marsden, and J. Banks, "Understanding Alternative Food Networks: Exploring the Role of Short Food Supply Chains in Rural Development," *Environment and Planning* 35 (2003): 393–411.

9. D. L. Barkley and P. N. Wilson, "Is Alternative Agriculture a Viable Rural Development Strategy?," *Growth and Change* 23, no. 2 (1992): 239–253.

10. Enderton and Bregendahl, "2013 Economic Impacts of Iowa's Regional Food Systems," 5.

11. Ibid., 9.

12. Ibid., 10.

13. Ibid., 15.

14. U.S. Department of Labor, "Health and Safety Topics," https://www.osha.gov/SLTC/meatpacking.

15. For more on occupational injuries in meatpacking, see https://www.osha.gov/SLTC/meatpacking/hazards_solutions.html and https://www.splcenter.org/20130228/unsafe-these-speeds.

16. "Food and Agricultural Industries," in *Compilation of Air Pollutant Emissions Factors*, sec. 9.5.1, https://www3.epa.gov/ttnchie1/ap42/ch09/final/c9s05-1.pdf.

17. D. Fink, *Cutting into the Meatpacking Line: Workers and Change in the Rural Midwest* (Chapel Hill: University of North Carolina Press, 1998).

18. Stull and Broadway, "Killing Them Softly"; Fink, *Cutting into the Meatpacking Line*; E. Schlosser, *Fast Food Nation: The Dark Side of the All-American Meal* (Boston: Houghton Mifflin, 2001).

19. D. D. Stull and M. J. Broadway, *Slaughterhouse Blues: The Meat and Poultry Industry in North America* (Belmont, CA: Thompson Wadsworth, 2004), 63–64.

20. P. J. Carr and M. J. Kefalas, *Hollowing Out the Middle: The Rural Brain Drain and What It Means for America* (Boston: Beacon Press, 2009).

CHAPTER NINE

1. M. A. Grey, "The Industrial Food Stream and Its Alternatives in the United States: An Introduction," *Human Organization* 59, no. 2 (2000): 143–150.

2. M. A. Lappé, E. B. Bailey, C. Childress, and K. D. R. Setchell, "Alterations

in Clinically Important Phytoestrogens in Genetically Modified, Herbicide-Tolerant Soybeans," *Journal of Medicinal Food* 1, no. 4 (1998): 241–245.

3. J. A. Magaña-Gómez and A. M. Calderón de la Barca, "Risk Assessment of Genetically Modified Crops for Nutrition and Health," *Nutrition Reviews* 67, no. 1 (2009): 1–16.

4. G. Flachowsky, H. Schafft, and U. Meyer, "Animal Feeding Studies for Nutritional and Safety Assessments of Feeds from Genetically Modified Plants: A Review," *Journal für Verbraucherschutz und Lebensmittelsicherheit* 7, no. 3 (2012): 179–194; J. L. Domingo and J. Giné Bordonaba, "A Literature Review on the Safety Assessment of Genetically Modified Plants," *Environment International* 37, no. 4 (2011): 734–742.

5. https://www.nass.usda.gov/Surveys/Guide_to_NASS_Surveys/Chemi cal_Use/2014_Corn_Highlights/#pesticide.

6. For 1996 data on both corn and soy, see http://www.ers.usda.gov/amber -waves/2015-may/managing-glyphosate-resistance-may-sustain-its-efficacy -and-increase-long-term-returns-to-corn-and-soybean-production.aspx#.V9 BzcD9El2A. For 2012 data on soybeans, see https://www.nass.usda.gov/Surveys /Guide_to_NASS_Surveys/Chemical_Use/2012_Soybeans_Highlights/.

7. R. H. Coupe and P. D. Capel, "Trends in Pesticide Use on Soybean, Corn and Cotton since the Introduction of Major Genetically Modified Crops in the United States," *Pest Management Science* 72, no. 5 (2016): 1013–1022, 1016.

8. Swenson, "Measuring the Economic Impacts of Increased Fresh Fruit and Vegetable Production."

CHAPTER TEN

1. For a discussion of the division between the alternative and conventional food systems, see M. A. Grey, "The Industrial Food Stream and Its Alternatives in the United States: An Introduction," *Human Organization* 59, no. 2 (2000): 143–150.

2. M. S. Carolan, "Social Change and the Adoption and Adaptation of Knowledge Claims: Whose Truth Do You Trust in Regard to Sustainable Agriculture?," *Agriculture and Human Values* 23, no. 3 (2006): 325–339.

3. See, for instance, L. Lengnick, *Resilient Agriculture: Cultivating Food Systems for a Changing Planet* (Gabriola Island, BC: New Society Publishers, 2015); D. Liverman and J. Ingram, "Why Regions?," in *Food Security and Global Environmental Change*, ed. J. Ingram, P. Ericksen, and D. Liverman, 203–211 (New York: Taylor and Francis, 2010).

Index

aerial spraying, 172, 186, 188, 202

Agent Orange, 173

agrarian, 14, 15–17, 29, 38, 120, 157, 177, 197–98, 200; and alternative agriculture, 19–20; economics, 20–21; Thomas Jefferson, 15–16, 17, 18. *See also* farmers' independence; rural culture

agribusiness, 8, 17, 140, 175, 188, 209; agricultural research, 34–35; corporate farm ownership, 10; Monsanto, 172–73; and policy, 32, 37, 171, 173, 174, 180

agricultural commodities, 7, 10, 44, 132, 177. *See also* corn; soybeans; pork

agricultural knowledge: of consumers, 13, 21, 23, 28, 120, 121–23, 132; of farm interns, 134, 140–41; of farm volunteers, 140; of farmers, 21, 52, 123, 142, 206. *See also* agricultural literacy; consumer knowledge

agricultural literacy, 124. *See also* agricultural knowledge

agricultural research, 5, 10, 14, 28, 29, 33–35, 37, 49, 50; on CSAs, 6, 11, 21–22; farm to school, 86–87; farmer-led, 42; on farmers' markets, 23–24, 25, 27; future needs, 205–6; GMOs, 174–75, 193; social science, 17–18, 121, 171; on volunteerism, 131

agriculture, narratives of, 13–14, 15, 17

agritourism, 4

alternative agriculture, 11, 17, 21, 34, 124, 134–35, 170, 178, 207; compared with conventional agriculture, 5, 8, 15, 37, 45, 147, 180, 194, 201; values, 20. *See also* agrarian; commodity production

amaranth, 150

American Farm Bureau Federation, 8, 201

Amish, 152, 155

anthropologists, 19, 206; and the study of agriculture, 8, 16, 17, 122, 129, 149

anthropology, research methods, 5, 11–12, 128, 151, 155

apples, 92–93, 95, 99–100, 102

aquaculture, 147

asparagus, 12, 58, 101, 115, 156, 167, 168

Bacillus thuringiensis, 194

basil, 150

beef, 3, 7, 32, 41, 44, 71, 88, 184, 191; grass-fed production, 45, 47–49, 129, 135–36, 185, 192–93; processing, 72, 73–75, 145

bees, 187–88, 202

beets, 58, 183

beginning farmer, 11, 31, 37, 52, 115, 134–35, 203, 206, 208; education, 43, 48, 139, 141; and farmland

rental, 49–50, 52; general support
for, 38–45; loans, 141; tax credits for
renters, 38
bell peppers, 22, 58, 92, 113
berries, 4
Berry, Wendell, 16
bok choy, 107
broccoli, 58, 186
butchering. *See* poultry processing

cabbage, 2, 12, 57, 58, 85, 115, 155,
167–68, 183
cantaloupe, 88, 113, 114
capitalist markets, 29
carrots, 12, 14, 31, 58, 85, 98, 124, 125,
150, 158, 183, 185, 202
cash rent, 46, 49–50. *See also* crop
share; farmland rental
Cedar Rapids, Iowa, 63, 65, 66, 67,
68, 70, 79
Charlotte's Web, 142
cheese production, 4, 54, 75–76, 199.
See also goat cheese
chemically intensive agriculture, 35,
201
chemicals, 9, 10, 32, 50, 54, 56, 67, 87,
104, 144, 186–87. *See also* pesticides;
Tsunami 100
cherries, 61
Chicago Board of Produce, 90
Child Nutrition Act, 83, 85; 2004 reauthorization, 87
Child Nutrition and WIC Reauthorization, 84
Christmas trees, 147
civic agriculture, 6, 21, 29, 121–22,
124, 140
commodity production, 7, 20, 32, 37,
38, 39, 40, 42, 135, 172, 182, 205,

207; support organizations, 8. *See
also* conventional agriculture
Community Food Security Coalition,
84, 85
community supported agriculture
(CSA), 2, 3, 10, 13, 23, 24, 31, 53, 92,
93, 96, 103, 172, 185, 187, 188, 197,
198, 201, 209; challenges, 2, 22–23,
32, 36, 202; collaborative, 45; CSA
shareholders, 4, 22, 55, 59, 106, 129,
130, 140; definition, 4; delivery, 55,
60, 61, 183; extension support for,
39, 40; history, 54–55; income, 58,
119, 139; and institutional sales, 116,
206; in Iowa, 55, 60, 128; packaging, 55, 58, 59, 60, 104, 183, 199;
promotion, 61–62, 68; shares, 58;
strategy, 55, 56–62, 179, 190, 194;
stress, 59–60; versus farmers markets (*see* risk). *See also* agricultural
research; farm intern; insurance:
benchmarks; volunteer farm labor
competition, 71, 178–79, 180
confined animal feeding operation (CAFO), 9, 191–92. *See also*
confinement
confinement, 4; manure management,
9–10
conscientious consumer, 53, 122, 143
consumers, 2, 4, 14, 28, 132, 134, 142,
158, 166, 168, 170, 197, 201, 205, 206,
209; African American, 24; civic
engagement of, 22, 121, 131; demand, 28, 54, 61, 62, 66, 79–80, 175;
direct-to, 7, 8, 52, 72, 73, 74, 76, 80,
81, 93, 135; knowledge, 21, 25, 66,
67, 116, 120, 162, 170, 183–84, 185,
198, 202; low-income, 23; power of,
3, 5, 198; tastes, 64, 66. *See also* agri-

cultural knowledge: of consumers;
farmers' market: attendance; relationship: producer-consumer; risk:
for consumer

consumption, fruit and vegetables, 28

conventional agriculture, 3, 7, 32, 35,
37, 39, 49, 158, 182, 204, 207; critique, 13, 14, 16–18, 19, 172; differences with alternative agriculture,
45, 135, 147, 171; and rural development, 144–45. *See also* relationship: conventional and alternative
agriculture

corn, 4, 9, 10, 32, 40, 50, 113, 114, 145,
172, 177, 178, 184, 186, 187, 190, 192,
200, 207; hybrid seeds, 189; open
pollinated, 188–89. *See also* genetically modified organisms (GMOs)

corn syrup, 176

corporate farms, 10. *See also* farmland
ownership: by corporations

corporate interests, 18, 20, 33, 36. *See
also* land-grant universities: corporate ties

crop rotations, 9, 11, 190–91

crop share, 46, 47, 49–50. *See also* cash
rent; farmland rental

CSA. *See* community supported agriculture (CSA)

cucumbers, 58, 155

custom farming, 45, 47, 56

dairy, 4, 7, 28, 34, 47, 54, 71, 72, 79, 85,
91, 92, 151, 185–86, 188, 203, 212. *See
also* cheese; direct marketing; milk

debt, 32–33, 43, 46

delivery, 83, 104, 155. *See also* community supported agriculture (CSA):
delivery; farm to school: delivery

Department of Education, 83, 89, 90

Dietary Guidelines for Americans, 115

direct market farmers, 6, 7, 31, 32, 43;
production, 8, 11, 37; relationship,
20

direct marketing, 3, 4, 12, 50, 53, 54,
57, 72, 93, 151, 171, 183, 199, 201,
203, 207; appearance of, 69–70,
80; challenges, 22, 204–5; dairy, 75;
meat, 52, 73, 123, 135. *See also* farm
to school

diversity, on farm, 7, 41, 43, 45, 56, 61,
83, 116, 151, 194–95, 200, 201, 205,
206, 209

E. coli, 77–78, 88

efficiency, 56, 128, 130, 133, 140, 149,
162, 208

employee incentive plan, 157

employee investment in work, 160–62,
165, 167–68, 170

employees, 12, 27, 71, 78, 90, 107, 108,
114, 119, 130, 132, 134, 136, 143–44,
155, 156–58, 160, 171, 186, 199; interactions with employer, 120–22, 124,
149, 169; in large-scale industry,
149–50; perception of customers,
166; satisfaction, 142. *See also* farm
labor

employer, 119, 124–25, 143, 156. *See also*
employees; farm labor

equipment, 4, 8, 9, 32, 40, 41, 45, 47,
50, 56, 59, 91, 106, 107, 152, 169, 182,
202; access, 38; dairy production,
54, 76, 77–78, 79, 199; harvesting,
104; sharing, 172, 189–90, 195

extension, 2, 8, 37, 39, 40, 52, 58, 198,
201, 202, 208. *See also* Iowa State
University Extension and Outreach

factory farm, 10

family farm, 17, 33, 46, 120; definition, 10

Farm Bill, 83, 84, 85, 172. *See also* policy

farm income, 4, 10, 55, 56, 58, 114, 119, 136, 162, 192

farm intern, 6, 120, 122, 123, 131, 132–35, 140, 199; and civic engagement, 134, 200–201; as future farmers, 134–35, 140–41. *See also* agricultural knowledge; farm labor; volunteer farm labor

farm labor, 7, 26, 29, 32, 33, 59, 76, 104, 106, 117, 148, 155, 170, 200–201, 207, 209; access, 119; and agricultural knowledge, 122; lack of study, 120, 141–42, 205–6; management strategies, 12, 75, 79–80, 116, 125–28, 140; profitability, 126–27, 128; social aspects, 121, 133, 140; training, 122, 136, 209. *See also* employees; farm intern; volunteer farm labor

farm scale, 4–5, 7, 10, 32, 36, 37, 39, 43, 44, 45, 52, 65, 76, 93, 104, 106, 116–17, 119, 124, 129, 134, 142, 151, 170, 172, 176, 179, 180, 184, 190, 200, 202, 205, 206, 207, 208; and community enhancement, 1, 16, 18, 25, 177, 181

Farm Service Agency (FSA), 43–44, 203

farm succession, 42

farm to school, 4, 81–82, 90, 116, 150, 197, 198, 203, 207, 208; barriers, 86–87, 98, 108, 112–13; critique, 86; delivery, 83, 87, 89, 91–92, 93, 98, 100, 111, 113, 114; farm visit, 103–7;

funding, 102; grower checklist, 103, 105; Iowa, 11–12, 88–89, 95–96; national programs, 85; policy, 84, 95; research, 86, 87; volunteer, 86, 110–11. *See also* apples; institutional purchasing; institutional sales; labor, school food; school kitchens; sweet potatoes; vegetables

farmer education, 52, 134; conferences, 32, 40, 41; workshops, 32, 43, 48. *See also* land-grant universities; Practical Farmers of Iowa (PFI)

farmer fair, 83, 96–97

farmers, age of 37–38. *See* farmland ownership

farmers' independence, 2, 16, 19, 29, 120, 141. *See also* agrarian

farmers' market, 2, 3, 12, 13, 22, 31, 45, 55, 92, 93, 116, 120, 130, 148, 151, 158, 169, 175, 183, 198, 208; access, 23–25, 26; attendance, 23, 63, 197; challenges for producers, 57, 58, 91, 161, 202; economic impact, 28; managers, 24, 27, 171; numbers of, 4, 119; packaging, 68–69; policies, 69, 70–71, 72–73, 79; producer strategies, 56, 65–71, 104–5, 122, 206; regulations, 53–54, 69; scales, 68–69; social benefits, 6; vendors, 65, 67, 70. *See also* consumers: knowledge; direct marketing; risk

farmland, 31, 180, 182; access, 31, 47

farmland, prices, 8, 12, 33, 46, 172

farmland ownership, 17, 18; by age 37–38, 46; by corporations, 33, 45–46, 186; out-of-state ownership, 37

farmland rental, 8, 12, 31, 38, 46, 48–49, 50, 201; to alternative producers, 49, 52; tenant landlord relationships, 51–52. *See also* cash rent; crop share

farmworker income, 18

Federal Post Roads Act, 33

fennel, 150, 158, 159

fertilizer, 9, 33, 44, 55, 144; in organic production, 191. *See also* chemicals; pesticides

field day. *See* Practical Farmers of Iowa (PFI)

flood, 56, 128, 130, 154

food justice, 23–24, 25–26. *See also* social justice

food processing, 6–7, 19, 25, 54, 122, 144–45, 148, 151, 207–8, 209; license for, 105, 106, 107, 150

food safety, 87–88, 89, 100, 103, 106, 203. See also *E. coli*

food service. *See* farm to school; institutional purchasing

fruit, 4, 7, 26, 27, 28, 58, 59, 71, 85, 99, 102, 112, 113, 152, 175, 194; in CSAs, 60–61, 62

garlic, 106, 154

gender discrimination, 20, 144, 149

genetically modified organisms (GMOs), 35, 172, 173, 174–75, 188, 189, 193–94

geographic preference, 84, 85, 90

global food system, 1, 25, 26, 173, 176, 199, 201, 204

goat cheese, 76–80, 185, 192, 193

Goldschmidt, Walter, 8, 146, 177

Goldschmidt Hypothesis, 17–18

Great Depression, 82

green beans, 58, 66, 68, 87, 126

greens, 66, 67, 68, 70, 85, 101, 103, 104, 106, 108, 109, 122

grocery stores, 12, 15, 22, 26, 61, 68, 70, 93, 100, 162, 176, 183, 184; as local food purchasers, 80, 103, 113, 115, 117, 129, 148, 150, 161, 167, 180

Growing Power, 24

harvest, 4, 12, 55, 56, 135, 141, 152, 156, 169; by hand, 105, 125–26, 127, 130, 200; mechanical, 116, 186, 189; salad greens, 104; sprouts, 108, 155, 158–62; watermelon, 113; wheatgrass, 151, 162–66

Hatch Act, 34

hay, 9, 45, 47–48, 50, 56, 177, 184, 186

Hazard Analysis and Critical Control Point (HACCP), 87, 88, 100

Healthy, Hunger-Free Kids Act, 85, 114

herbicide, 35, 193. *See also* chemicals; pesticides

heritage farm, 56

High Mowing Organic Seeds, 1

high tunnel, 104, 106, 111

hogs, 9, 32, 135, 145, 178, 191. *See also* pigs; pork

Homestead Act, 33

horseradish, 58

industrial agriculture, 5, 8, 13, 29, 106, 124, 180, 182, 194, 199, 201, 202. *See also* conventional agriculture; factory farm

insecticides, 187, 193–94. *See also* pesticides

inspectors, 8, 53, 71, 108, 109, 171, 199, 203; dairy production, 76–79; meat processing, 72–73, 145

institutional purchasing, 11, 81, 100, 148, 208. *See also* farm to school

institutional sales, 4, 43, 91, 93. *See also*
    farm to school
insurance, 43, 56; benchmarks, 44,
    50; federal crop insurance, 19, 203;
    health, 150, 169, 200; lack of poli-
    cies for vegetable producers, 44,
    113–14; liability, 105, 109
Iowa agricultural history, 8, 29,
    32–33, 145
Iowa agricultural industry, 35, 37, 72
Iowa Beef Packers, 149
Iowa City, Iowa, 68, 79, 180; farmers'
    market, 63, 65, 67, 69–70, 71
Iowa Department of Agriculture and
    Land Stewardship (IDALS), 28, 56,
    63, 71, 88–89, 90, 92, 96, 101, 102,
    103, 108, 187
Iowa Department of Agriculture and
    Land Stewardship Weights and
    Measures Bureau, 71
Iowa Department of Education, 83,
    89, 90
Iowa Department of Human Ser-
    vices, 89
Iowa Department of Inspections and
    Appeals, 108, 109
Iowa Department of Public Health,
    89
Iowa Farm Bureau, 58. *See also* Iowa
    State Farm Bureau
Iowa farm size, 10
Iowa politics, 16
Iowa State Farm Bureau, 34
Iowa State University (ISU), 6, 34–35,
    39, 103, 105, 172
Iowa State University Extension and
    Outreach, 8, 31, 32, 43, 44, 203;
    Beginning Farmer Center 42, 48;

support for organic, 35–36. *See also*
    extension
Iowa value of agricultural production,
    8–9

kale, 66, 68, 107, 122, 126, 183
Kingsolver, Barbara, 3
kohlrabi, 13, 58

labor, school kitchens, 88, 98–99, 113,
    114. *See also* farm labor; volunteer
    farm labor
labor unions, 145–46
lamb, 73, 135
land-grant universities, 39, 134, 140;
    corporate ties, 34–35, 123; Land-
    Grant College Act, 33–34
Leopold Center for Sustainable Agri-
    culture, 6, 39, 60, 148, 151, 157, 179,
    194
lettuce, 40, 58, 66, 68, 85, 95–96,
    98–99, 100, 101–3,104, 105, 106, 107,
    108, 109–13, 114, 115, 212
livestock, 2, 4, 7, 9, 38, 41, 47, 56, 71,
    72, 85, 105, 145, 175, 177, 181, 185,
    187, 191, 200, 205. *See also* beef; hogs;
    pigs; poultry
local food, 10, 11, 12, 14, 15, 35, 39,
    40, 207–9; access, 23–24; advo-
    cacy, 37, 139, 151; as alternative
    to conventional, 3, 6–7, 8, 16, 19,
    45, 80, 171–72, 182–83, 184, 201–3;
    and civic engagement, 131; com-
    munity enhancement, 25, 121, 123,
    147, 157–58, 165–66; consumers, 5,
    13–14, 53–54, 61–62; cost of, 23, 87,
    93, 102, 103, 110, 115–16, 132, 180,
    184–85; definition, 3–4, 14, 22–23;

economic analyses, 6, 26, 28, 142, 147–48; expansion, 3, 4, 44, 169–70, 203–5, 206; farmers, 5, 29, 32, 43, 194, 198–99; financial support for, 32; in Iowa, 28; job creation, 26, 27, 148; and land use, 38, 42, 49–50; media attention, 61; movement, 2, 143; values, 5, 20, 179. *See also* agrarian; community supported agriculture (CSA); direct marketing; farm labor; farm to school; farmers' markets; farmland rental

Local Foods Connection (LFC), 61–62, 68

locavore, 3, 29, 204

Lyson, Thomas, 21, 22, 121, 122, 140, 170

machine in the garden, 16, 29

meat, 4, 7, 19, 54, 55, 56, 57, 71, 75, 199, 203; in school kitchens, 88, 100. *See also* direct marketing

meat processing, 145–46, 149, 206; custom-only, 72; locker, 29, 72, 198; social disparities, 149–50; state-inspected, 72. *See also* occupational safety

microgreens, 36, 101, 107, 150, 153, 158, 162. *See also* sprouts

Midwest Organic and Sustainable Education Service (MOSES), 1, 11, 40, 124, 133, 203

migrant and seasonal farmworkers, 120–21

milk, 75, 77; antibiotics, 78; regulations, 76; soy, 190. *See also* dairy

minimally processed foods, 85

Monsanto, 35, 172, 186. *See also* agribusiness; genetically modified organisms (GMOs); pesticides

Morrill Act, 34

Muscadine grapes, 147

mustard greens, 68

National Farm to School Network, 4, 81, 84, 85

National Farm to School Program, 84

National School Lunch Act, 83

National School Lunch Program (NSLP), 82, 84, 87

Natural Resource Conservation Service (NRCS), 31; grazing programs, 45

nitrates in water, 44

nitrogen, 186, 191

nutrition, 153; of children, 75; and farm to school, 95; and school lunch, 82, 83, 84, 85

Obama, Michelle, 82

obesity, 82, 85, 88

occupational safety, 146, 148–49

okra, 58

onions, 58, 85, 93, 106, 130

organic, 13, 14, 67–68, 91, 92, 106, 133, 150, 158, 160, 162, 172, 181; interactions with conventional farming, 185–86, 188, 190, 202; large-scale, 123–24; practices, 10, 35–36, 38, 52, 56, 65, 67, 70, 104, 129, 175, 180, 191, 201. *See also* Midwest Organic and Sustainable Education Service (MOSES)

packaging, 4, 12, 83, 87, 91, 93, 110, 114, 120, 172, 199, 203. *See also* community supported agriculture (CSA); farmers' market

pasture, 41, 45, 48, 50, 71, 129, 135, 136, 137, 182, 199. *See also* poultry

peaches, 58, 112

peas, 101, 106, 113, 160, 190, 191

permits, 78–79, 80

pesticide drift, 25, 181, 186–87

pesticides, 9, 187, 188, 193; 2,4–D, 173; fungicides, 186; glyphosate, 173, 174, 193, 194; malathion, 65; organophosphates, 193–94; pyrethroids, 193; Roundup, 172–73, 174–75, 189, 193. *See also* herbicides; insecticides

pigs, 9, 15. *See also* hogs; pork

Pioneer Hi-Bred, 35, 173, 177. *See also* agribusiness

plums, 58

policy, 5, 28, 29, 49, 147, 180, 206; federal, 18–19, 171–72, 175, 185, 190; immigration, 185; local, 25, 181; zoning, 181–82, 205, 207. *See also* agribusiness; Farm Bill; farm to school; land-grant universities; regulation

Pollan, Michael, 3, 15, 122

pollen drift, 174, 187, 188, 189

pork, 47, 71, 72, 73, 135, 145, 149, 173, 185. *See also* agricultural commodities; hogs; pigs

postharvest handling, 105, 203

potatoes, 2, 58, 93, 104, 105, 183, 185, 202

potentially hazardous food, 101

poultry processing, 11, 73, 74–75, 85, 145; on farm, 136–39

poultry production, 3, 4, 18, 41, 47, 54, 74–75, 91, 135; broilers, 137; pastured, 129, 139; turkeys, 191

Practical Farmers of Iowa (PFI), 11, 39, 208; farmer education programs, 40–42; field day, 135–39

prairie, 32, 33, 153, 197

processing. *See* food processing; meat processing; poultry processing

racial discrimination, 20, 24, 144, 149

radishes, 101, 150, 153, 158

raspberries, 58

regional food systems working group, 151

regulation, 20, 29, 52, 53–54, 68, 74, 80, 149, 152, 188; dairy production, 76, 78, 79. *See also* occupational safety; policy; school food: procurement

relationship: conventional and alternative agriculture, 5, 8, 171–72, 180, 185 194–95, 199, 201–2; cooperative between farmers, 41, 151, 188–90; producer-consumer, 3, 6, 21, 29, 53, 55, 66, 69, 70, 71, 80, 116, 121–22, 139, 199; rural-urban, 10, 180–82

rental agreements. *See* farmland rental

risk, 87, 91, 93, 99, 105, 113, 139, 154, 170, 172, 187, 202, 204; for consumers, 69, 161; farmers' markets vs. CSA, 63–64, 70, 91; of farmland rental, 49, 50, 52; shared with consumers, 55, 61

rural culture, 176–77, 178. *See also* agrarian; relationship: rural-urban

rural depopulation, 16, 50

rural economic development, 3, 14, 28, 143, 146, 198, 207, 209. *See also* agrarian; relationship; rural

culture; rural depopulation; rural social problems
rural economic development research, 144–45, 147
rural social problems, 157

salad spinner, 104, 109, 159, 160
Sara Lee, 19, 191
school food: budgets, 93, 116; federal reimbursements, 98; meat products, 100; procurement, 88, 89–90, 99, 100, 103; quality, 82, 91, 112–13; quantity, 101, 102, 109–10, 115; ready-to-eat, 105, 106–7, 109; requirements, 99. *See also* farm to school; institutional purchasing; institutional sales; United States Department of Agriculture (USDA): produce standards
school garden, 83, 197, 112
school wellness policy, 84
self-sufficiency, 152, 174, 178. *See also* agrarian; farmers' independence
Sensitive Crop Registry, 186
Small Pig, 15
snow peas, 159, 160
social justice, 86, 124, 209. *See also* food justice
soil, 2, 104, 111, 167, 168, 186, 194; conservation, 43, 204; health, 41, 49, 59; quality, 31, 32–33, 44, 113, 172, 190, 191–92; science, 40
Southeastern African American Farmers' Organic Network (SAAFON), 25
soybeans, 4, 9, 32, 113, 114, 173, 174, 176, 177, 178, 184, 185, 186, 187, 189, 190, 191, 192, 193, 194
spinach, 58, 59, 67, 88, 101, 107, 184

sprouts, 101, 150, 151, 153, 154–55, 156, 158–62, 163, 166, 167. *See also* microgreens
squash, 113
Stearns, Tom, 1, 2, 171, 204
strawberries, 57, 58, 61, 62, 101
subsidies, 19, 20, 33, 123, 132, 172, 173, 190, 204
suburban development, 171, 180–81
sugar snap peas, 58
summer squash, 58
sunflower, 150, 153, 155, 158, 175
Supplemental Nutrition Assistance Program (SNAP), 24
Swamp Land Act, 197
sweet corn, 16, 58, 135, 145
sweet potatoes, 12, 95, 115–16, 155, 167, 168, 201
Syngenta, 173

tatsoi, 68
tax credits for farmers, 38, 198, 207
taxes, 50, 58, 132, 146, 149, 181
tomatoes, 13, 21, 26, 36, 58, 66, 68, 88, 113, 127, 128–29, 183
Truman, Harry, 83
Tsunami 100, 104, 108, 110, 159
turnips, 186
Tyson, 19, 73, 149

Union of Concerned Scientists, 27
United States Department of Agriculture (USDA), 4, 10, 31, 53, 73, 108; census of agriculture, 9; chemical application reports, 193; Economic Research Service, 145; Food and Nutrition Services, 85; grant funding, 207; Initiative for Future Agricultural and Food Systems, 84;

produce standards, 92–93; Resource Conservation and Development (RC&D), 31, 43, 52, 96, 97, 100; statistics, 54, 63
U.S. Food and Drug Administration, 101

value chain, 179
vegetables, 4, 7, 26, 28, 40, 60, 61, 67, 68, 82, 123, 152, 175, 180, 184; grower, 43–44, 55, 64, 66, 71–72, 90, 125, 129, 133, 176, 185, 197; offerings in school lunch, 85, 98–99, 102, 112, 114–15, 200, 202; production, 41, 50, 52, 58, 189, 190, 194
venison, 72
vertical integration, 18–19
volunteer farm labor, 6, 27–28, 121, 123, 128–32, 140, 155, 200–1; and civic engagement, 124, 131–32, 134; and cost of food, 132, 209; economic benefits, 132; lack of skill, 129, 130, 131, 141, 161; in local food systems, 129; product quality, 139. *See also* agricultural knowledge; farm intern; farm labor; Practical Farmers of Iowa (PFI): field day

volunteers, 131, 166; at farmers' markets, 130. *See also* farm to school; volunteer farm labor

wages, 6, 120, 124, 139, 141, 143, 146, 147, 162, 170, 200, 209
walk-in cooler, 87, 105, 107, 108, 109, 154, 156, 160, 161
watermelon, 95, 112, 113–14
weather: effects on production, 96, 104, 105, 110, 112, 126, 127–28; and farmers' market attendance, 66
weeding, 59, 93, 130, 152, 155
weeds: palmar amaranth, 173; waterhemp, 173
wheatgrass, 150, 151, 153–55, 156, 158, 161, 162–66, 168, 169
wholesale, 93, 94, 104, 113, 116, 129, 150, 155
Women's Food and Agriculture Network (WFAN), 31
World Health Organization, 173

yield, 46, 50, 55, 113, 115, 116, 130, 141, 168, 172. *See also* insurance: benchmarks